Researching for the Media

Researching for the Media: Television, Radio and Journalism is an essential guide to researching for the media industry. It explains the role of the researcher and journalist within radio, television and journalism, exploring key areas of what to expect in the job.

Researching for the Media: Television, Radio and Journalism offers advice and instruction on practical, ethical and legal issues which can affect anyone working in these industries. Beginning with suggestions on how to think up ideas and how to devise treatments, through to general research methods and techniques and guidance on working on location at home and abroad, it uses real examples of good and bad practice from the industry. Written by an experienced researcher, writer and producer, *Researching for the Media* includes:

- tips on finding contributors from contestants, experts and specialists through to audiences and celebrities
- how to find photographs, picture and film clips, and the ethical and legal issues involved
- advice on finding and using music and copyright issues
- how the media use the internet and social media such as Twitter, Facebook and Instagram
- a discussion of risk assessment, codes of conduct, ethical behaviour and legal and safety issues
- a glossary of media terms, further reading and a list of helpful websites.

Adèle Emm has worked in a news agency, in film editing at the BBC, as a free-lance researcher at Thames and Tyne Tees Television, and as staff researcher and producer at Granada.

Media Skills

EDITED BY: RICHARD KEEBLE, LINCOLN UNIVERSITY

The *Media Skills* series provides a concise and thorough introduction to a rapidly changing media landscape. Each book is written by media and journalism lecturers or experienced professionals and is a key resource for a particular industry. Offering helpful advice and information and using practical examples from print, broadcast and digital media, as well as discussing ethical and regulatory issues, *Media Skills* books are essential guides for students and media professionals.

Researching for the Media

TELEVISION, RADIO AND JOURNALISM

SECOND EDITION

Adèle Emm

Routledge
Taylor & Francis Group

LONDON AND NEW YORK

First published 2001 as *Researching for Television and Radio*
by Routledge

Second edition published 2014
by Routledge
2 Park Square, Milton Park, Abingdon, Oxon OX14 4RN

Simultaneously published in the USA and Canada
by Routledge
711 Third Avenue, New York, NY 10017

Routledge is an imprint of the Taylor & Francis Group, an informa business

British Library Cataloguing in Publication Data
A catalogue record for this book is available from the British Library

Library of Congress Cataloging in Publication Data
A catalog record for this title has been requested

ISBN: 978-0-415-84355-3 (hbk)
ISBN: 978-0-415-84356-0 (pbk)
ISBN: 978-1-315-77899-0 (ebk)

Typeset in Goudy
by Keystroke, Station Road, Codsall, Wolverhampton

Printed and bound in Great Britain by
TJ International Ltd, Padstow, Cornwall

For Pasqualle

Contents

Acknowledgements

Danny Adams, Broadcasting Department, PRS for Music

Melisa Akdogan, freelance factual producer

Alamy, picture agency

BBC for use of extracts from the Editorial Guidelines

Councillor Jane Brophy

Kate Burns, journalist

Georgina Butler

Olivia Chapman, PRS for Music

Joanna Geary, Digital Development Director, *Guardian*

Richard Goldthorpe, Business Development Manager, British Pathé

Robert Hahn, Head of Rights, *Guardian*

Gillian Harrison, freelance travel writer

Andy Harrower, Head of Broadcast Licensing, PRS for Music

Greg Hughes, producer, Capital Radio

Mark Kelly

Susanne Kittlinger, BAPLA

Maine Film Office

Ofcom for use of extracts from the broadcast codes

Tania Pearson, PRS for Music

Naomi Pohl, Recording and Broadcasting Official, Musicians' Union, who was especially helpful with the music chapter

Network Rail

Nevada Film Office

Nic Stevenson, CAA

Michael Sweeney, Musicians' Union

1
What is a researcher?

If you watch programmes such as *Jeremy Kyle* or one of the popular talent shows, you may spot the researcher in the background with an intense expression clutching a clipboard to her trendy chest. And it is a 'her', because the trendy young male researcher has been promoted to the intense, trendy young producer/director with his feet on the desk barking orders. Recognise the stereotype?

Forget it. The researcher is the kingpin gopher, the bottom rung of the production ladder but a job in its own right. A police constable may never make it to sergeant and a researcher may never make it further up the production ladder but, because of the very nature of the job, this shouldn't matter. The same applies to a newspaper journalist. A reporter may start as the junior reporter on a local newspaper and, 30 years later, be the chief reporter on the same publication. However, with the rise of social media, the miniaturisation of technology and the contraction of budgets, several job designations have contracted so that more media professionals – whatever media they work in – have to be increasingly multi-skilled.

In radio terms, although the number of radio stations is expanding day by day, radio is, in many respects, the Cinderella of the media. Compared to television, there is a relatively small audience and the fewest number of listeners is for local radio. Because the audiences are so small, the budgets are miniscule; there is no money for pre-production and everything is required now. The result? Apart from at the BBC (and often there too), the producer on a radio programme does their own research.

As for those working in the press – the very job *is* research. Oh, and writing it up. I'm being flippant here . . .

A researcher and journalist should have two mottos:

- Give me a phone and I can find you anything.
- The impossible I can do now; a miracle takes a little longer.

I shall start by describing the personal attributes of a researcher – and remember, this includes anyone doing media research in whatever capacity.

Anyone conducting research is/has:

- well educated and informed with interests in a wide variety of subjects; a whizz at *Trivial Pursuit* and *Articulate* and who can answer lots of questions in quiz shows;
- curious, with the ability to ask pertinent questions and sound convincing even when they know nothing about the subject. By the end of the project, they are an expert. The get-out-of-jail-free is to admit to Professor Whatnot right at the beginning that they haven't a clue about the politics of Papua New Guinea but he is the expert and . . .;
- a good listener with the ability to précis accurately and take good notes (those on a journalism course may have learnt shorthand to help with this);
- an excellent memory;
- hard working and indefatigable. The hours can be appalling; a 105-hour week non-stop for three weeks including weekends is not unusual in television. Yes, the European Union Social Charter limits hours to a 48-hour week but middle management and the media are so far exempt. BECTU (Broadcasting Entertainment Cinematograph and Theatre Union www.bectu.org.uk) has, at the time of writing, just conducted research into 14-hour days for members working on factual television programmes. As a journalist will remind you, the news doesn't stop at 6pm. Council planning meetings are often scheduled for evenings and sporting events happen at the weekends. Wars and battles are won and lost overnight;
- fit, healthy, self-starter, assertive, reliable and responsible;
- excellent organisational and administrative skills;
- able to get on with and like people. All people. Rudyard Kipling's *If* sums it up. If you know to what I am referring and have looked it up, you are well on the way;
- meticulous and gives attention to detail;
- good computer skills, including fast and accurate typing;
- a facility with language as television researchers often write voiceovers, links and narration. Reporters write articles and radio producers write scripts. All media are verbal in some way and, depending on the production, scripts should read like something you'd say, not a report you'd hand to your accountant. On the other hand, if you are writing for current affairs and political programmes, the script should sound like the voice of authority. The same applies for a newspaper article; if it doesn't capture the reader's attention in the lead paragraph, they won't read further;
- the ability to get to the nub of an issue in as few words as possible;

- a sense of humour (for all those puns) and to survive in a fast moving industry;
- the essential social skills of drinking late into the night, partying until dawn and being back on location, in the office or radio studio bright eyed and bushy tailed at 7am.

As for what a researcher actually does, that is the million dollar question. Depending on the type of production and the size of the team, it is a pivotal position crossing many demarcation lines. Many of the jobs a TV researcher does correspond with jobs in radio and journalism.

I'll start by summarising the stages of programme making from pre-production. Radio and Newspapers follow.

Television

Pre-production

This is the commissioning, planning and organising element of programme making up to the actual shoot. During pre-production, the set is devised and built, the costumes designed, hired or made, the contestants and actors auditioned, special effects designed and produced and the programme planned in detail, bearing in mind that, as good ideas crop up, the programme is inevitably amended.

Pre-production can take an inordinate length of time. A feature film or historical drama may be in pre-production for several years. However, the escalating use of accountants results in squeezed budgets and increasingly tight pre-production schedules.

The first person assigned to a production, often because it is his/her idea, is the producer closely followed by the researcher and the director. The production team consists of the producer, director, researcher, production assistant (PA), and, in drama, sitcoms, etc., the scriptwriter. There are other ancillary roles such as assistant (occasionally associate) producer, executive producers, line producers, etc.

The jobs of the production manager, location manager and assistant director often overlap depending on the size and requirements of the production and in some situations, the role may be taken by the researcher.

Design departments include the set/production designer, props, costume, graphics, make-up and wardrobe departments who start working during pre-production and often continue through the production stage as well.

All of the above liaise with the director.

Production

This is when the programme is recorded on location or in a studio.

Feature films expect to shoot the equivalent of 1½ minutes of screen time a day; in other words, a feature film shoot usually lasts 10–16 weeks or more depending on the overall length and the budget. Television drama, on the other hand, shoots an hour's drama over 11 days or less if possible. Soaps such as *Coronation Street* record three half-hour episodes a week, more when working towards the Christmas break or for a special.

In the 1990s, one quiz episode was recorded a day but now, up to four are recorded. Why? The same number of studio crew is required in one day to make four shows as is required to make one. Simple. Also, when a programme like *The X Factor* goes out live on ITV1, it is common for extension programmes, such as *The Xtra Factor*, to continue on ITV2.

Chat shows and daytime current affairs like *The One Show*, *This Morning* and *Today* are usually transmitted live although they will have pre-recorded inserts.

Others are recorded *as live*. 'As live' means the programme is taped in real time but pre-recorded a few hours or a day before. There are several reasons for this, a common one being that the TX (transmission) time is unsociable (a bank holiday, 3am) and costs a fortune in wages. The benefit of recording as live is that, although each take is 'for real', should there be any serious faults (technical or editorial), the take can be rewound and re-recorded. There is no editing on an as live programme.

A daily *live* programme such as *This Morning* or *The One Show* has a separate production team assigned to Monday or Tuesday and throughout the week. Effectively, once the pre-production period is over (perhaps as little as a month or less to set up pre-recorded items), the team works a rolling schedule culminating in their day's edition.

Here, pre-production merges into production. Imagine being on week 4 of a 16-episode fashion show. The first three programmes have been transmitted, episode 4 is in editing, episode 5 onwards is being shot but no-one has more than the vaguest idea of the content of programme 12 onwards. This happens. Depending on one's attitude, it's very stressful or an adrenaline roller coaster.

Post-production

Once filming is over, it is technically in post-production. This is when editing takes place (where the shots are put in the correct order and mistakes cut out), special effects added (sound re-recorded, mixed and dubbed) and a master edit produced.

For live programmes, there is no post-production although the programme will be recorded whilst being transmitted to fulfil regulatory demands. Currently, Ofcom states in its 'Procedures for investigating breaches of content standards for television and radio' that the output must be kept by broadcasters for 42 days after the broadcast. Recordings of television programmes must be kept for 60 days except in the case of BBC1, BBC2, ITV1, Channel 4, Channel 5 and S4C, in which case recordings must be kept for 90 days. This is done automatically and includes radio programmes.

TX (transmission)

This is when the programme goes out. The word is used in both radio and TV.

Radio

The BBC must not be confused with commercial radio which, to exist, sells advertising air time. Depending on the radio station, the BBC can concentrate on broadcasting more factual and current affairs programmes as well as longer news bulletins, music and drama. It will therefore specifically employ researchers whereas research for commercial radio is conducted by the individual programme producer who must ensure the programme stays on brand. Because radio is a more compact medium than television, there is a smaller range of jobs. Personnel moving from radio to television are often horrified to find how many extra people are needed.

The BBC is funded by the licence fee and does not have advertisements. This statement may appear simplistic but has a fundamental effect on radio output and the jobs in the BBC and independent radio stations. In other words, people in independent radio sell air time to advertisers and the *traffic* department schedules advertising and promotions to maximise effectiveness and revenue.

Programme making in a commercial station is almost a secondary activity which is why so many independent radio stations play music interrupted by (inane) chat. Although it is cheap and relies on minimum production personnel, it must, of course, deliver to the target audience or the advertisers won't buy air time. As the news is usually provided by IRN (Independent Radio News) for most commercial radio stations in the UK, there is no need for journalists. The producers for independent radio stations invariably do their own research although a station assistant may be employed to help out.

One important difference between people working in radio and those in TV and newspapers is that, especially for the BBC, anyone working in radio must speak clearly and have a good microphone voice – often tested at interview. Unlike television, which only appears to employ the beautiful people, those in radio can be more homely in appearance. Regional accents are no longer frowned on even in the BBC and the BBC Pronunciation Research Unit advises on difficult and controversial words in any language free of charge to BBC personnel and anyone making programmes for them. The radio researcher is more likely than their television counterpart to conduct their own interviews, edit them, script and edit promotional material such as trails, although with the surge in multi-skilling in the media this is increasingly happening in television. Even researchers working on the flagship Radio 4 are expected to do this. If interviews are conducted over the phone, researchers may well set up the technology.

Newspapers

The boss is the editor who is responsible for the content of the newspaper and can be sued (alongside any journalist working on an article) for libel, conspiracy, perverting the course of justice, etc. Heads of department include, for example, the features editor, news editor, picture editor and head of rights who report to the editor.

The sub-editor checks accuracy and spelling and writes the headlines, etc. and is increasingly responsible for the layout of the newspaper, although nowadays it is common for journalists to write the articles directly into layout software programs. For small local newspapers, one sub-editor may oversee several different papers.

Reporters/journalists find, research and write articles and features for newspapers. On local newspapers, they may also write advertising features on behalf of commercial businesses. There are a decreasing number of staff photographers working on newspapers to cut costs – also because of the proliferation of smartphones and the public supplying their own photos. A local newspaper may only have one photographer whose jobs are scheduled in a diary. For nationals, more are employed but the general public also supply photos on breaking or unexpected news events. It is increasingly common for reporters to be encouraged to take photos when reporting on a story.

The marketing and advertising departments are important as they earn revenue for newspapers by selling advertising space. As a day's newspaper output can be printed in a few hours, several newspapers share printers.

Genres

Researchers work on a variety of programmes. Some genres overlap in radio and are familiar to journalists too:

- documentaries and documentary scenes/docu-soaps/infotainment;
- light entertainment/quizzes/game shows;
- music;
- sport;
- children's programmes;
- magazine/daytime/chat shows;
- news, current affairs and politics (mainly employ journalists);
- drama (few dramas employ researchers as such).

The researcher's role

This is what researchers, radio producers and journalists do:

- suggest ideas;
- suggest treatments;
- find contributors (newspapers, radio, TV) and interview them. 'Mind' them in studio or on location (e.g. celebrities, experts, MPs, contestants, documentary subjects). For TV and radio, this may also include auditions;
- assessing and inputting UGC (user-generated content – tweets, Facebook, email, blogs, text messages, photos and YouTube, etc.) into programmes and newspaper articles;
- verify the accuracy and source of UGC;
- keep in touch with social media in order to access breaking news;
- check the spelling and details on interviewees' and contributors' names;
- find and check facts;
- find statistics and confirm their accuracy;
- set and verify quiz and competition questions and act as scorekeepers;
- find locations and go on recces (short for 'reconnaissance'; see Chapter 8);
- organise hotels, restaurants, travel arrangements, etc. for self, contributors, interviewees and crews;
- supervise and organise the personal props of programme contributors;
- pay expenses (when applicable) to contributors;
- book specialist equipment in consultation with film, outside broadcast and broadcast crews;
- find prizes, props and costumes;
- write links, voiceovers, narrations;
- act as on-screen or audio reporter on short items;

- find film clips, photographs and pictures, check copyright and organise their transfer into the correct format;
- suggest atmospheric music;
- research, direct, shoot/record and edit items for TV, radio and online;
- organise ISDN lines;
- operate equipment in radio studios;
- organise photographic shoots;
- take photographs;
- edit or supervise editing, including devising edits (the cutting order or the EDL – edit decision list) although, controversially in some quarters, TV increasingly uses edit producers.

Phew! Many of these mirror other jobs but the larger and more prestigious the programme or newspaper and the larger the budget or access to expenses, the less likely you are to take on some of the responsibilities in the list above. However, on local newspapers, documentaries, cable and satellite stations (where the budget is virtually non-existent), you may do everything from research, shoot, take photos, edit and dance the polka at the same time. All for £13,500 a year. And would anyone be mug enough to research, direct, produce, shoot and edit a satellite station's entire output? Or spend their evenings at a local council meeting, stand on the sidelines of a chilly local football pitch or meet distraught parents? Of course they are. For free – although the unpaid internship system is currently under governmental review. For the experience. Because they have direct editorial control. Because they are desperate for a job in the industry. Someone else will do it for less (or for free) and it's a good place to begin a career. Because it can be exciting and because no day is ever the same.

Generally speaking, however, the researcher is responsible for offering ideas, finding contributors and suggesting angles by which a pretty ordinary idea can be recorded in an unusual, novel and interesting way.

For a journalist, the main responsibility is similar; find a news story, the 'witnesses' or interviewees and write it up in an accurate and readable way. The key here is finding the stories in the first place.

In the words of Chris Cowey, the renowned music programme executive producer, a researcher needs the Four Is:

- Innovation;
- Imagination;
- Intelligence; and
- Integrity.

This also applies to a journalist. He adds that a good researcher is extremely hard to find and harder to keep because, in this day and age where a researcher's job is not regarded as a be-all and end-all, either they are poached by other programmes or they become a producer. A journalist is in a slightly different position because the job is, in some ways, 'for life' but there are opportunities to move between media and to change from local to regional and thence national newspapers.

The beauty of working as a researcher or in journalism is that no two jobs are ever the same. In the 'good old days', a researcher might find themselves working for six months on a chat show followed by a music programme and then a year's contract on current affairs where a different subject is tackled each week. However, now that freelance contracts are the norm, it is more likely you will be pigeon-holed within a genre. The issues ensure that every day has its own challenges.

In a nutshell, a researcher and journalist is a jack-of-all-trades with opportunities to specialise in their preferred genre depending on their background and interest.

A brief note about contracts

Until the 1990 Broadcasting Act, most jobs in the media were permanent 'staff' jobs where an employee worked for the same company until they retired or found a job elsewhere. Since then, the majority of jobs in film, television and radio are fixed-term contracts, usually of a few months' duration. Journalists are a little luckier as there are still staff jobs available. Having said that, many journalists eke out a living writing on a freelance basis. If they write an article which isn't published, they don't get paid. Simple as that.

Production personnel, including researchers, cannot assume that any fixed-term contract will be renewed and must expect to work where a job is available. Inevitably, this means frequent moves. Until recently, the majority of the work was in London. Many media professionals resent moving south with its exorbitant house prices and inherent problem of insecure short-term contracts. Leeds, Birmingham, Nottingham, Southampton, Bristol and Glasgow are large media centres but the largest centre outside London is MediaCityUK, Salford. The BBC relocated many of its production departments there, including drama, children's and sport, and several media companies followed, including Granada and the *Coronation Street* set.

Most media newcomers obtain their first job at independent production houses and in cable television. These tend to be based in cities although cable stations are now setting up in larger towns where rents are cheaper. Contracts and pay are short and low.

Radio stations are, by their very nature, more regional and localised. Competition for jobs is less fierce than in television but fierce enough! On the whole, for most independent radio stations, there are fewer jobs in production and most people work in marketing and promotions. By independent, I mean non-BBC. Greg Hughes, a producer at Capital FM, believes that most radio journalists start in radio rather than migrate from local newspapers or television.

For journalists, there are plenty of local newspapers on which to 'cut your teeth'. However, with the decline in newspaper sales, a local newspaper may have only three journalists working there. It is not unusual for a local journalist in a newspaper group to supply articles for several newspapers and it can be 'dead man's shoes' getting the first job.

The downside of short-term contracts is the instability. The upside is that, if you find routine tedious and savour change and new challenges, this is perfect.

A note on ethics

A global and dangerous statement is that a producer and editor often want what is impossible. The researcher and rookie journalist is in the unfortunate position of having to provide something the producer doesn't know they want until they see it. This sounds harsh but is reality and can result in ethically questionable results, especially in an age when time is minimal.

*   In December 1998, the ITC fined Carlton Television £2 million for setting up drug runners in a *Cutting Edge* documentary on the Columbian drug trade.
*   In 1999, Nottingham Council took Channel 4 and October Films to court for paying schoolchildren to sit in doorways and act as prostitutes while the cameras rolled.
*   *Vanessa* and *Trisha* were discredited for hiring fake guests. *Vanessa* was axed in June 1999. *The Jerry Springer Show* from the USA was revealed for winding up its guests until they 'fought' on set. *The Jeremy Kyle Show* is often criticised for spurious practices (e.g. *Daily Mail* article, May 2011).
*   In September 2012, Ofcom investigated allegations that two teenage children watching their mother's audition in *The X Factor* would be subjected to bullying because her performance was transmitted on television.
*   Rupert Murdoch's empire (News International), which includes the *Sun*, the *Sun on Sunday* (formerly the *News of the World*) and *The Times*, was accused of conducting police bribery and phone hacking between 2005 and 2007 although it was later revealed that these practices had been taking place much earlier. The scandal exposed the antics of private

investigators and journalists hacking into the phones of politicians, the British Royal Family and celebrities in the pursuit of personal and salacious stories with which to sell papers. At first, it was thought that only phones of people in the public eye had been attacked until it was revealed that the voicemail of 13-year-old murder victim Milly Dowler had been intercepted (2002), with the result that her parents believed she was still alive. Phones of the victims of the 7/7 London bombings (2005) and those of deceased British soldiers had also been accessed. The fallout was considerable. Several prominent people resigned, among them Sir Paul Stephenson, the Commissioner of the Metropolitan Police, and News International executives Rebekah Brooks and Tom Crone. After advertisers boycotted the paper, the *News of the World* was closed in July 2011 to be replaced by the *Sun on Sunday*. Several journalists, including Rebekah Brooks (the former editor of the *Sun*), and various police officers were arrested; some have since been jailed. Perhaps the most important repercussion for the press was the Leveson Inquiry (official website, www.levesoninquiry.org.uk) to investigate the culture, practice and ethics of the press. The Inquiry has made several suggestions as to how the press should be regulated, how it should conduct itself in future and on accountability and sanctions.

As production schedules tighten to save money, the researcher and journalist has less time to supply or interview a controversial new guest with an outspoken, outrageous viewpoint. If a guest has come up with the goods before, do you use them again? Even if their face has appeared on three different talk shows with a different spin on each? Do you pay them a fee for something they neither care in nor believe? Do you ask people to do something for ratings which you know is ethically dubious?

The answer, of course, is no and yet the researcher has to deliver at all costs or their contract isn't renewed. Yet, if the programme is discredited and axed because of fixing, the researcher has lost their job anyway.

After the *Trisha/Vanessa* debacles, the BBC issued guidelines that all guests on factual programmes must sign an honesty declaration exonerating the production team should the guest prove fraudulent.

Years later and production times are even tighter, with the October 2012 BECTU survey highlighting exploitation in working hours and how this affects the health and safety of the staff. My point here is that, under such conditions, there is not enough time to be scrupulous about the ethics of the content within the programme. This doesn't condone the harassed researcher cutting corners and taking the easy way out but it does explain it.

Culpability and recrimination?

Does it matter if the responsibility lies with you, the producer or the editor? If the producer or editor overrides what you have provided in all good faith, and if you have acted ethically and to the best of your ability, it is the producer's and editor's ultimate responsibility. Just ensure you have proof to cover your back when blame is apportioned.

Working in the media involves long and, according to the BECTU survey, excessive hours. However stressful the job, it can be exciting, satisfying and fulfilling. It's like the old army joke: you get the chance to go to many places, meet both influential and ordinary people – and shoot them! On camera.

Further reading

Chater, Kathy, *Production Research: An Introduction* (Media Manuals), Focal Press, 2001. Kindle edition, 2012
Fleming, Carole, *The Radio Handbook* (Media Practice), 3rd edn, Routledge, 2009
Keeble, Richard, *Ethics for Journalists* (Media Practice), 2nd edn, Routledge, 2008
Keeble, Richard, *The Newspapers Handbook* (Media Practice), 4th edn, Routledge, 2005
Kellison, Cathrine, *Producing for TV and New Media: A Real-World Approach for Producers*, Focal Press, 2011
Orlebar, Jeremy, *The Television Handbook* (Media Practice), 4th edn, Routledge, 2011

Websites

BBC: www.bbc.co.uk
BBC College of Production website has profiles of a researcher and articles on TV research: www.bbc.co.uk/academy/production
Channel 4: www.channel4.com
Creative Skillset: www.creativeskillset.org
IRN, Independent Radio News: www.irn.co.uk
ITV: www.itv.com
Leveson Inquiry: www.levesoninquiry.org.uk
Ofcom (Office of Communications), regulatory body: www.ofcom.org.uk
Radio Academy: www.radioacademy.org

2
Ideas

There are no new ideas in the media; everything has been done before. Your task is to find a different way of doing it, to find a new angle, give it a new treatment. Take talent shows for instance; what started out as, amongst others, *Opportunity Knocks* became *New Faces*, *Pop Idol*, *The X Factor*, *Britain's Got Talent* and *The Voice*.

With hundreds of channels of television on air 24 hours a day and hundreds of radio hours to fill, let alone the pages in a newspaper, anyone who can whistle up novel, interesting, exciting, sexy ideas will never find themselves out of work. But where do these ideas come from?

This is the hardest part of any creative job. Some people are just naturally inventive and creative. Others work hard at it. I remember a conversation with a colleague about a one-minute package for a television charity appeal for the Samaritans. 'Just have a BCU (big close-up) of a ringing phone,' he replied. 'And don't answer it!' Simple, effective and *cheap*.

Copyrighting ideas

Ideas in general cannot be copyrighted. Inevitably, most ideas have been thought of before but try telling someone that. Television and radio stations are always taking calls from members of the public insisting that they 'spoke to someone at your television studio last week/month' with the same idea and format that they are now seeing on screen. Even though the programme has been in production for months and was put forward to the commissioning editor a year previously, the caller still argues that their idea has been stolen.

Formats *can* be copyrighted and several television companies, notably those producing game, quiz and light entertainment shows, buy and sell formats. Endemol is a prime example: in 2013, ITV commissioned a version of *Stars in Their Eyes* called *Your Face Sounds Familiar* created by Endemol's Spanish division and sold across the world. The same year, Endemol acquired the international format rights to *The Common Denominator*, a game show devised in Israel. *University Challenge* was originally a radio quiz from the USA.

Media people are unprincipled enough to pinch ideas and pass them off as their own, resulting in job interviewees or colleagues in a pub refusing to divulge their precious idea in case it is screened with someone else's credit or the appointment goes elsewhere. At the job interview, this strategy misfires if the second best idea is mediocre. Media moguls always insist that you should offer your best ideas at interviews but I leave this up to you to decide.

Exclusivity

If creativity and good ideas are so difficult, is it surprising that television and newspapers (radio less so) constantly demand the scoop, the first airing of the video, the exclusive interview, the rights to publish extracts from a celebrity's autobiography, the hitherto unseen footage?

There are no easy answers, but there *are* strategies. To have ideas, you must be interested and open to everything. The media consume everything; it is easy to lose sight of what is going on around you because you are too busy making programmes or writing articles.

Keep up to date and be informed

If your reply to the interview question 'And what are your hobbies?' is 'I haven't any', you have a problem. Job applicants are commonly turned down because they have no outside interests. People with diverse activities, no matter how unusual or anorakish, are more creative with more to draw on. The more they do, even if it isn't television or radio experience, the more likely they are to have ideas.

It is vital to know what is going on in the world, especially if you are working in the media. How can you work on the news if you don't know the names of the main politicians in the current government?

Read magazines and newspapers such as *NME*, *Look*, *Pick Me Up!*, *Woman*, *Nuts*, *Closer*. Even *Beano* if you must. Listen to the radio, and not just Capital or Radio 1 but Kerrang! and Radio 5 live. As for newspapers, the *Sun* won't tax your brain but you'll know what the editor thinks the public wants. Don't forget the qualities; it is the pinnacle of someone's success if they get a job here: *The Times*, the *Guardian*, the *Independent*, the *Daily Telegraph*. *i* (from the

Independent stable) at 20p a copy at the time of writing must be the best value in the high street. Know the issues of the moment and keep up with them. Who's in? Who's out? Who wants to be in? Who are the movers and shakers in politics, the arts and the business world? What's on at the cinema but, crucially, what is being filmed today for distribution next year? And who is tipped for the big time?

You can never know too much, however trivial and irrelevant it may appear. As your life changes, go with it. After having her children, Esther Rantzen used her experience to make programmes about birth, babies and children's issues and set up ChildLine. After I had my daughter, I worked on similar programmes. The tragedy of this anecdote is that because so few women in television juggle a career with bringing up children, and as most women around me were single and childless, by merely giving birth I became an expert. Radio and journalism are perhaps a little more forgiving to working mothers but it is still a hard existence. Again, use your new knowledge to conceive those ideas. Mumsnet. com is an excellent example!

Idea sources

Brainstorming

My daughter tells me that this term is no longer politically correct but it still appears to be in common parlance so here goes.

Even something as banal as the British obsession with the weather can become a valid topic. The method of brainstorming involves thinking around the subject in as silly or serious way as you can. The rules are simple. Nobody laughs and all suggestions are jotted down. All sorts of treatments crop up and many can be adapted to suit a particular programme or newspaper article.

Weather forecasting by folklore for a lifestyle programme or newspaper article this month. Cue a dotty expert who foretells a dreadful winter because the daffodil in his garden faces east. Photograph the daffodil for the newspaper. Include the famous clip when Michael Fish got it wrong in 1987 for television.

Turn the idea around and you get an item about how not to get flu in winter – a phone-in of granny's fail-safe way of keeping the bugs at bay by wearing mustard plasters on her corns.

In *Blue Peter*, the weather becomes 'infotainment'. Canadian Inuit children surviving extreme conditions with, of course, location filming. For a Christmas special, include reindeer.

Other examples include 'The World's Ten Worst Meteorological Disasters' or 'Why Take Aspirin For a Cold?' and the celebrity chat 'How I Nearly Died of Flu!' All of these could be for multi-platform use. You'll think of more.

There is an anecdote on the BBC College of Journalism website telling of a newspaper editor who challenged his staff to walk 500 metres down a road and find more stories than him. He looked at the litter, the parked cars, the number of new cars and traffic wardens, the building construction, etc., all of them providing further investigation for a story.

Crowdsourcing

Although not strictly a method which someone in the media can use as inspiration for ideas *per se*, a variation on brainstorming is 'crowdsourcing' which I first encountered at Granada TV although the name had not been coined at that time. Granada TV opened itself up for everyone to offer programme ideas. I remember a floor manager being extremely excited by the prospect of one of his ideas going into production.

In the latter end of 2012, the BBC opened up an online noticeboard, *iCreate*, by which all staff, from engineers to safety officers to production personnel, could suggest ideas for any genre. 'Winning' ideas included *Mr Mum* about a single father which was being made into a 30-minute pilot for radio. Wish fulfilment *Make My Dream* was commissioned as a segment for *The One Show* with the possibility of it being a full series. According to *Broadcast* (14 December 2012), the BBC was aiming to improve its ideas and increase the skills of its staff. Other crowdsourcing software is being developed by Universal Music and the US branch of Amazon which is trying to break into content for VOD (video on demand).

In *Broadcast* (26 July 2013), celebrity chef Jamie Oliver, who owns production company Fresh One Productions, was convinced that, because of the current lack of broadcast originality, content will be initiated and funded through crowdsourcing by 2014.

Crowdsourcing is increasingly used to raise money for projects, especially independent films and theatre productions. The term used here is 'crowdfunding'.

Newspapers and magazines

Years ago, I went on a novel writing course which included 'how to think up ideas'. The course leader made us riffle through newspapers and magazines (another form of brainstorming) and think of ideas for ourselves. Anything is permissible, from looking at the personal columns to the NIB (news in brief) and the celebrity pages. A journalist friend of mine once asked me how I got my ideas for a show and I replied, 'from newspapers!' She was not impressed. Television and radio researchers and producers are constantly pinching ideas from the papers. This helps the broadcast industry no end but, as my journalist friend pointed out, doesn't help her!

The futures/planning desk

In newspaper offices and TV and radio station newsrooms, the futures desk keeps a diary on what is happening over the next few months. In a small local newspaper office this might be the journalist's personal diary.

Sports events are fixed months, often years in advance. We know that the Olympic Games will be staged in 2016 in Rio de Janeiro and in Tokyo in 2020. The winter games are also scheduled years in advance. Wimbledon is *always* held in the last week of June and the first week of July. The Football Association draws the fixtures and announces dates well in advance. Other sporting information is sent by the governing bodies to the futures desk in the form of press releases to be entered into the futures diary.

Events such as Christmas, Halloween, Guy Fawkes Night and Easter are annual. Radio, television and newspapers all base items around these themes because it's already in the audience's agenda and, frankly, because it's easy. How often has *Blue Peter* made variations of Advent calendars and Easter bunnies? What's the best frock for a Christmas party and how to lose weight in the new year? These topics are in every radio and television programme or magazine throughout December and January.

The Queen's birthday (jubilee for 2012–13), Crufts Dog Show and Wimbledon are regular items. Why? Because everyone knows when they take place and therefore they become ideas: what is being worn at Ascot this year, youngest person entering a dog in the show, how to improve your tennis skills.

If you can think of ingenious ideas and treatments, apply for a job.

Press releases and churnalism

Press releases are brief documents usually one side long outlining the main points of an approaching event. They are sent out by organisations wanting publicity, preferably free, to national and local newspapers offices, national and local radio and television stations. The intention is for it to be used as a newspaper article or television and radio item.

Examples of when press releases may be sent out are:

- the publication date of the latest novel by a blockbusting writer;
- the opening of a new play;
- special awareness health days or months, e.g. non-smoking day or breast cancer awareness month;
- changes in government policy;
- changes in social security and welfare payments;
- the Royal Mail's new postal charges, stamp designs or last postings for Christmas;
- a local Brownie pack advertising a bravery award;
- a company expanding employment;
- a school or college where a student has achieved something special;
- a local sporting event;
- the opening of a children's hospice;
- a local street carnival;
- a pop group signing records in a high street store;
- a national television company auditioning for a talent show.

It can be seen immediately how such press releases provide content for myriad items in television, radio and newspapers. In many cases, the press release is advertising something low-key but, although it isn't a huge occasion, it instantly appeals to the local newspaper journalist, radio and TV news station – if not the nationals as well.

The lazy journalist – unfortunately it's all too easy – just changes a few words and the press release appears virtually in its original form. In this electronic age, when these press releases are sent by email or a hashtag on Twitter, all the journalist need do is a judicious copy/paste. Churning out press releases as new content is what is referred to as 'churnalism', a term popularised by Nick Davies in his book *Flat Earth News*. And for the writer of the original press release, often a highly paid professional, this is exactly what they wanted – free publicity.

However, in the words of a local journalist, 'What's the point of being here if I'm just copying and pasting something someone else has written?' She added that a press release has its useful side: the names and addresses, contact numbers and the story itself.

Press releases by their very nature are the same format although the writing style depends on the source and style of the writer. The information consists of:

- the event;
- the organisers;

- the location;
- general background information: names, ages, the gist;
- when it takes place;
- contact name and number for further information.

For anyone setting up an item from a news release for newspapers, TV or radio, the first step is to contact the organiser.

Embargoes

An embargo is occasionally put on a press release. In other words, the organising body requests that the information is released *after* a certain date or time. The recording of the Queen's Christmas Day Speech is covered by an embargo clause and, in one famous incident, the *Sun* printed the speech several days early, provoking considerable outrage. What happened? Effectively nothing but there is always irreparable damage in trust between, in this case, the Palace and the press. In future the Palace, or whoever's embargo was broken, may refuse to work with certain journalists, damaging that person's career.

Personal contacts

Don't underestimate the benefit of your own hobbies and interests when devising ideas. The old maxim exhorting you to write about what you know is good advice. Use your own background as ideas. If your Saturday job was at Tesco, it may throw up an idea for a topic. It also provides invaluable personal contacts and insight. Whenever possible, use them.

A school friend who trampolined for Leicester is a mine of helpful information. One phone call will gain leads of who to speak to at the trampolining club, the governing body and phone number, how much headroom is required (vital in studio) and suggestions of different ways to tackle the item. 'When I was trampolining, I never saw . . .' becomes the new angle. The new angle could answer the question 'What did you never see when you were trampolining?' The old boys' and girls' network is alive and well in television, radio and the press.

Working in the media hermetically seals you from reality. Friends from 'outside' keep you in touch with the world. A simple chat in the pub can produce ideas for a game show, medical documentary, an *I'm a Celebrity . . . Get Me Out of Here!* challenge or even a feeling for what Joe Public thinks about certain issues. File the ideas in your smartphone for use later or keep a handful of index cards in your wallet or handbag.

User-generated content

This is now a media essential. The *Guardian*, for instance, is developing its role by integrating UGC into its story telling and content. It is not alone.

Local journalists hold 'surgeries' at accessible locations such as libraries where residents can offer up stories. Television programmes such as *The One Show* have webpages for the public to contact them with ideas; *Surprise Surprise* advertises on television for ideas and newspapers actively promote themselves in the papers and online.

It is increasingly common to see video clips and photos recorded on mobile phones in the media and Twitter is increasingly used to share ideas.

Storyful (www.storyful.com) calls itself the 'first news agency of the social media age' and, in its own words, separates the 'news from the noise', providing UGC stories to many media companies such as Channel 4 and Reuters.

The problem with UGC and citizen journalism is that of veracity and verification, explained throughout the book.

Twitter

All journalists at the *Guardian* have professional public *Guardian* Twitter profiles. According to Joanna Geary, the *Guardian*'s Digital Development Director, there are four reasons for a journalist to use a Twitter account:

- if you have solid connections with people, for instance some of your readers or other contacts, they may tip you off on something. Useful for news gathering and exclusives;
- as an alert system – trending, community and following especially in breaking news and news gathering;
- appealing to an audience to confirm a rumour – a way of verifying that a story is true;
- using advanced search techniques to identify something you are interested in.

She has a caveat, however. It is no good blanket tweeting everyone with bold questions, etc. You must have soft skills, small talk and introductions or you won't get anywhere.

All media professionals follow contacts appertaining to their own speciality. For instance, political journalists follow MPs who publish their own news on Twitter. Others keep in touch with the police, fire brigade and hospital tweets. They all use Facebook Follow.

Hospitals, police, fire brigade, armed services, local councils, etc.

These organisations routinely use press statements to release information to the media. By their very nature, they are the lifeblood of the daily news and are contactable via their press office, public relations departments and Twitter. Contact details are on their websites.

Unless you are working on the news itself, it is unlikely that a general researcher would use these services to initiate ideas unless you develop an interesting idea from an unusual press release.

A local reporter pointed out to me that, when contacting a police press department to find out about a crime, you must have the date and time otherwise the press office has too much data and too many incidents and will fob you off. The police have their own Twitter account.

A more junior police officer might talk to you when the press officer won't but take care. There are more implications than you just losing your contact if s/he gets into trouble. There have been many recent cases when police officers have been prosecuted for selling stories to the press. You could compromise a court case, leading to contempt of court whereby both of you end up in prison – with your name in the paper for the wrong reasons. See Chapter 10.

Many local journalists phone the fire brigade every day for incidents in their area.

The armed forces are often more than willing to work with high-profile light entertainment (LE) programmes and newspapers and regard media involvement as positive public relations and self-promotion. Any idea involving the army, navy or air force is well worth exploring. What helps is that, once they have agreed to co-operate, everything works like clockwork with guaranteed professionalism. However, at the time of writing, the government was dramatically reducing the armed forces and, with their commitment abroad, it is highly unlikely that they will have the capacity to work with the media in anything but the most basic of items – the changing of the guard and hospital recuperation spring to mind.

One of the many jobs a local journalist does is attend council meetings. Planning meetings often involve residents opposing plans, thus providing an opportunity for newspaper stories. Local councillors frequently contact journalists via their Twitter accounts.

Treatments

A treatment is how an item is tackled. Take the closing of a common cold centre. For the national news, its treatment is a serious interview with an eminent professor and the Minister of Health. A regional newspaper might tackle the angle of job losses and interview employees and the local MP. A documentary would focus on the scientific and medical angle of the common cold and *This Morning* might, to use a previous idea, include a light-hearted phone-in on old wives' cures. The same story but different audiences and different treatments in studio or location, some humorous whilst others are serious.

One of the best treatments I saw was for a children's animal programme. The item was about the bee dance where bees waggle their bottoms to indicate to other bees where to find the pollen. This could have been tedious – narration over stock-shots of bees and flowers. Instead, it was a musical montage with two presenters dressed in dirty macs greeting each other in a large meadow. Removing their coats to music, they revealed dinner jacket and tails and waltzed 1930s style through the flowers accompanied only by sound effects and comic book bubble box captions. Brilliant.

Location or studio

It's no good suggesting taking someone to see an acre of rainforest in Belize if the programme is studio based. I once worked on a wish fulfilment programme with a minimal budget where all wishes had to be fulfilled in studio. Without notifying them of this, the public were asked to send in ideas. Most were greedy and uninspiring, along the lines of 'I want to travel first class on the Orient Express' (so do I) and did not meet the requirements. There was no second series.

This doesn't mean that a location idea can't be adapted for a studio although, unless the treatment is brilliant, it can fall flat on its face.

I fell into the trap in my first researcher's job. 'Let's have,' I said enthusiastically, 'indoor fireworks in studio.' Fortunately, I had enough sense to test the idea on camera beforehand. There we were, the producer/director, the head of cameras and the TV company safety officer standing round as a chap from the firework company duly brought out some worryingly small fireworks from a worryingly small suitcase. Three minutes later, the politest phrase I heard was 'damp squibs' which is why you rarely see indoor fireworks on television although you will see firework effects on shows such as *The X Factor*. They are different. The River

Thames Millennium Wall of Fire in London had the same effect as my fireworks.

In other words, ideas and their treatment must be appropriate to the programme format but they must also be effective, innovative, imaginative, exciting and visual – pretty close to those four indispensable Is!

Further reading

Boyd, Andrew, Stewart, Peter and Alexander, Ray, *Broadcast Journalism: Techniques of Radio and Television News*, 6th edn, Focal Press, 2008

Chater, Kathy, *Production Research: An Introduction* (Media Manuals), Focal Press, 2001. Kindle edition, 2012

Davies, Nick, *Flat Earth News*, Vintage, 2009

Randall, David, *The Universal Journalist*, 4th edn, Pluto Press, 2011

Websites

BBC College of Journalism: www.bbc.co.uk/academy/journalism

BBC College of Production: www.bbc.co.uk/academy/production

Channel 4 Producers Handbook: www.channel4.com/producers-handbook

Facebook and Facebook Follow: www.facebook.com

Sport England, the governing body for all sport: www.sportengland.org

Storyful, news agency for social media: www.storyful.com

Twitter: www.twitter.com

3
General research

Media research is nothing like academic research unless a researcher is hired for their specific expertise on, say, archaeology. Fifteen or 20 years ago, a huge amount of media research took place over the telephone; now the majority is electronically based, via the email and the internet, for example. The phone is still enormously important especially since mobiles have taken over the world. An essential element is 'getting into the field' although many researchers never leave their desk. As for books, there is often little *book* reading although reference to source material, directories and other written sources is essential.

Primary research

First-hand research is the original source: locating an eye-witness for the journalist, speaking to the expert on the phone, going on a recce to find a location or where the action is taking place – all this is primary research and doing everything from scratch is the media researcher's bread and butter.

Secondary research

This is 'second-hand' source material such as old newspaper and magazine reports, and reading around the subject on the internet or in books.

Both primary and secondary research have a role to play. However, in secondary research, someone else has done the original spadework and the secondary resources may include mistakes and personal opinions. Not everything you read in the newspapers or see on television is true! Whenever possible, secondary research should be verified – and verified several times.

Starting your research

Finding the first lead is the hardest part, especially if the topic is something you know nothing about. One of the challenges of working in the media is its very uncertainty; researchers and journalists often work in areas where they have no background whatsoever. However, due to short-term contracts and factual programme producers demanding a researcher with a demonstrable background in the subject, this is becoming increasingly rare. Employing uninformed people for the job may initially appear unprofessional but researchers and journalists are highly educated graduates and, for a magazine or current affairs programme, it is impossible to employ someone with an expertise in everything. Specialisation, yes, omniscience, no. I have worked on fly-fishing stories, scrap metal dealing, pig washing, Swedish refuse collection, deep sea survival et al. – none of which I knew anything about until I made the programme. I am no expert on any of them but know considerably more than I did – even if I'd rather not.

Because of time constraints, most preliminary research nowadays takes place over the phone or on the internet and occasionally *all* research is done by phone. It is unfortunate but meeting people prior to recording is a luxury nowadays. *The Jeremy Kyle Show* advertises a helpline number at the end of each show manned by a researcher. The potential contributors phone up and are interviewed by the researcher prior to going to the studio. All the information is taken down and 'used as evidence' during the show. Sometimes, the first time the production staff see the contributors is when they arrive in studio.

Finding the first lead is a matter of luck, judgement, experience and knowing where to start. Finding someone to talk to in the first place directs you elsewhere, each lead suggests further invaluable information. See Chapter 4. All names, leads, contact numbers and email addresses should be noted down.

Note taking

Good note-taking skills are essential if only to remember everything that has been said. The verification of quotations, facts and information is *crucial*, especially as it could end up being evidence in a case of law.

There are different ways of keeping the notes; the least useful is scraps of paper or loose leaves which can get out of order at best and lost at worst. Journalists use notebooks. Many researchers still use large, hardback A4 margined and lined notebooks. They are an adjunct to the contacts book and a useful place to jot down names and phone numbers before transferring them into the contacts book. Comments, recce notes and general research can be written here and it is harder to mislay a hardback A4 book.

Many journalist training courses teach a form of shorthand, usually Teeline. There is a debate over whether or not shorthand is important in today's digital world where one can record interviews on various digital devices. The National Council for the Training of Journalists (www.nctj.com – see the journalism qualification page) still advocates the use of shorthand because, as I know well, it is hard to whizz backwards and forwards through an electronic device to find the relevant information or quotation and it is much easier to scan your notes – written in shorthand or, in my case, appalling handwriting. The police, by the way, are changing to a digital record which can ostensibly be used in court.

Whichever form of note taking you subscribe to, the key point is *accuracy*. Just as a policeman's notes are crucial, so may your notes be. Many a job or a reputation (more important?) has been lost because of inaccuracy.

The contacts book

This is the essential tool in any creative's bag. Effectively, it is a list of all the contacts you have made or 'borrowed' from someone else.

In this electronic age, there are lots of ways of keeping names, addresses, phone numbers and email addresses. Journalists often still prefer the paper address book. I keep mine in a large A4-sized address book, hardback and *very* thick.

Those with an electronic bent may prefer an electronic device: palm-top, Blackberry, iPad, etc. One radio producer I spoke to saves his contacts on cloud on his Mac laptop but his contacts are duplicated on phone and iPad. Others use Outlook or a similar database.

Very few researchers or reporters photocopy their contacts book. However, a contacts book is so important that I have never heard of anyone losing it. Media people nowadays are more security conscious than MI6 and do not leave their laptops at Paddington station!

Some contacts are so sensitive that they should never be disclosed. After working a few years in the industry, you'll have confidential numbers which cannot be bandied around. It is not merely a matter of security but the wider issue of privacy. Because of the Data Protection Act, personnel departments can't reveal phone numbers and nor should reporters or researchers. If you are worried that your electronic system is insecure, even with a password, use a paper-based system for the really sensitive contacts – but don't lose the book.

Whichever system you use, record all names, phone numbers and email addresses in the contacts book even if you don't use them or consider them useful for the future. You may not phone them today but it's surprising how often you want them later. The paper system is easier to keep up to date as it merely involves jotting down names whilst holding the phone in the other hand. Store:

- home phone numbers;
- mobile numbers;
- work numbers (especially direct lines);
- email addresses.

It can be helpful to note addresses as well, but as speed of contact is crucial, phone numbers are more useful.

- Every time you get a lead, write in the name and number.
- Don't forget to include what people do, e.g. clog dancer, stamp designer, astronomer, expert on molecular chemistry, MP for Sunderland.

A double-entry system is invaluable; list the clog dancer under 'clog' as well as under the surname. When filming or reporting in Lowestoft, enter useful names under L for Lowestoft and T for Tourist Information, P for Police and so on. This sounds simplistic and doubles the work but finding someone or something quickly is essential. Names are quickly forgotten under tight deadlines and fast-changing projects but 'he lived in Lowestoft' or 'he was a clog dancer' won't.

Media job advertisements often stipulate a 'good contacts book'. Not only does the contacts book follow your career, making life easier as researcher, producer, journalist or editor, but it also gets you the job.

On *Today*, Radio 4's flagship, and other news and current affairs programmes, the researchers, producers and journalists keep politicians' and Cabinet ministers' home and mobile phone numbers together with experts such as academics, businessmen and government press officers.

Light entertainment producers and researchers hold celebrities' phone numbers and those of agents and record companies' A & R (artists and repertoire) representatives. Those working on radio music programmes, the same. Eccentrics and experts are also useful. Generalists collect an eclectic mix because they never know what they will work on next.

The contact book of a journalist depends on their specialism. Obviously, one working in sport holds contacts for managers, sports' clubs, athletes and sporting bodies whereas a local reporter will have completely different numbers in their books.

And how are these numbers found?

- Time and experience.
- Producers, researchers, journalists and editors who have worked in similar fields.

- Agents and managers (who rarely give them out for the same reason as personnel departments).
- Contributors themselves. After all, you may need to phone them to explain changes of plan and so forth.
- The phone book/internet.

You will rarely find any but the most obvious phone numbers on the internet. The Capital Radio phone number on the internet is its public phone – there is also an ex-directory one. Direct line numbers require additional digging. Many people, especially celebrities, are cagey about revealing personal numbers. The reason is obvious; to protect their privacy. Some unscrupulous journalists hound them for stories and all celebrities live in fear of being stalked. No wonder; presenter Jill Dando was shot dead in 1999 and in November 2012, a stalker threatened to castrate Justin Bieber.

Telephone numbers

There is always the phone book – but which one? BT no longer has the monopoly on phone services and not everyone has a landline nowadays so if the person you want is not on BT, this is a problem. BT's paper-based *Phone Book* is organised into three sections: a classified directory at the front, business listings in the middle and residential numbers at the end. Companies must have a BT line to be listed here so if they don't, they won't be in the book. The larger display ads in the book cost a little more to the listed company. Because of cost considerations, most firms are only issued with one *local* phone directory but a central library holds them all – although who knows for how much longer.

The paper version of *The Phone Book* has its uses of course, but in this digital age, most people search for phone numbers via Directory Enquiries on the phone itself or the internet.

118 telephone directory services are heavily advertised. You know them: 118118, 118500 and 118404 are obvious examples. These are premium services and extremely expensive. At the time of writing, 118118 was 79p per call on a landline plus £1.79 per minute with a minimum 60 second charge. For 118500 owned by BT, calls at the time of writing were 62p per call plus £1.99 per minute from a BT landline. Mobile phone charges for both companies may be dearer. Justifiably, production companies and newspaper offices dislike their employees using this service as it escalates the bills. Mobile phone companies have their own directory enquiries, but again, these are expensive and not always efficient. Also, why should you (unless you have a company mobile) pay to find a phone number for business reasons?

The internet has its own directory enquiry systems, sites like www.bt.co.uk, www.bt118500.com, www.192.com, www.118.com, www.yell.com and others. For members of the general public these services are useful and often free. Directory enquiry websites require a town as they cannot do a global search. If you haven't a clue where the person or company you are seeking is based, this is a major problem although there are ways around it. See below.

No directory enquiry service will give out ex-directory numbers and you won't get numbers from rival phone companies.

Electoral registers

More useful are the websites which use the electoral register as the basis of their database.

All citizens of the UK over 18 are legally obliged to register themselves on the electoral register every year in order to vote in elections. The maximum fine for not doing so is currently £1000 although prosecutions are rare. The electoral registers are public documents compiled by local authorities and available for perusal in local libraries and town halls. They are organised in constituencies on a street-by-street, house-by-house basis. They are paper based and published locally so there is no centralised database. Anyone wishing to view the electoral register may find that they are supervised whilst they do so. By law, only the current year's register can be inspected and photocopies cannot be made. This makes it difficult to conduct, say, a search for someone living in Exeter when you are based in Leeds. It is time consuming and frustrating running one's eye over a list of streets in the hope of spotting the relevant name and the chances are high that, even if the name is there, it will be missed.

Fortunately, the internet has made an electoral search easier but with some constraints. Examples of online websites are www.192.com and www.people tracer.co.uk. Some genealogical websites such as www.ancestry.co.uk and www.findmypast.co.uk also have electoral registers online, generally at an extra cost. This service may throw up all relevant (and similar) names in your search. For common surnames, you will need a location or the database has too many results and won't work. A potential snag is that this system works on official names – in other words what is listed on the electoral register. Not everyone is known by their first name and nicknames are, obviously, not listed. This doesn't help if people work under a pseudonym, for instance, a stage name or maiden name.

www.192.com is the most well known and, like all of these, is a subscription service which means that, although you might find the name, unless you pay, the information is unavailable. One of the advantages of electoral role databases is that a search for an uncommon surname may throw up all the people in the country with that surname and a guide to their age range. However, to access the actual information itself, you pay.

The Representation of the People Act 2000 made provision for an *edited register*, where people who want anonymity can opt out of their name being published. The electoral register is sold commercially to marketing companies, for instance, and this Act ensures that only the edited register can be used by them – just like ex-directory in the phone book. Anyone who has opted out will be more difficult to find. The paper-based version viewed in the town hall is the *full* register.

The other major drawback of the electoral register is the fact that it is out of date as soon as someone moves house. The main registration period for the electoral register is between August and October of any given year. A *rolling registration* system means that it is now possible to add a name to an electoral register at other times of the year. Unfortunately, not everyone does this and the information in www.192.com, etc. will only show the address that is officially on the electoral register.

Yellow Pages and local business directories

All internet directory-based companies mentioned previously have commercial company databases as well. Because businesses subscribe to these, such internet directories are free to use for commercial and business companies. Hard copies are, of course, delivered to the doorstep and it is often easier to use these than online versions although, of course, being printed, the details are more likely to be out of date than those listed online. These directories are invaluable for local business numbers rather than London head offices and the local firms may be more willing to help you than the head office. The most well known of these directories are *Thomson Local, Yellow Pages* and, of course, the first section of *The Phone Book*.

Depending on which directory is used, another advantage is the first few pages where maps, lists of local government offices and post offices can be found.

Using the telephone

In the age of the mobile phone and Blackberry, people spend hours texting their friends although to actually use the phone to *find* information or to *speak* to an expert initially makes them twitchy. They'd rather spend ages seeking an anonymous webpage which, once located, doesn't reveal the required information.

There's no replacement for speaking to real people. It irons out ambiguities and gets immediate specific answers. If not, at least you can ask the person at the other end to suggest another contact and give you their number.

If phone phobia is the result of being unsure what to ask, jot down the questions first in note form to prevent the 'parrot fashion' approach that sounds pompous and false. A good phone manner and the ability to prise out answers come with experience. Established journalists are expert at this and often get people to admit something over the phone that, in the cold light of day, they wish they hadn't. It is much easier to get a scoop or a confession over the phone or face-to-face than any other way. Emails give the person time to consider their reply, think up a spin, evade the question or delete the email entirely.

In my experience, I have found that the public believe who you say you are and take you on trust if you phone them first. Paradoxically, turning up on spec has less credibility even when armed with a press pass or ID card. Isn't it annoying when someone ignores you to answer a ringing phone? Even when the number is displayed and the recipient can tell who is phoning, they take the call and ignore you! Yet *anyone* can claim *anything* over the phone.

In December 2012, 2Day FM radio presenters Mel Greig and Michael Christian phoned the King Edward VII Hospital in London from Australia pretending to be the Queen and Prince Charles concerned about the Duchess of Cambridge's pregnancy. They got through to the ward and spoke to a nurse. The result, as you are aware, was that the nurse who originally took the call and put it through to the ward, Jacintha Saldanha, later committed suicide. Yes, an extreme example but it happens. In 1998, Steve Penk, live on Capital Radio, phoned Tony Blair in Downing Street pretending to be William Hague, the then leader of the Conservative Party. It was some minutes before Tony Blair realised. According to Steve Penk in an article in the *Guardian* in February 2007, it may be harder to pretend to be someone famous on the telephone nowadays and there is a huge question about the ethics (especially following Saldanha's suicide) but the phone is still very effective.

Incidentally, impersonating someone is fraud.

However, in the age of emails, the person on the other end of the phone often wants the questions written down and emailed to them. Be prepared for there to be no answer – it is not unusual for a busy person to get over 300 emails a day and it is easy to delete them. If there is no reply after a few days, what do you do? Phone them, of course.

Facetime on smartphones uses wi-fi and therefore is a free-to-use video-call although, of course, both callers need to have a smartphone. The South Manchester Messenger Group, at the time of writing, used GChat for conferencing between the different newspapers and it may be that you find this or other instant talk systems useful.

The more time spent on the phone, the easier and more efficient you are. Boringly, practice does make perfect.

Hacking

Much has been written in the press about hacking after the *Sun* and *News of the World* came to prominence with several prominent media professionals and former police officers losing their jobs and being prosecuted. The *News of the World* closed. There is not enough space in this book to discuss the ethics of hacking but take precautions against having your digital systems hacked. Use antivirus software and reputable operating systems and, of course, don't attempt to hack into anyone else's system. Keep your contacts book safe. (See Chapter 10.)

Skype

Skype is a wonderful Estonian invention, a technology via which you can see and hear someone at the other end of a computer anywhere in the world in real time and for free. Interviewing and talking to people via Skype becomes more common by the day. There *are* disadvantages, time zones being one. Both Skypers have to be on the computer at the same time which involves prior arrangement if one correspondent is, say, nine hours ahead or behind the other one. Finding someone's Skype address is another issue, especially for common-place names.

It is common for Skype audio tracks to be used in broadcasting, especially radio; Radio 1, for instance, uses Skype for online interviews as do some BBC local radio stations. The audio matches ISDN. Obviously, this opens up a debate about how far radio is becoming visualised not just with Skype but with studio webcam content transmitted on the internet.

The personal approach

Journalists work in the community. TV and radio researchers occasionally need to go into the field. During the 1980s miners' strike, no-one would talk to me over the telephone, let alone agree to be filmed. I drove 200 miles north to the picket lines to find someone. Depending on how the rest of the media has treated them, seeing you in person may make them more amenable. Whilst researching the second edition of this book, I found that some people wouldn't answer emails or answerphone messages. Again, I physically went to get an appointment. It worked.

Always be professional and behave politely, sympathetically and impartially to your contacts. A bit of humour helps. On many occasions, the first contact with a journalist or researcher occurs at times of serious stress and trauma. Yours might be the friendly face in a bewildering world. It is not uncommon for a television or radio researcher to become close friends with their contacts. For journalists, the relationship is different. In all cases, though, don't forget that people may refuse to be filmed or interviewed because of previous treatment received at the hands of unscrupulous media professionals or because they are too upset. There's a fine line between pushing it too far and unethical intrusion. All regulatory bodies such as the NUJ, BBC, Ofcom, *Guardian* Editorial Code and Channel 4 have rulings about this and it is touched upon many times in this book.

Interviewing skills over the phone and face-to-face

This section is purely concerned with how to glean information for research purposes, not how to conduct an interview for the newspaper, television or radio.

Before you speak to anyone, you need to be sure what you want to achieve. Picking up the phone and pausing when you get through gives the wrong impression, especially if the person at the other end of the phone is very busy. Even more so if they are high-powered. Jot down a list of key words and questions beforehand and if, during the course of the conversation, other things spring to mind, jot them down to ask later. Two questions at once, in other words multiple questions, are difficult to answer.

Remember:

- be courteous;
- use the familiar questions: Who? What? Where? When? Why? Which? and How?
- what do you *need* to know?
- what does the producer/editor/crew *need* to know?
- what does the reader/viewer/listener *want* to know?
- listen; don't do all the talking;
- if they answer your next question before you ask, don't ask it; merely confirm the gist;

- don't get bogged down taking notes whilst you are talking; brief notes should suffice;
- if you don't understand, say so; if you want clarification, repeat what they have said in your own words and check they agree;
- confirm essential facts; get them to spell names and addresses;
- is there anyone else they recommend you to talk to? Can they give you a contact number?
- thank them for their time and information;
- write up the notes immediately.

Email

Remember, email is not just a communication system between friends. It is also used to contact MPs, official bodies, agents and chairmen of international conglomerates – although the chance of you having direct email contact is low as an assistant or secretary may intercept the message. In a word, many emails must be formal. It's no good emailing the Prime Minister with 'Hi, how's it going, mate?' and expecting him to subsequently appear on a TV programme.

As a rule of thumb, compose the email as if it were a formal letter. Be brief and to the point and use bullet points if necessary.

Emails to you may well specify conditions such as forbidden topics. Emails may come from someone other than the person you initially contacted so don't delete them indiscriminately; that unknown name may be the answer to your initial request. Periodically check your junk mail. I've found crucial emails hidden away there months after I've forgotten about them.

Print up any important email messages for reference. File email addresses in your contact book.

Other research sources

Clippings services/media monitoring

In-house libraries of large media companies, for instance the BBC, used to run a clippings (sometimes called 'cuttings') service. Each day, the library staff searched the newspapers and magazines, cutting out articles on current issues, celebrities and businessmen, stamped them with the date and title of the newspaper and filed them in folders. Any company employee could theoretically borrow the files although there may be an in-house charge for the service. This service, however, is disappearing because of the internet. The downside is the difficulty of accessing information prior to the World Wide Web.

Media monitoring, however, is still in existence and there are agencies which routinely monitor media output for public relations (PR) companies and other agencies. The data are generally supplied electronically. From 1 April 2009, all companies receiving clippings from magazines, newspapers and journals from agencies via hard copy or digital clips must be licensed by the Copyright Licensing Agency (CLA) because of copyright. It is also likely that they need a licence from the Newspaper Licensing Association (NLA).

The NLA lists all newspapers associated with them (plus links) as well as access to newspaper content. A clipsearch service allows searches of over 140 newspapers and access to foreign newspapers from the year 2006. As always, many of the NLA services are via subscription.

Media monitoring services also exist in America and the North American Conference of Press Clipping Services (NACPCS) has a list of media monitors in the US who may be useful for foreign sources although, as usual, it is not free.

Newspapers

It used to be that all newspaper offices held back-copies where anyone could riffle through them. No longer. Should your research require you to view archive newspapers themselves, certain libraries hold microfilm or microfiche copies of newspapers such as *The Times*, the *Guardian* and local newspapers such as the *Manchester Evening News*. You can usually drop in and literally wind your way through them although to ensure access to a reader when you want it, it is better to book one in advance. This is all well and good if you want a general view of what Newport Pagnell, for instance, was like in 1872 but, as there are rarely indexes, it doesn't help you find a specific person or event unless you know the actual date concerned.

Local newspapers are generally found locally (no-one expects copies of *Northampton Chronicle and Echo* in Carlisle). Many libraries enable you to photocopy the newspaper from the microfilm reader for a small charge. There are, of course, copyright issues in photocopying newspapers but it is permissible for *individual* research.

National newspapers are increasingly digitised and accessible online, e.g. *The Times* which is subscription only. If your production office or newspaper does not subscribe to this resource, libraries do and *The Times* online can be accessed for free at most libraries.

The British Newspaper Archive is a joint venture between the British Library and brightsolid Online Technology to digitise up to 40 million newspaper pages over the next ten years. It will mean that names and events can be searched for online rather than wading through issues. Already online, it is a subscription service ostensibly geared towards genealogists and family history researchers.

The famous British Library newspaper archive, previously held in Colindale, north London, was moved to Boston Spa, near Wetherby, West Yorkshire, between November 2013 and 2014. Many novelists mourned its move because it was possible hitherto to flick through original newspapers.

For the new arrangements, see the British Library entry below.

LexisLibrary (formerly LexisNexis) is a well-known online legal database with a comprehensive collection of cases and documents. However, it also has access to most national and local newspapers including *The Times, The Sunday Times, The Times Educational Supplement* and *The Times Higher Education Supplement.* One documentary producer I spoke to when researching this new edition praised LexisNexis above all other sources. Again, it is a subscription service. Many universities are linked to the LexisLibrary UK but you need to be a current student or staff member to use it.

A useful source for those working in the BBC is the Genome Project, a scheme in which the *Radio Times*, first published in September 1923, has been digitised and catalogued so that the entire BBC history can be accessed through the internal network, Gateway. At the time of writing, features and longer-length articles were not available. It is hoped that the project will eventually be available to the general public but whether or not all the material will be depends on copyright restrictions. It will be a tremendous resource for social history and programme information but using it in media terms will involve negotiating fees with the BBC.

Books

Books are not generally the first port of call for anyone working in the media. Often there isn't time before transmission or publication to read them. However, documentaries and heavy-weight programmes with a longer pre-production schedule or an in-depth newspaper feature may require substantial background information although with the decreasing pre-production time involved nowadays, there still may not be enough time for any more than a superficial internet search.

Libraries are under considerable budgetary restraint nowadays with contracting opening hours. Up-to-date specialist reference books are, on the whole, more likely to be located in larger branches of high street bookshops than in the library. An internet search and express delivery might be the answer. Check with the producer or editor if they will justify the expense.

If you are working on a chat show, you might want a copy of the celebrity's biography or autobiography for research purposes. Often their management company will supply a free copy, especially if the reason the celebrity is on your show is to promote the book in the first place. Remember that the information in the book is a glossy version of the celebrity's life . . . an unauthorised biography contains the salacious in order to sell it!

Forty-two thousand books can be found online on Project Gutenberg, the first producer of free e-books. The books available are those for which the copyright has expired in the USA and include favourites such as *Little Women, Pride and Prejudice, Gulliver's Travels* and *A Tale of Two Cities*. Although it is useful for a free version of such classics, whether it is useful for media research depends on what you need. It is worth checking if the classic you want is there. There are other Project Gutenbergs around the world, e.g. Australia.

Google Books acts in a similar way to Amazon or Waterstones insofar as there is a search bar for topics but it goes a little further. You can type in a name or a subject and a list of books will be produced. For instance, I typed in Hannen Swaffer, a famous political journalist in the 1920s to 1950s, to find a couple of books about him plus highlighted extracts. If the book is out of copyright or in the public domain, you may be able to see the entire text or download a copy as a PDF file. It is also possible to locate a copy of the book. You will need to create a free account to receive more information than the bare minimum.

Another archive which may be useful is www.archive.org. This is a digital library of internet sites providing free access to researchers, historians and the like and includes, amongst others, e-books, videos, music and a link to the Gutenberg project.

There are, however, some indispensable books for people working in the media. *Whitaker's Almanack* is arguably the most useful. Published annually, it includes facts and statistics about the infrastructure of the UK plus information about the world hard to find under one cover anywhere else. Just a snapshot of the entries shows how essential this directory is:

- calendar for the year and forthcoming events;
- the Royal Family: their private secretaries, the kings and queens;
- the peerage with lists;
- Parliament: the MPs, election facts and figures and by-election results;
- government: local, regional and public bodies;
- European Parliament;
- law courts and offices: ombudsman services, police and prisons;
- defence: salaries and pensions;
- education;
- health;

- countries of the world with facts and statistics about them;
- astronomy;
- important events of the previous year.

Libraries

Some larger newspaper offices may have their own in-house libraries with directories, encyclopaedias and dictionaries kept for general reference although, because of the space required and the internet, they are becoming increasingly rare.

The commercial and reference sections of the local library are a helpful resource although opening times are increasingly restricted. Librarians will do research for you over the telephone and this is a free service but remember, they have a responsibility towards the general public as well.

Books and directories held in the reference sections of local libraries cannot be loaned out.

The useful thing about libraries is that they are a wonderful repository of older books and standard reference texts. If the timescale permits, the interlibrary loan system can order up books for you from anywhere in the country. It might take several weeks for some books to come from the other end of the country but I have had books arrive within days. Books can be renewed online as well as over the phone but fines are incurred for books returned late.

Archives

For profound and specialised research, archaeological or historical documentaries, etc., you may wish to delve into archives. Family history programmes such as *Who Do You Think You Are?* are an example although the production team uses specialist genealogists on the programme. Start with the local university or main library. Local record offices may be useful, including the Public Record Office at Kew or, as a last resort, the British Library at St Pancras.

Forums

Self-help forums are useful for people with similar issues or problems. Although they may not give you a creditworthy answer (much of the material is opinion), they may lead to somebody who can.

The British Library

The British Library is an unsurpassed, world-renowned depository for over 150 million items and three million are added every year. Under the Legal Deposit scheme (in English law since 1662), a copy of all UK print publications, books, newspapers, magazines, etc. must be given to the British Library and five other libraries should they request it. It also holds over 260,000 journal titles, eight million stamps, 310,000 manuscript volumes and over four million maps. There is a sound archive and newspaper archive as mentioned above.

The collection is housed in two locations: the main repository at St Pancras, London, and Boston Spa near Wetherby, West Yorkshire. The famed newspaper library was moved from Colindale, north London, to Boston Spa to preserve over 750 million pages of local, regional and national papers and periodicals where they will be housed in purpose-built storage. A dedicated newspaper reading room at St Pancras will permit digital and microfilm access. If there is no digital copy, originals can be transported from Boston Spa to St Pancras within 48 hours if the original is in a good enough condition to travel.

There is no browsing of books in the British Library. This is a research facility and not for public reference; the material is far too precious and, in many cases, fragile. Anyone wishing to research here must prove that no other library can supply the required information.

In order to access the material, it is necessary to have a reader's pass organised through the Reader Registration Office. It is also necessary to check that the resource required is in the library by referring to the online catalogue. It takes ten days to issue a pass. It is possible to pre-register online but lost, stolen or expired passes must be renewed in person at the Reader Registration Office. Identification documents and proof of address must be presented in person even if you have pre-registered. You will still have to discuss your reasons for using the British Library so there is no guarantee that a pass will be issued. If it is, it is valid for between one month and three years.

For security and preservation reasons, most of the library's collection is housed in closed access storage and must be ordered up for viewing. This takes an hour or so with a deadline of 4pm for viewing the same day. The majority of the collection is in St Pancras but, for material stored in West Yorkshire, expect to wait up to one working day (48 hours for original newspapers) before the material is available. Pencils only are allowed in the rare books and manuscripts reading rooms, and rare and fragile material is viewed at desks close to a staffed enquiry point.

The internet

A huge number of sources and resources have become accessible simply because of the World Wide Web. Too much, perhaps. It is increasingly difficult to wade your way through the internet to find what you're looking for.

However useful a research tool, the internet is not a be all and end all and there are several pitfalls. The most common assumption is believing that everything on the internet is copyright free and accurate. Nothing is further from the truth.

Anyone can have a webpage on the internet, a Facebook page, a Twitter account, a blog which can be filled with whatever the author fancies. The content can be their opinion, not fact based at all. Also, unless the author took the photos themselves (in which case they own the copyright together with, for instance, Facebook), drew or owns the rights to the pictures or the music, they may not have permission to use them.

The copyright issues of pictures, photos and music are of no importance if you are merely seeking information, but the *accuracy* of that information is. A company will not publish how awful an employer they are, how they cheat their customers or pay no tax to Inland Revenue – although when reading their company accounts, this may become apparent.

Official sites are likely to be reliable but even these have their own agendas, their own spin on events and what they want you to be aware of. These sites do, however, offer contact addresses and phone numbers and may link to other sources and sites. It is also more likely that official sites have permission to publish copyright material but just because *they* do, it doesn't mean you can too. As for accuracy, although official sites should (?) get it right, the lies about the use of weapons of mass destruction in the lead-up to the Iraq invasion in 2003 challenge this. And then, of course, there is WikiLeaks.

In June 2013, whistle-blower Edward Snowden exposed the extent of US and UK security services' monitoring of search engines such as Google and Yahoo. Since then, the use of search engines such as DuckDuckGo, Startpage and Ixquick has increased. The implications of online surveillance and tracking have yet to be revealed but, whatever topics being researched, remember *all* searches can be tracked unless on search engines such as DuckDuckGo.

Specialist companies exist to manipulate entries to the top of a search engine page or to limit damage by putting negative information on, for example, page 137 so no-one finds it.

No-one knows how many pages there are on the internet although it runs into billions. It is tempting to browse through all the listings, printing off at random huge numbers of pages which *may* be relevant and handing them to your producer or editor. This is not helpful. Nor is it helpful to email a huge number of links to sites. One short, sweet and to the point link is good. A few high-lighted notes gathered from various websites with the relevant links next to them for verification are useful. As the saying goes, less is more.

When asked for specific information, find that and nothing else. Extraneous information is irrelevant and extremely irritating, especially when you are always up against a deadline. Act as editor. Don't expect the presenter, writer, producer or news editor to waste their precious time doing your job. In the end, it is your job that goes.

Verification of internet sources

The suffixes to web addresses are a useful hint to the source of the website and their likely accuracy. The country domain, e.g. uk, is at the end of the URL (uniform resource locator). Unfortunately, although the following are the official classifications, it is by and large easy to purchase any domain at all. Proceed with caution . . .

There are others but the main ones are as follows.

- .ac – academic. A university or college. The information should be accurate and reliable as an academic source depending on the academic status of the author. Student articles are less trustworthy. The information is only as accurate as perceived knowledge at the time, e.g. the flat earth debate . . .
- .co – anyone can register a .co name. Although respectable companies use this domain, be aware that anyone else can too. The more prominent a company, the safer the site.
- .com – commercial. Officially a commercial company but, like .co, can be purchased by anyone. Accredited institutions are more reliable than oddbod.com.
- .edu – education. An educational institution in the USA – university or other level. Student work is not necessarily trustworthy.
- .gov – government. A government-maintained website. The information comes direct from the government or local authority so is officially endorsed. Statistics should be relatively safe but there may be political bias. Beware dictator-led countries and those with no free press.
- .mod – military, e.g. the army and navy.
- .org – organisation. Usually non-commercial organisations such as chari-ties and trade unions but not always. Can be accredited to any organisa-tion in the world including highly political groups with an agenda. Trustworthiness depends on their bias.

- .net – network infrastructure. Internet companies.
- .sch – school. Content may be from the school or the pupils. The accuracy of children's work is questionable.

Credibility checklist

There is no regulatory body checking the accuracy of information on the internet.

- Check the URLs as above.
- Is there an email, contact address and contact name?
- Has the webpage been updated regularly? If not, the information may be outdated.
- Online journals and magazines: the more well known and reputable, the more reliable and credible. Good academic journals have bibliographies and citations.
- Can you check the information another way, e.g. via links and citations?
- Check the byline or author. If they are accredited academics or journalists they will be more reliable than 'unnamed' writing from home.
- Non-profit organisations (charities, the BBC) may be more reliable than for-profit organisations – with caveats, of course.
- Non-internet sources (e.g. text books) may be more reliable than the internet.

Public domain

Anything no longer under the term of copyright is deemed to be in the public domain, for instance, Shakespeare's plays. However, the typeface, layouts and notes of the Penguin (or any other published edition) version of *Hamlet* are still governed by copyright. Quoting from Shakespeare or Dickens, for instance, is fine; both have been dead for well over 70 years!

Example of research methods

A researcher is often required to find statistics along the lines of 'What is the percentage of left handers in the UK?' or 'How many women have eating disorders?'.

Questions like this are, to be frank, often badly phrased and as soon as you start 'Googling', you realise there is no simple answer. Ask a question and get another one in return. Male or female? Over what age? Living in which part of the country? And so on.

Assuming you have never done anything like this, where do you start? The following are suggestions; there are plenty of other routes.

- How about official government departments? The Office of Population Censuses and Surveys (the OPCS, commonly known as the Census Office) cannot help. The OPCS covers demographic data which, because the census takes place every ten years, means its information and statistics may be up to ten years out of date. You might try the Department of Health.
- Google it. A quick search reveals studies from various academic institutions. One in 14 women has an eating disorder in pregnancy. An estimated 5% of girls in the UK have an eating disorder, etc.
- Contact academia, university statistics departments or medical institutions. These may have been thrown up by the Google search. The trick is to find the expert. Much of the information on Google might be reports from years ago. Start with the most local university and work out.
- Is there an association or charity covering your topic? An Eating Disorder Society? Check the search engines. Societies and charities often compile research statistics and are always a useful source of information. The statistics may already be on their websites.

Remember, you may need to corroborate your figures and prove their accuracy. You may even need to credit the source. Jot down all names, phone numbers and web addresses. Make notes. No-one can remember everything.

The computer will keep track of which site you have been on, but still keep a note of the main websites. Remember, the statistic you read today may be changed tomorrow after more research or further information is input onto the website. It may be expedient to print up the relevant pages and store them safely.

The more research of this nature you do, the easier it becomes as you pick up tips and shortcuts and file names in the contacts book.

Departments of state, government agencies and quangos

Finding phone numbers for these is not as easy as it used to be simply because of the amount of content on websites and the fact that the government would rather the general public downloaded information, forms, etc. than contact them direct. That's my impression of government websites nowadays. So much information on government websites makes them incredibly unwieldy.

The easiest way to get any sensible answers is to contact the Press Office. But which Press Office?

- The Prime Minister's Office (www.number10.gov.uk)
- Foreign and Commonwealth Office
- Treasury
- Home Office
- Ministry of Defence
- Business, Innovation and Skills
- Work and Pensions
- Ministry of Justice
- Education
- Communities and Local Government
- Health
- Environment, Food and Rural Affairs
- International Development
- Scotland Office
- Energy and Climate Change
- Transport
- Culture, Media and Sport
- Northern Ireland
- Wales
- Cabinet Office

The springboard for any of these offices is www.number10.gov.uk. You can follow them on Twitter, Facebook and Flickr, all of which may give you some news or ideas for your programme or newspaper. Getting hold of someone to speak to is a different matter but the phone numbers, addresses and other contacts are all on the website. When you get through, be sure to ask for direct lines! A directory such as *Whitaker's Almanack* (discussed earlier) may provide leads.

Quango is an acronym for quasi-autonomous non-governmental organisation, in other words, public service bodies run as private businesses. Examples of these include the Competition Commission, Ofcom, the Office of Fair Trading, the Arts Council, UK Sport, the BBC and English Heritage. There are dozens of them – all with their own websites.

Copyright issues

There was a lot of media coverage in 2012 on the copyright issues of Facebook and Instagram and the pressures of public opinion forcing them to change their policies. Copyright and piracy issues are dealt with elsewhere in the book but the copyright issue cannot be overstressed. Anything creative is likely to be covered by the copyright law, including music, pictures and text on the internet, in books and newspapers. Whatever the source, anything broadcast or published in newspapers *must* have the copyright status checked beforehand. See other chapters for specifics.

Accuracy

- The information found in books and newspapers is only as accurate as the work that went into it. Far be it from me to raise suspicion about secondary research, but please be aware that not everything is accurate. How many times have you read a wrongly spelt name or incorrect age in a newspaper?
- People have their own prejudices, bias and agendas and often interpret material in their own way.
- The more eminent the source, the more likely it is that the information is correct but, whenever possible and time permitting, double-check your facts.
- Wikipedia should be viewed with reservation but is a base to start from with external links, books and citations.
- Most newspapers and the BBC prefer facts to be checked and verified from three different sources.

The BBC, Ofcom, newspapers' Editors' Code of Practice and the National Union of Journalists (NUJ) all refer specifically to the importance of accuracy. If there is a problem, it is better to find out before transmission/publication or the implications can be enormous. At the very least, you will be writing, publishing or broadcasting an apology; at the worst, your company will have sanctions taken against it and you will be looking for another job.

Further reading

Beaman, Jim, *Interviewing for Radio* (Media Skills), 2nd edn, Routledge, 2011
Boyd, Andrew, Stewart, Peter and Alexander, Ray, *Broadcast Journalism: Techniques of Radio and Television News*, 6th edn, Focal Press, 2008
Brooke, Heather, *Your Right to Know: A Citizen's Guide to the Freedom of Information Act*, 2nd edn, Pluto Press, 2006
Dolowitz, David, Buckler, Steve and Sweeney, Fionnghuala, *Researching Online*, Palgrave Macmillan, 2008
Flemming, Carole, *The Radio Handbook* (Media Practice), 3rd edn, Routledge, 2009

Hanna, Mark and Dodd, Mike, *McNae's Essential Law for Journalists*, OUP, 2012

Harcup, Tony, *Journalism: Principles and Practice*, 2nd edn, Sage, 2009

Hennessy, Brendan, *Writing Feature Articles*, 4th edn, Focal Press, 2005

Hudson, Gary and Rowlands, Sarah, *The Broadcast Journalism Handbook*, Longman, 2007

McGuire, Mary, Stilborne, Linda, Hyatt, Laurel and McAdams, Melinda, *Internet Handbook for Writers, Researchers, and Journalists*, Guilford Press, 2003

McLeish, Robert, *Radio Production*, 5th edn, Focal Press, 2005

Owens, Jim and Millerson, Gerald, *Television Production*, 15th edn, Focal Press, 2012

Quinn, Frances, *Law for Journalists*, 3rd edn, Longman, 2011

Rudin, Richard and Ibbotson, Trevor, *Introduction to Journalism: Essential Techniques and Background Knowledge*, Focal Press, 2003

Singleton-Turner, Roger, *Cue and Cut: A Practical Approach to Working in Multi-Camera Studios*, Manchester University Press, 2011

Smith, Jon and Butcher, Joanne, *Essential Reporting: The NCTJ Guide for Trainee Journalists*, Sage Publications, 2007

Whitaker's Almanack, published annually by A & C Black

Websites

British Library: www.bl.uk

British Newspaper Archive: www.britishnewspaperarchive.co.uk

Channel 4 Producers Handbook: www.channel4.com/producers-handbook

Copyright Licensing Agency (CLA): www.cla.co.uk

Google Books: www.books.google.co.uk

Guardian Editorial Code: www.theguardian.com/info/guardian-editorial-code

Internet Archive: http://archive.org

The Knowledge, film, television and commercial production directory: www.the knowledgeonline.com

Mandy's Film and Television Production Directory: www.mandy.com

Newspaper Licensing Agency lists media monitoring agencies: www.nlamediaaccess.co.uk

North American Conference of Press Clipping Services lists American members: http://nacpcs.com

Pinterest: www.pinterest.com

Press Association: www.pressassociation.com

Project Gutenberg, 42,000 free books online: www.gutenberg.org

Twitter users, a guide to the law by the BBC: www.bbc.co.uk/news/magazine-20782257

Whitaker's Almanack online: http://whitakersalmanack.com

4
People

I once answered an internal phone call at nine in the morning that started with 'Adèle, have you ever been in a car crash?' and ended 'Are you free for half an hour? We're on air in ten minutes and there aren't enough people in the audience. We're desperate – come and be a bum on a seat.' Can this happen today? Probably not – someone in a tabloid newspaper would write a headline 'Television producer plays victim in own TV show!' So, you must ensure it doesn't. The media have never been under such a spotlight as they are today. And it is the journalists among you whose job is to expose the stories.

Finding people for programmes or newspaper stories is the major role in any creative's working life. News and current affairs need witnesses and experts, chat shows require celebrity guests and quiz shows, talent shows and reality shows need contestants. The current fashion for documentary series and docu-soaps, such as *The Only Way is Essex*, *Junior Doctors* and *Your Life in Their Hands*, 'cast' programmes beforehand. Lifestyle programmes and magazines need people with gardens, houses, antiques to make over or highlight – and even people to make over as in *Snog, Marry, Avoid*.

For the journalist, it is a little simpler; find someone with something pertinent to say who was there at the time or can add expert opinion. As journalists in the BBC and Sky file reports for a variety of platforms (television, radio and the internet), the quest is virtually the same. Those working in radio need to suggest stories and find contributors but in less time! A few hours are often the only given notice. At least you don't have to worry about what they look like or send a TV crew when a satellite car suffices.

The brief is simple: find someone willing to take part who won't freeze on camera or mic, has something valid to say and a personality to match. The audience doesn't even need to like them. Casting someone in the role of villain, someone for the viewer to love to hate, is as televisually important as star making. Star making, so much a consideration nowadays, is covered later in the chapter.

Locating contributors for television programmes or newspaper articles can't be done from books. However, experts write books and research papers and this is a source which, although not an immediate solution, may lead to someone who could be useful. Once you have winkled out a name, speak to them personally. The best practice (the BBC's Editorial Guidelines endorse this) is to vet potential contributors in person – production schedule permitting. For those working in newspapers, a phone contact and quotation via the phone or email is enough for inclusion in an article – but keep accurate notes of what they said by shorthand in your notebook, recorded or the email itself. The *Independent* claims (26 March 2013) that Boris Johnson was sacked from *The Times* for inventing quotations.

Some programme schedules are so tight nowadays that it is impossible to meet every contributor. Daytime chat shows such as *This Morning* and *Jeremy Kyle* are examples of such tight production schedules where it is common for researchers to book virtually everyone over the phone. *The Jerry Springer Show* followed a checklist along the lines of 'How much do you weigh? Do you have a tattoo or other disfigurement?' The viewer gets the impression that the more outlandish the contributors, the better – and the ratings confirm this. How many people watch *Jeremy Kyle* for the verbal and physical fisticuffs?

It is customary for production companies to insist that contributors sign clauses in which they confirm their status and identity. This is still no guarantee that the contributors are genuine; the most determined imposter is hard to detect but the policy goes some way to getting the researchers (and the programme) off the hook when corroborating programme credibility.

The policy is not infallible. A BBC *Everyman* programme was hoodwinked in 1999 by a *Sun* journalist answering a newspaper advertisement and masquerading as a barmaid 'addicted to love and sex'. Although an honesty clause had been signed, the programme makers independently went through a number of checks to verify her story. These included checking her mail at her flat during filming to ensure it corresponded, checking her name with *Spotlight* (the actors' directory) to ensure she wasn't an actress, talking to 'friends' to authenticate her story and asking if they could film at the pub where she worked. This she turned down in order to 'protect her job' (BBC news release, 29 June 1999). Unfortunately, even after such stringent checks, the programme was dropped prior to transmission because they discovered the 'barmaid' was a fraud.

For checking the status of business men and company directors, try DueDil at www.duedil.com which searches Companies House for free although you will have to register.

The BBC Editorial Guidelines (Section 3.4.7, Accuracy, finding contributors) says that they should be interviewed and checked by more than one member of the production team, amongst other checks including documentary evidence that they are who they say they are, and that they declare any criminal convictions or political affiliation. Contributors may be checked through the Criminal Research Bureau (now DBS, the Disclosure and Barring Service). This still may not have exposed the *Sun* journalist . . .

Chat shows and radio phone-ins

Generally two types of people contribute to chat shows and phone-ins: members of the general public with a story embellishing the theme of the day and the celebrity guest.

Celebrity guests

The casting department is an established route for booking actors for television and radio drama and they are responsible for drawing up contracts and negotiating Equity rates. Researchers are never involved. However, for light entertainment, children's shows, chat shows, etc., finding celebrities and actors often becomes the job of the researcher although sometimes specialist talent producers are employed. Whoever is responsible has the added advantage of knowing exactly what the programme requires in terms of personality, style and content. For radio it is, of course, the producer. In newspaper terms, the role lands in the lap of the specialist reporter or editor: the fashion editor, show business editor or whoever.

Depending on one's view, this job could be regarded as the best or worst in the media. For those who regard it as the *best* in television, the job of celebrity booker is paradise and in some shows one person has the sole responsibility of booking them although it is more common for several researchers on a show to suggest and book celebrity guests. An up-to-date knowledge of celebrity tittle-tattle and gossip is crucial.

- Now is the time to subscribe to *Hello!*, *OK!*, *Chat* and other gossip magazines.
- Get on the mailing list for publishers, theatres and record companies, email and print.
- Keep up with musical trends from what's on at *The Proms*, which groups are in the Top 10 charts and who's touring and where.
- Watch television soaps and light entertainment.
- Go to the cinema and theatre.
- Subscribe to *The Stage*, *Music Week*, *Cinema One* and any other specialist industry journals.

- Read the sports pages, fashion pages and the *What's On* guide in the local paper.

Who's in, who's out and who is up and coming?

Match the guest to the audience of your show and the budget. Guests themselves are self-limiting. You may be under the impression that huge Hollywood stars and pop groups don't get out of bed for an audience of less than several million but persuading an agent or manager that your show or newspaper is *influential* might convince them that, even without the huge audience, it's worth their client appearing on your programme or being interviewed for your newspaper to boost the book, film or public image. Some stars will appear on your show because it sounds fun – *Graham Norton*. Others because it may boost sales or put money in their pockets. Let's face it, minor celebrities desperate to keep in the public eye appear on anything! The question is, do you want them on *your* show? Can you afford to be choosy?

Finding guests who are approved of by even the fussiest of producers (those disliking minor celebrities nobody has heard of) can be a daunting and dispiriting task. Pulling off a coup, though, gives a huge boost to your self-satisfaction, esteem and career.

Thesps, turns, celebs, artistes and *guests* are synonyms used. Although not rude, the first two are the least polite and I don't recommend using them in the hearing of humourless guests or agents. Those with a sense of humour don't care and use ruder expressions to describe themselves. *Thesps*, incidentally, is short for thespians (actors) and *turns* usually refer to variety acts such as jugglers, vents (ventriloquists) and singers.

It goes without saying that demand influences price. The more popular the potential guest, the more work they have (film, theatre, television), the harder they are to book and, for drama especially, the higher the fee. For chat shows and one-off appearances in light entertainment (LE), the cost is often irrelevant. What is more important is whether the celebrity wants – or has time – to take part.

There are exceptions to this. Some guests appear on television or radio for free simply to promote their book, new single, film, TV series or theatrical tour. The trick is to get them on your programme *first* before everyone is sick to death of them. For newspaper journalists, the trick is to write a different angle for the article.

Working with famous people can involve the tact of a siege negotiator. Some celebrities are brilliant on-screen but impossibly temperamental. Others are tremendous value if kept away from the pre-recording booze. Some are notoriously unreliable and, at the last minute, fail to arrive. Some won't talk to anyone lower than a producer. Others only travel by plane even if that's the most inconvenient way to get to the studio. Some expect the backstage to be cleared before they go on and others must be the centre of attention, telling appallingly tasteless jokes in warm-up. Others are excruciatingly shy.

Then again, some of the biggest stars are delightful to work with, buying the entire crew presents at the end of production.

In short, beware the following difficult celebrity guests:

- the demanding and temperamental;
- those who can't talk without a script;
- the snob, the alcoholic, the sexist and the sexual predator. After the Jimmy Savile and Stuart Hall scandals, this had serious repercussions.

On hearing rumours, phone a colleague and ask their opinion. It may be too late to make replacements or the guest may be so sensational in principle that the production team are prepared to take a risk, but at least you are forewarned and can prepare a strategy for how to deal with them. The Jimmy Savile consequences are discussed in the children's section later in this chapter.

Agents and managers

Agents and personal managers represent actors and a host of celebrities, including sporting stars, television presenters, variety acts, weather presenters and people from shows like *Big Brother* who come to the fore by appearing in a TV programme. For a fee, usually 10% or 15% of their income, an agent manages their client's career, negotiates fees and acts as intermediary between client and employer.

For films, theatre productions and television or radio drama, casting agents negotiate the contracts on behalf of the production company. For one-off appearances in television or radio programmes, the researcher, assistant producer or producer may make the booking but the casting department usually sends out the contract.

It is possible to go direct to the celebrity, although this is potentially problematic, especially if the cold caller doesn't know the celebrity personally. Actors often prefer all work to go via their agent and many agents are upset if their clients are approached individually as it can lead to double-booking. Most celebrities inform their agents anyway to avoid conflicting dates although some are only too happy to keep the full fee! For best practice, all approaches should be via the agent. In an emergency, a researcher or producer with an hour to magic up a replacement guest will, of necessity, phone a celebrity direct if they know them personally.

Agents' books change constantly. They take on new presenters and actors, shedding the less popular, uneconomic ones. Agents occasionally poach each others' clients although this is unprofessional and understandably frowned upon.

Finding agents and managers

How do you find out who represents whom and their phone number and email?

The main directory for *actors*, *dancers*, *presenters*, *stunt artists* and *walk-ons* is www.spotlight.com. Updated daily, *Spotlight* is an online database of 40,000-plus professional performers as well as directors, cameramen, choreographers, fight directors and casting directors. Casting agents, who must prove they have cast a production in the past, can subscribe to *Spotlight*. The interactive subscription includes access to the online database and, if the subscription is one year or more, hard copies of the book. The book consists of several large volumes showcasing actors under separate sections – lead and character actors for instance. The subscription service is for casting directors, actors and agents as it highlights up-and-coming productions requiring casting. Subscription charges are found on the *Spotlight* website. There can be more than one user for a subscription service of one year or more.

Another directory is www.thehandbook.com with 30,000 celebrity contacts including actors, novelists, sporting stars, etc. Again, this is a subscription service costing £15 a month (at the time of writing) but is more for PR.

There are other ways of finding agents. The Google search can be a soulless task as you may get all the gossip, the IMDB and Wikipedia sites before finding an agent who may not be the one you want. It is possible but time consuming. A better service is provided by Celebrity Intelligence and Celebrity Bulletin. Further information about these is given later in the chapter.

It is not unusual for celebrities to have different agents: one for TV and radio, one for corporate events and personal appearances (after-dinner speaking and such like) and one for literary purposes, e.g. books, scriptwriting.

Larger agencies such as Curtis Brown not only represent actors but also have a literary agency representing writers, playwrights and presenters, amongst others – a cross-over service so that any actor writing a kiss-and-tell autobiography can 'keep it in the house', so to speak. It means that a famous screenwriter can be represented for both their film and literary works.

Many sporting personalities, variety acts (vents, jugglers, comedians, contortionists, etc.), singers and other non-specific celebrities may be in *Spotlight* but it is common to find them under their own name.com. A reputable website has a link to the agent unless they represent themselves. It may take some time to get a response and some are run by fan clubs and therefore of no particular use to you.

A useful agent/PR guru is Max Clifford's company, MCA. This press and public relations company represents celebrities and, indeed, ordinary people swept into the media circus by events outside their control. There are similar firms, but this is the most well known.

For *footballers, cricketers* and *sportsmen still playing*, the first approach is via their club although many have another representative for non-sporting appearances. For anyone retired from the game, it is a matter of finding who represents them. A lot are on the after-dinner speaker circuit and one of the larger agencies is IMG (also a production company) started by the late Mark McCormack (once regarded as the most influential man in sport). The local TV, radio or news-paper sports desk may have a contact. Remember to keep all numbers in your contact book.

For *athletes* still competing and younger sportsmen (Olympic hopefuls, for instance), try Sport England or the relevant governing sporting body. Again, the local sports desk may be helpful. However, if the athletes are under 16, refer to the rules governing children found later in the chapter. Another source is the sports promoters. For boxing, for instance, the first port of call is Frank Warren's office although at the time of writing, his influence on the sport was allegedly declining. Former sports personalities who have taken to performing in pantomimes often have a theatrical agent as well.

According to Roy Hudd (Radio 4's *Midweek*, 21 August 2013), there has been a renaissance in the former *variety acts* – jugglers, vents, contortionists, magicians and other speciality acts (colloquially *spesh* acts) – on the comedy circuit! They were increasingly rare and reliant on the vagaries of fashion but now crop up on talent shows such as *Britain's Got Talent*. The comedy circuit is, according to Roy Hudd, regaining the flavour of the old music hall – but for how long? As proved by Simon Cowell, they were ripe for discovery but their existence is precarious, which is a shame. Think how they are treated on *Britain's Got Talent*! Finding them is a matter of persistence. Wikipedia has a list of, for instance, caricaturists or ventriloquists but, in many cases, these are the most famous (many of them dead) and you still have to get hold of them. Scouring live venues is hit-and-miss. LE production personnel do this as a matter of course, trawling the Edinburgh Fringe and other venues to discover acts. Contacting the specialist magic shops and suppliers is an option. Finding a ventriloquist for next week is a challenge unless you know one. The same goes for other performers. There *are* agents who specialise in these but beware the children's entertainer syndrome; the semi-professional, little better than Great

Uncle Harry, adding a few quid to his pocket by entertaining children on Saturday afternoons.

Acts such as *jugglers*, *contortionists* and *escapologists* often make a living as street entertainers but are increasingly found on the comedy circuit. If you spot one, get their details, but such performers are nomadic by their very nature and work Europe-wide where takings are better. Again, the jugglers' supplies shops (usually in London) are a source – after all, they're selling the kit. For magicians, try the Magic Circle, the magicians' professional body. In my experience, contortionists on local agents' books are little better than good gymnasts although the current crop are more exciting.

Once you have contacted one variety act, should they not be entirely what you are looking for, ask them for suggestions and contacts. One ventriloquist will know plenty of other specialist acts as it is a small world – and getting smaller. Facebook, blogs and Twitter all help.

Comedians have agents too. The more famous the comedian, the more likely they are to have exclusive representation – in other words, only one management company. The two biggest agencies at the time of writing are Avalon and Off the Kerb, both companies also owning media production companies. These two agencies represent their clients for live and broadcast and it may be that their clients have other agencies for corporate events or books. Most comedians have their own websites which should divulge an agent. Check it is their website and not a fansite which, although it may provide an agent's details, may be out of date.

Another source for finding agents etc. is *The White Book*, an events production directory. Type in 'juggler' in the search engine (free to use), and you get a list of suggestions although it will only consist of just that, a name and no method by which to contact them although other entries are more comprehensive and link to agents. However, having got a name for your juggler or contortionist, you can Google them. A hard copy of *The White Book* (at the time of writing) costs £90 and lists all the jugglers *and* their contacts. The book is updated annually.

Don't forget Facebook and Twitter

There are thousands of hopefuls awaiting their big break and talent programmes like *Britain's Got Talent* and *The X Factor* exploit this. Agents exist for unknown singers and dancers too but the quality is variable and it may be worth asking the casting department for suggestions. Stage, music colleges and drama schools are excellent sources. Equity and the Musicians' Union have lists of reputable establishments and reputable drama schools are listed in Drama UK, an amalgamation of the Conference of Drama Schools and the National Council for Drama Training. Local stage schools bend over backwards for broadcast and press publicity. The casting department, who has close contacts with all drama schools, sets up auditions but, to be honest, few researchers are involved in finding new faces unless they are working on a talent show – in which case the production office will be *deluged* with wannabes and agents.

Bands, singers and *groups* with recording contracts are contactable via their labels. Most recording companies are London-based but some large influential ones are in the provinces. The recording companies' A&R (Artists and Repertoire) department's responsibility is to look after the company's signings and they go to any lengths for media publicity. They accompany the band, often organise travel arrangements and keep an eye on clothing, behaviour and any other problems likely to be encountered. Basically, they act as minders for the band. Some groups have managers touting the media stations for appearances and publicity and, once the group is to appear, take the same function as the A&R department in that they organise all travel and other arrangements. Issues involving bands and musical acts are discussed in Chapter 7.

Authors (including actors, presenters, sports personalities, explorers – anyone famous who has written a book) are contactable through the publisher. If an actor writes a book, this effectively circumvents their agent. When a publisher promotes a book, a publisher's representative may well accompany the author with the publisher taking responsibility and paying for the travel expenses (ultimately coming out of the author's royalties). This is not always the case, so check first. To find the publisher, go online. www.Amazon.co.uk is quick. Publishers' addresses and phone numbers are found online or listed in *The Writers' and Artists' Yearbook* but once you have found the publisher, getting the contact number is a cinch.

Where are they now? The media are all-consuming monsters, idolising one day, discarding the next. Once-household names disappear off the face of the earth or at least off the airwaves and can prove most elusive to trace. Agents drop them from their books and the casting department hasn't heard of them in years. These are the people who crop up in the bankruptcy courts spotted by a keen-eyed journalist scanning court lists. Finding these is largely a matter of luck and graft. A former agent may have kept in touch on a friendship basis; the gossip columnists on the national papers might know. Blogs, Facebook and Twitter might throw it up. The social network community is worth a try. If they appear in the obituary columns, you are too late.

Foreign celebrities are contacted in very similar ways. Many larger agencies have a US branch and most have USA and European contacts. Start with your UK sources and contacts and work out from there. There is also Celebrity Intelligence.

Celebrity Intelligence at www.celebrityintelligence.com is a diary subscription service used by, for instance, the BBC, ITV, national newspapers and several radio stations as highlighted on their home page at the time of writing. It was also recommended to me when I was doing my research for this edition of the book. It combines the celebrity diary with a contacts service and the home page has a quick contact list for any celebrity currently making news. The diary is emailed to subscribers daily; the website is updated live throughout the day and any change in celebrity representation is highlighted four times a week. Information can be supplied by tweets, apps as well as email via the website or phone. Celebrity Intelligence provides contacts for agents, managers and publicists not only for mainstreamers but also diverse characters such as WAGS, socialites, models, reality stars and international personalities of note from the UK and USA, etc. The subscription rates depend on how many logins the client requires. Depending on the budget, subscription to this service might be helpful for those elusive Hollywood stars and non-mainstream celebrities for whom finding an agent or contact proves difficult.

There are other diary services available such as Celebrity Bulletin (www.fens.com) providing a subscription service for a twice-weekly (Monday and Thursday) celebrity diary and a Celebrity Bulletin Contact Service. In other words, they email you an international diary of who's in the country, from where and why, plus contacts. The diary is available to three users per subscription. The Celebrity Bulletin Contact Service provides contact numbers for 400,000 celebrities including actors, musicians, athletes and media personalities around the world. There is a database, an email and phone service (available at the time of writing from 10.00 until 17.00 on weekdays for up to ten personalities a day). At the time of writing, this service costs from £125 per month for the database and bulletin to £2925 for access to both the Celebrity Bulletin and the Entertainment Combo for up to five users for a year.

If this type of service can't help and you really have no idea how to contact someone but have seen them on television, in a newspaper or heard them on the radio, phone the production company or newspaper which should supply you with the agent's name and number. It occasionally happens that a celebrity has no agent. Under these circumstances, the production office or newspaper will contact them for you and ask permission to give out their number. For reasons of ethics and data protection, it is doubtful if the production company will reveal a personal number straight away.

Lists of agents can be obtained from their governing body, the Personal Managers Association which can be found at www.thepma.com.

Booking celebrity guests

Once the agent has been located, it ought to be a relatively easy process to book a programme guest or a newspaper interview. Unfortunately, it isn't. Clients hire agents to find the best jobs and remuneration. Theatrical agents, especially those representing 'serious' actors, often consider a one-off appearance on a quiz show as tawdry, cheapening the credibility of the actor involved. For smaller agencies and those preferring the personal touch, one agent handles all offers of work. Other celebrities have different agents representing different fields, as discussed above.

Agencies have many clients on their books and it often happens that, trying to cast guests for a particular series, the same agent is contacted several times with requests for different people. They are not impressed!

There is no mystique to booking someone. The negotiations usually follow the same procedure:

- the date and time the celebrity is required;
- the programme – what it is and how the celebrity will be involved; or
- the newspaper or magazine and the focus of the interview;
- the fee.

If, according to the agent's records, your target is free on the date stated, the agent will phone the celebrity and ask if they want to take part. Like the rest of us, celebrities have lives away from the spotlight and, just because they are free, it doesn't mean they will take part; hospital appointments, their son's sports day or a trip with friends may take priority. Whereas an important film part will induce them to drop everything, appearing on a chat show doesn't have the same appeal unless they need the money or exposure.

An actor or musician working away from home is not an automatic refusal unless they are abroad. Someone can be considered a potential guest because they are filming or performing 'just down the road'. For regional newspapers, this is a gift; a quick interview with an interesting, famous person. In these circumstances, it is worth contacting the stage or film producer first instead of the agent as they must give the go-ahead anyway. Producers are pretty amenable about extra publicity especially if the newspaper article is published while they are still in town. Whether or not the guest *can* appear depends entirely on the schedule. Once the production is up and running, theatre performers are free during the day except for matinees and can be tempted to pick up an extra fee or the publicity. This depends on the person involved: some are too tired during a stage run or tour to take on anything else, others find living in a strange city palls after a while and are only too pleased to widen professional contacts.

Be prepared for rebuffs and setbacks. Don't take it personally. Many agents decline (suspiciously quickly – did they approach their clients?) and a few are patronising while they do so. Others are only too willing to help and are approachable in the extreme. Booking celebrities is a small world and word gets round as to which agent is easy to work with and which celebrity is capricious.

After a while, experience tells you that:

*   some celebrities, especially actors, won't appear at all. They are either too busy, live abroad or their agents won't let them. If you succeed in getting one of these on your show or newspaper, congratulate yourself;
*   some performers are on exclusive contracts and *cannot* appear, however much the project might interest them.

Journalists requesting interviews should follow the same procedure. Because a newspaper interview is quicker than appearing on a radio or TV programme, any celebrity appearing in your area as promoted in, for instance, Celebrity Intelligence can be contacted via the hotline in the event diaries.

Negotiating fees

Equity sets recommended minimum production fees for its members but this covers *performance*. If the celebrity is to perform during their appearance, all further negotiations should go via the casting department in order to prevent major misunderstandings; there are too many legal pitfalls which the casting department has the experience and knowledge to avoid.

The Equity agreement does not cover personal appearances when an Equity member is being themselves and the researcher (producer in radio) may well negotiate the fee. This is normally via the agent although on a few occasions I have discussed it with the celebrity themselves. How much is offered depends on the programme budget; the producer sets the limit. Should an impasse occur, consult the producer because if one guest is appearing for less than expected, more money is in the kitty. Again, the producer may regard the potential guest as such good television that they are prepared to up the stakes. In some cases, once the researcher has confirmed the availability of a potential guest, the producer takes the reins, negotiating the fees and other contractual issues.

The casting department draws up contracts. Long gone are the days when a guest insists on being paid cash-in-hand to avoid income tax and agent's fees. If this is suggested, speak to the producer. The Inland Revenue is hot on issues like this nowadays . . .

Travel expenses and other incidentals are normally paid and, according to the guest's status, train travel may be first class. Check the budget. Having said that, no-one expects a big star to travel standard class and anyone suggesting it might find the guest refuses to come. Airfares are commonly barred unless the distance is considerable or there are time constraints.

However, everything is negotiable and some well-known celebrities happily drive as long as the second-class train fare covers their petrol. Other celebrities, especially in London or big cities, are collected by taxi. It is often the researcher's remit to co-ordinate this.

Where a guest is *promoting a product* (book, film, tour, single), the fee may be waived and travel expenses funded from someone else's budget – namely the record company, film distributor or publisher. Film clips, copies of the book, photographs and other sundries are supplied in the hope that they will be screened, talked about, shown on the radio webcam, photographed for the newspaper, etc. Because copyright is in the hands of the promoter, royalties may be waived although in the case of promoting a new film, an on-screen credit is usually mandatory. Check first. The use of film clips and music is discussed in later chapters and you must refer to Ofcom and BBC Editorial Guidelines about on-screen promotions.

It is increasingly common for performers to have 'promotion' built into their contracts, for instance in the BBC/Equity Agreement 2013. In this case, you may find that a performer arriving at your studio or for a newspaper interview is covered by this clause in their contract and won't expect to be paid although their travel may have to be negotiated. This is very common when a stage play is on tour or an author is promoting their book. Check Celebrity Intelligence and Celebrity Bulletin and facilitate. Be aware that not all performers are happy about such contracts and may be a little reserved when interviewed although this, of course, could be their natural temperament.

General public contributors

Experts

For reasons of impartiality, local television debates and current affairs programmes (e.g. the BBC's Radio 4 flagships *Today* and *PM*) feature differing and opposing views. The contributors holding informed opinions tend to be experts: a politician, doctor, lawyer, historian, businessman, representative of a self-help group and so on. The researcher locates them. For newspaper articles and features, the journalist locates the expert.

In a society where the establishment is still dominated by white, middle-class, middle-aged men, the challenge is to avoid just such a panel. There has been much criticism that many news programmes have low ratios of female to male participants, with research showing that in the week beginning 15 July 2013, Radio 4's *Today* had a ratio of 14 men to one woman (6am to 7am on 16 July), *Channel 4 News* had a ratio of 6:1, *BBC News at Ten* 5:1 and *ITV News* 3:1 (*Broadcast*, 30 August 2013). Tokenism should be avoided especially if the token woman, for instance, is not particularly strong. Aim for a good mix.

There is a current campaign for the BBC to employ more female experts and in January 2013, an Expert Women's Day was held where female experts went to the BBC's Academy to promote themselves and their expertise to commissioners and editors. There is now a BBC database of 200 female experts covering a wide variety of subjects and who can be used as potential presenters, interviewees and contributors. Notwithstanding, much criticism (Harriet Harman amongst others) bewails the fact that few women over 50 appear in the media at all.

Finding a *politician* is easy. Getting them to appear is more difficult and depends on their attitude, the topic for discussion, their availability and the programme or newspaper. Members of the Cabinet are the hardest to pin down because of their schedule and overwhelming preference for appearing on influential national flagships like *Today, The News* or a national broadsheet. If you are working on this type of programme or for a national broadsheet, apart from fitting in with their schedules, there should be little problem.

Otherwise, it may be easier to aim for a local politician with a lower profile. The constituency office number is found via a quick search on the internet or in the phone book. Emails can be sent either via their local office or direct to the House of Commons although a phone call may have a faster response. Politicians are extremely busy and, first off, you are likely to speak to the MP's researcher or assistant.

Members of the European Parliament are also relatively easy to 'book'. There are 73 MEPs in the UK and a quick search on the internet will find the nearest. From there, you will find email links, addresses and phone numbers, including their EU office number. Bearing in mind that MEPs spend a lot of time travelling and working between Strasbourg, Brussels and the UK, finding a time when they are available to be interviewed might be difficult to co-ordinate. The downside of MEPs in a programme or newspaper article is that few members of the general public know who their MEP is and fewer appear to care.

Depending on the content of the programme or article, it may be obligatory to balance views with someone from an opposition party or parties.

Prominent politicians and certainly those in the Cabinet expect a list of questions beforehand, usually emailed prior to their agreeing to participate. There are several reasons for this. Should the question involve facts and figures, they need to research these first. Also (excuse my cynicism), for unpalatable or controversial questions, the official spin is ascertained beforehand. Politicians have been known to veto certain topics. A presenter tackling a vetoed topic on the radio or television is courting an on-air row, politicians storming off in a huff and future boycott from both politician and party. Good for ratings, yes, but if a non-biased ethos is integral to the programme, this is a serious consequence and may lead to repercussions within the television or radio station.

Once a general election is declared, the appearance of members of Parliament in studio and newspapers is strictly regulated. Effectively, they are now *constituency candidates*, prospective members of Parliament, and are restricted under the Representation of the People Act 1983 and the Political Parties, Elections and Referendums Act 2000. This comes into force from '*the date of the dissolution of Parliament or the announcement of dissolution in the case of a parliamentary election, the issue of the writ at a by-election, or five weeks before polling day for local government elections*' (Representation of the People Act 1983).

The rules can be found in Section Six, Elections and Referendums in the Ofcom Broadcasting Code. The programme editor on a news and current affairs programme will be aware of such restrictions and politicians do, of course, appear all the time after a general election has been called. The main point is that '*special impartiality requirements in the Communications Act 2003 and other legislation relating to broadcasting on elections and referendums, are applied at the time of elections and referendums*' (Ofcom Broadcast Code, Section Six, Elections and Referendums).

Effectively, a candidate cannot appear on a radio or television programme as a news presenter, interviewer or presenter of any sort during the election period. Also, if you have a candidate on your programme, you must also, for the legal requirements of impartiality, include other views and perspectives – in other words, candidates from the other major parties.

There are rules covering a referendum as well so should you be interviewing an MP during the time a referendum has been called, refer upwards to your editor or producer.

A problem arises if a politician is booked to appear on a programme before an election is declared. For instance, I once booked a politician who had, as a single woman, adopted a child and she agreed to talk on a chat show about it. Between agreeing to appear and the studio recording, the election was declared. We were all aware of the upcoming election but the speed of the declaration surprised even her. This appearance was permissible because she appeared as herself with no reference to standing as a prospective member of Parliament on a *non-political programme*.

The actual wording from Section 6.7 in the Ofcom Broadcasting Code is:

> Appearances by candidates (in UK elections) or representatives (of permitted participants in UK referendums) in non-political programmes that were planned or scheduled before the election or referendum period may continue, but no new appearances should be arranged and broadcast during the period.

We had adhered to that implicitly. When in doubt, refer to the relevant guidelines.

Doctors can be contacted via the British Medical Association (BMA) which is happy to help. For something more specific, such as a neurosurgeon, the Royal College of Surgeons will give you the name of the society in whose specialism you are interested. The Royal College of Physicians will put you on to a neurologist and so on. The main colleges are in London but Scottish colleges are based in Edinburgh and Glasgow.

The nearest hospital might help; contact the press office. You might even try your own GP and don't forget contacts within your own team or newspaper. Be warned, doctors are extremely busy and most need advance notice.

Lawyers are contactable via the Law Society. As always, if you have your own personal contact, don't be bashful about using it. At the worst, they can refuse; at the best, they can say yes or suggest someone else.

I am lumping together *academics* and other professionals like astronomers, historians and sociologists. Universities and colleges, the Royal Observatory at Greenwich and specific professional associations can be contacted for leads. Finding an expert is relatively easy but their televisual and radio quality can be hit and miss. The reason why the same face or voice crops up time and again is because the production team are playing safe, well aware that their expert will perform to order and give good value. It may be lazy but it is expedient. The Expert Women's Day initiative may change this, or merely add a new set of familiar but female faces . . .

When an expert is required *now*, the contacts book is crucial. Note the name and expertise of each contributor with their numbers (mobile, home, direct line at work, email) and file them.

There are associations, charities and agencies for virtually everything and these are invaluable for spokespersons from the world of business through to self-help groups.

The general public

Cue Andy Warhol's 15 minutes of fame; the chat show with an audience of millions and the chance to spill the beans about meeting a burglar face-to-face, the car accident that saved a life, the boyfriend who slept with mother and brother. The deeply personal to the deeply boring. The sublime to the ridiculous. You must find the people with the stories. And the show is tomorrow. Or this morning!

There are several established, reliable and reputable methods for finding guests. A researcher uses a combination of them.

A common one is the end-of-show request. Usually this takes the form of an on-screen slide with the programme logo and a voiceover (usually the presenter) requesting people with ideas and opinions on the next topic to phone in, email, tweet, etc. The contact number, email and Twitter addresses are given. The researchers contact the potential contributors as soon as possible by phone. Social media like Twitter are useful for promoting a 'buzz' and getting more response.

Another common method is via the webpage. The BBC's *The One Show* has a link whereby potential contributors and storylines can be suggested to the programme and again, the researchers contact the person who made the suggestion. The more interesting the suggestion, the more likely the researcher is to take up the idea.

Another method, less common nowadays, is the newspaper advertisement. For this to be effective, there must be ample pre-production time, making this an established method for documentaries rather than chat shows. Depending on the programme budget, an advert is placed in several newspapers or journals aimed at potential contributors. The downside is that many people take too long to summon up the courage to reply whilst others hoard newspapers so long that responses appear months after the ad originally appeared.

By negotiating with listing magazines such as *TV Times* or with local journalists, it is possible to 'advertise' free and gain pre-transmission publicity by turning the request into a newspaper feature: the 'fancy yourself on TV' approach. New programmes often do this because there is no current programme on which to request more contributors.

Whichever method is chosen, a contact name, number and email address, together with a short description of the type of person or story required, must be included in the text. It is unwise to use personal phone numbers and good practice to connect the phone to an answerphone for out-of-hours calls. For emails and Twitter, the company email and Twitter account must be used for security reasons. This filters out crank calls and aids potential contributors who cannot use the phone during the day. Always leave a final date for responses.

Expect a large number of time wasters, cranks and trolls.

Trawling magazine and newspaper articles often throws up suitable people but is a matter of luck and spotting the article at the right time. As mentioned in Chapter 2, if a newspaper inspired a programme topic in the first place, inclusion of the featured person is an added bonus. It is a good idea to file unusual hobbies or stories and refer to the file at frequent intervals.

Contacting people from articles involves phoning the relevant newspaper or magazine and asking for the journalist who wrote the original article or the picture desk editor (if a photograph has been printed) for the contact name and phone number. Although some newspapers are cagey about revealing names and addresses, most are happy to pass on the information to fellow professionals (so much for privacy and confidentiality). Occasionally payment for the contact number is requested. This tends to be from freelance journalists or a news agency scrabbling to make a living. Whether or not the payment is made depends on the programme budget and how desperate the producer is for the contributor.

Use contacts from people working on other programmes. Swapping names and addresses between production teams is a well-trodden method but relying on a source of overexposed controversial contributors is bad practice and to be avoided at all costs. If used judiciously and scrupulously, swapping contacts for programme guests is legitimate. By chatting to fellow professionals who have used the contributors before, you can confirm how well the guest performs and their value to the programme. *The Jeremy Kyle Show* is not averse to using the same contributors again should a development arise in the original story and the advantage to the production team is that they know how the contributors will react on camera and the audience already has an emotional response to them.

Selection process for general public contributors

Not everyone is suitable to appear on television or radio. Put another way, some people are better than others. Who to choose depends on how good the other potential contributors' stories are, how well the person talks and how you actually feel about them. A lot of it is gut feeling. The more sensational and provocative the story, the better the television and radio (the same goes for newspaper stories of course) but, for balance and mix, include the mundane as well. Also, the more sensational and outrageous, the more chance the story is invented. *This Morning* doesn't just rely on the sensational; it wants everyday items and views as well. When *The One Show* requests stories on its website, the contributor might be self-determining. The same goes for radio stations and newspapers' surgeries.

Depending on the subject to be covered, the questions to ask potential contributors are:

- name;
- age;
- their story;
- town where they live/come from;
- phone number, address and email address;
- are they free and willing to come along to the recording or to speak on air?

Programmes aim for a balance of age and gender but this is prescribed by the subject matter itself; a programme on prostate cancer is unlikely to feature women unless they're older and accompanying their husbands.

On-screen arguments make good television. A contributor may be chosen simply to offer extreme and oppositional views, however frivolous, prejudiced and specious their point. Beware. The BBC and Ofcom regulate taste, decency and offence to public feeling in their programme codes and editorial guidelines. It is also important to ensure that contributors are not coached or pushed or improperly induced into saying anything which they know not to be true or do not believe to be true.

The residence of the contributor is an issue depending on the location of the recording studios and whether or not the programme is made for local or national transmission. A local programme (radio and television) has contributors from around the region; the listener doesn't want to hear someone from Billericay if the radio station is in Birmingham. However, for a networked programme, the viewer in Carlisle won't be interested in it if all the contributors are from Croydon.

A consideration to bear in mind is how the contributor gets to the recording studio. It is great television to have someone from a northerly Scottish isle and a strong regional accent, but the amount of time they spend on the train and whether they arrive in time for the recording must be considered. Chat shows are cheap, cheerful and made on a shoestring budget. Some programmes pay travel expenses, some don't. The cost of transporting someone from one end of the country to the other is a drain on the budget especially if hotels and planes are included.

The producer, however, might be so desperate to include someone that they consider Skype or other similar technologies and transmit this way. Be aware that the BBC gets many complaints about poor transmission quality and drop-out when using Skype, etc.

For radio, of course, distance is no obstacle. Nor is what the contributor looks like although with studio webcams and Skype, radio is becoming increasingly 'visual'. What *is* important is what is said and how it is said. For phone-ins, the request for contributions is transmitted on air and the producer awaits the response, choosing contributors for their topic, articulacy, relevance and what has just gone on before, all of which is subjective. Now that local radio has an internet platform, some contributions may not even be local but the producer can decide if the listeners would wish to hear it. Emails and tweets are intercepted by the producer and handed to the presenter for broadcast.

Never confirm anyone over the phone without checking with the producer or editor first unless you are absolutely sure about who else is on the show or you are in sole charge of who appears in a particular programme. This way, the balance of the programme is ensured and will not be one-sided. Unless you are totally certain, always leave the option of backing out by promising to phone back. For newspaper journalists and radio producers, the balance of the article and the show is your responsibility so the decision is yours anyway.

Talent shows

Talent shows have been a mainstream of television virtually since it was invented, regardless of the title: *Opportunity Knocks, New Faces, Britain's Got Talent, Stars in Their Eyes, Pop Idol, The Voice, The X Factor* and even *Big Brother* – the same idea, just different titles. People perform, there is a vote, a loser and a winner. Finding people to take part is easy. It's persuading people that they have *no* talent that is the difficult bit!

In the past, advertisements were placed in newspapers, listing magazines and public places such as libraries and sports centres. Now it's generally on-air promotions with online applications. Thousands apply. The task of the production team is to whittle them down to a manageable number. It is not generally known that not everyone, for instance, gets an audition for *The X Factor*. There is a pre-selection process even for the thousands who turn up for the audition. How this is done depends on the programme and the production team. For some shows, tapes are requested and selected people auditioned. For others, it is entirely the online application process, much as it is for quiz and game shows. The more interesting the application and back story, the more likely the production staff will see the applicant.

Preliminary auditions are held. These are often recorded and, in the case of *The X Factor*, the auditions are an integral part of the show itself. We all want to laugh at the no-hoper who thinks they are 'the next big thing'. Other programmes use the audition tapes as a prelude for selection; with so many applicants, a necessary *aide-mémoire*. Travel expenses are not paid; there are too many people.

The decision on who to choose is down to the taste of the production team and, depending on the programme format, the presenters or judges. Certain considerations may apply such as where the person comes from (local newspaper support raises ratings), their age and gender (you don't want a programme filled with women or people under 20 unless that is the programme's unique selling point). The balance of the show has to be considered. For instance, *Britain's Got Talent* has been criticised for having too many singers and not enough variety acts so more variety acts might be shortlisted.

Once the contestants have been chosen, the rest of the show is in the hands of the programme format. Who continues in the show depends on the audience or judge vote. The researcher's role is restricted to looking after the contestants and any other programme requirement.

Quiz and game shows

Production companies who specialise in quiz programmes often employ contestant co-ordinators whose entire responsibility is advertising for and picking contestants and co-ordinating travel arrangements. Everything, in fact, to make the contestant acquisition efficient. Elsewhere, researchers take on this role.

Quiz shows have specific contestant requirements. *Eggheads* requires teams of five. *University Challenge* wants teams of four from the same university. *Pointless* wants pairs. *Surprise Surprise* wants people who deserve a prize. For general knowledge shows like *The Chase* and *Mastermind*, individuals are picked although they may work as a team for part of the show itself. The brief here is a range of age, gender, class and occupation. For dating shows like *Take Me Out* and *Dinner Date*, the contestants are (presumably) single, attractive and personable. Some shows prefer the eccentric, others the strictly conventional.

For a not yet entirely explained sociological reason, women and ethnic minorities are under-represented on quiz shows although this is improving on the lighter quiz shows. You only have to watch *University Challenge* and *Mastermind* to appreciate there is a gender and ethnic imbalance. It isn't because they aren't picked, it's because fewer apply in the first place. In early episodes of *Who Wants to be a Millionaire?* critics and viewers alike commented that few contestants were women and even fewer black. It can be noted, however, that the Chasers in *The Chase* (at the time of writing) include a black and Asian Chaser but only one woman. The disabled and elderly are also under-represented. It remains one of the major challenges for the researcher to find good, competitive female and non-white contestants.

Who Wants to be a Millionaire? revolutionised the contestant search. The potential contestant phoned a premium rate phone line, answered a simple question and was picked at random by computer. The cost of the calls helped fund the prize money.

Nowadays, contestants are generally advertised for at the end of a programme and initial applications are done online via the 'Be on a Show' page on www.itv.com, www.bbc.co.uk or commercial 'talent' spotting websites such as www.starnow.co.uk. The BBC occasionally asks potential contestants to email for an application form but other applications are done entirely online. New programmes without a broadcast history merely put the information on the ITV or BBC websites and await the applications. For *Mastermind*, there is an online *Mastermind* style quiz to try at home with an application form at the end. There is always a deadline date by which applications must be received. For activity or more specialised programmes, the production team may advertise in sports centres or specialist magazines to attract potential contestants who may not be the usual type to want to appear on television. For *Million Pound Drop Live* contestants are recruited from the online play-along website and the application is made online.

The application form requests the usual information – age, gender, marital status, location, occupation – and often has a clause saying that you must not work for or have worked for the television production company producing the show – so none of us need apply! It will also request information about hobbies and unusual facts about you (to be revealed, for instance, at the last stage of *Take Me Out*). For fitness programmes, there may be questions on level of fitness, sport played and at what level. Many applications require photographs. Thousands of people apply to take part in popular programmes, especially ones with high-value prizes, and the number of applications can be daunting. From here, you, the researcher, whittle down the potential contestants and contact the ones who sound more fun or have a tale to tell.

Because so many people are desperate to get onto television, potential contestants may misrepresent themselves. A common question in online application asks if they have a criminal record. Regulatory bodies are concerned that a programme will be discredited should a criminal, especially one with a history of violence or fraud, win something valuable on television. Presumably this person would lie . . .

The contestant tour, if programme schedule and budget permit, is one way to whittle them out. If time is at a premium, the final selection takes place over the telephone.

The contestant tour

Contestant tours are expensive. Even for the lone researcher or producer operating in a hotel conference room armed with a digital camera, there are travel and hotel costs. For talent shows like *Britain's Got Talent* the contestant tour is part of the production itself, filmed and transmitted, thus offsetting the cost.

The venue is generally in a city or large town in each of the major regions. Hotels are a popular choice because they are well known to the general public but for large productions like *The X Factor,* venues like theatres are chosen. Hotels supply coffee and sweets (at a charge) which is of considerable benefit when the selection process involves being cooped up between the same four walls today and all day tomorrow.

At this initial stage, potential contestants are not reimbursed for travel costs or for taking time off work.

Such tours involve considerable travelling between venues and there are several schools of thought as to the best method. Should you:

- travel to the next location after finishing the last audition, i.e. travel when tired but enjoying a relatively late start the following morning; or
- travel the following morning and risk traffic jams, getting lost and setting up in a hurry?

On the whole, researchers and producers organise their own schedules and there are strategies for reducing stress:

- whenever possible, if going long distances, take the train and consider flying (if the budget runs to this) and car hire;
- ensure the schedule isn't ridiculously tight.

Of course, if you are working alongside Simon Cowell and the judges on a big-budget talent show, part of the appeal of the audition tour for the hordes of bystanders and auditionees is watching the judges (who have stayed the previous night in a hotel) arrive.

If your company has a travel desk or production manager, they can order train tickets and book hotels. Few production companies sanction first-class travel for production staff unless their name is Simon Cowell.

The selection process itself depends on what is required for the show. Tasks can range from chats (those amusing anecdotes), a general knowledge or IQ test to, as in talent shows, a full-scale audition.

There are a few guidelines on how to behave:

- you are representing the production company and must be polite and professional at all times;
- under no circumstance can you snigger at anyone's performance (if Simon Cowell does so, that's his prerogative);
- nor can you turn up in Bermuda shorts and Hawaiian shirt. That researcher lost his job.

Tours are exhausting for everyone on the production team with considerable travel, a succession of late nights, a different impersonal hotel each day and mass catering. It can be very dispiriting. They meet a lot of ordinary (and extraordinary) people together with the 'tone deaf' singer for a talent show and the complete ignoramus for a general knowledge quiz. Faces merge into each other; the stars stand out but it is difficult to remember the rest.

Once the contestants are chosen, it is expedient to include reserves to cover illness and other possibilities. Reserves often live relatively locally to the recording studios and it is essential they fully understand that they may not make it into the programme.

Once the contestants are selected, they are given a recording date or dates and their travel to the studio is arranged. Nowadays several episodes of a quiz are recorded in one day and contestants should be warned that they might have an overnight stay. When contestants are likely to appear in several consecutive programmes, they need to bring a change of clothing for each programme. It is usually the researcher's job to inform them of this.

Contestants are not media professionals and it may be their first time on television although some people list appearing on quiz shows amongst their hobbies. Everyone should be treated with courtesy and respect.

Reality shows

By reality shows, I mean programmes like *24 Hours in A&E*, *Brit Cops/Cop Squad*, *An Island Parish*, *UK Border Force* and *The Only Way is Essex* and *Made in Chelsea* – two programmes which, arguably, are not 'real'.

The former programmes are recorded with a minimal camera crew simply because of the situations which they portray. (For *24 Hours in A&E*, multiple fixed rig cameras are used.) For many of these shows, the key is to get the permission to film first and the permission of the people likely to participate. 'Casting' this type of programme is literally down to who gives their permission although the production team prefer to include the more charismatic and interesting members of the public they encounter within the subject matter they are recording.

One of the features of this type of programme is the number of people whose faces are concealed. This is either to respect their confidentiality and safety (police working under cover, for instance) or because they have not given their permission to be filmed. For more discussion on this, see 'Persuading someone to be filmed' later in this chapter.

The amount of footage filmed in this type of programme is extraordinary. A shooting ratio of 300 to one is not unusual – that means 300 hours of rushes to one transmitted hour. This puts pressure on the editor, the producer/director and often the researchers in actually scanning the footage to choose the best extracts for programme inclusion. The same happens in programmes like *I'm a Celebrity . . . Get Me Out of Here!* and *Big Brother* where a large number of fixed cameras record non-stop and the production team must find something worthy of broadcast. What is picked depends on a variety of criteria, the most obvious being how interesting it is – conflict scores highly as does the 'yuk' factor, tastelessness and sexual intrigue. Whether or not it is transmitted depends on considerations such as the watershed, the time of transmission and repeats. Ofcom's rules are specific:

> . . . broadcasters must ensure that material which may cause offence is justified by the context. Such material may include, but is not limited to, offensive language, violence, sex, sexual violence, humiliation, distress, violation of human dignity, discriminatory treatment or language (for example on the grounds of age, disability, gender, race, religion, beliefs and sexual orientation). Appropriate information should also be broadcast where it would assist in avoiding or minimising offence. (Ofcom Broadcast Codes Section 2, Harm and Offence 2.3, http://stakeholders.ofcom.org.uk/ broadcasting/broadcast-codes/broadcast-code/harmoffence/)

The Only Way is Essex differs from the verité style of the *24 Hours in A&E* genre in that contributors are chosen like actors in a play and many storylines taking place are semi-scripted/pre-devised beforehand. The contributors in this type of programme become celebrities in their own right, appearing in chat shows, film premieres and publishing their autobiographies. Contributors are chosen for their character, their occupation, what they look like, what they say, the way they react with the others and their age. This genre is aimed at a younger audience and the contributor reflects this. The production company may pay expenses to compensate for loss of earnings but, on the whole, it is unlikely to pay much and not at all if it can get away with it. The first series of MTV's *Living on the Edge* did not pay and I have been told anecdotally that when several contributors asked to be paid for series 2, they were replaced. If you are working on this type of programme, check with the producer before you mention *any* money at all.

Documentaries

The main difference between someone appearing on a half-hour chat show and taking part in a similar length documentary is that a documentary takes considerably longer to film. Anyone appearing in a documentary gives up a lot of their time, potentially exposes themselves to the world and has more to gain – and lose.

A documentary is, by its very nature, supposed to *document* reality. This is not the place for a media debate on the issues of reality except to confirm that most documentary makers try their utmost to present the truth as they see it. It is important that the programme team do not impose their own viewpoint over the opinions of the contributors. Nor should they intentionally misinterpret or misrepresent what people say (refer to Ofcom and BBC Editorial Guidelines). Controversies do occur. A trailer for a 2007 documentary, *A Year with the Queen*, was edited to make it look like the Queen had stormed angrily out of a photo shoot, resulting in the resignation of the Controller of BBC1. Allegations that it had tarnished the relationship between the Palace and the BBC were also made.

It is surprisingly common for production crews to get personally involved in the lives of their subjects although, in the majority of cases, this happens with emotional topics or when the documentaries are filmed over several months. During the filming of a series about couples undergoing fertility treatment, a producer/director found herself pregnant and agonised about revealing this to the women who were now part of her daily life. Professionally speaking, perhaps programme makers should draw a line between themselves and their documentary subjects. In some extraordinary way, you must be prepared for an umbilical cord making you feel responsible for how someone comes across on screen and their subsequent welfare.

For documentaries, it is best practice to meet people beforehand. What do they look like? Do they talk well? Are they nervous? Will the audience feel attuned and sympathetic to them?

It is virtually impossible to know beforehand how well someone will work on television. Their confidence and how articulate they are at the initial meeting are good indicators but fallible. I have met wonderful people who fell apart in front of the camera and others, initially shy and reticent, who came across as quietly confident and well informed. Usually, however, the initial gut feeling is an accurate indicator.

Finding people in the first place depends on the type of documentary and its topic. If it is based on a situation such as a driving school, trawl through several driving schools, getting speculative permission first. It is a bit chicken and egg – does one get permission to film first or find suitable people? There is no hard and fast answer, it depends on the circumstances.

When 'casting', meet more people than you intend to film so that you can whittle down the unsuitable ones and have reserves for those who inevitably back out.

Aim for a variety of age, class, race and gender. The types represented by the Spice Girls, One Direction and other manufactured groups are an example of somebody for everybody. Try not to fill the programme with eccentrics but involve a few 'normal' people as well. The major ingredient of a docu-soap is the people and their stories which is what makes them work. Avoid stereotypes – although it could be argued that they make for a better programme; the audience likes having its prejudices confirmed. Sociologists and critics, however, question the use of stereotypes in television and docu-soaps in particular. *People Like Us*, a 2013 fly-on-the-wall documentary on BBC3 about Harpurhey, Manchester, was criticised for showing a distorted view of the residents of the town. Newspapers reported how the contributors were appalled at their depiction in the programme and the local MP, Graham Stringer, added his voice to the protests. In the face of this, the BBC replied that the programme focused on the resilience and resourcefulness of the young people in the programme. All I shall say on this matter is that this is an example of how careful a production team needs to be when making this type of programme.

Visit prospective contributors in their own setting. If they are comfortable in their own surroundings, this gives a better idea of their personality and reaction to appearing on television. It also offers an insurance policy to validate their identity and corroborate the honesty clause should one be required. Another important issue is checking locations in order to film them in their own territory. The producer of *People Like Us* will have done this.

Why do people commit themselves to being filmed? The star-maker fixation is where teenagers don't aspire to a job, they just want fame. The 'this will change my life and make me famous' concept is a major reason for signing up for a year on a tropical island or having every minute of the day recorded for three months in a 'social experiment'. For some, it worked; for instance, the personalities in *The Only Way is Essex* or Jane McDonald, who, since appearing in *The Cruise* in the 1990s, has appeared regularly on *Loose Women*. These are exceptions. Most people who take part in a documentary are never heard of again in media terms although it may change their life in ways which we, the viewer, do not know about.

A researcher, however, must be aware that anyone taking part in a documentary risks, as a consequence, the breakdown of their marriage, their business folding or losing their job. But it is not entirely the researcher or television itself that should bear the brunt of the responsibility. The people taking part are not entirely innocent bystanders. It is, however, the programme makers' responsibility to ensure that the subjects know what they are letting themselves in for and that their life may be irrevocably changed and not necessarily for the better. Ofcom and the BBC Editorial Guidelines give advice on what you must tell a contributor before recording.

For further information, tips and details on organising contributors for filming and recording, refer to Chapter 8.

Persuading someone to be filmed or interviewed

It occasionally happens that someone has a particularly pertinent story or viewpoint but is unhappy or unwilling to be filmed or interviewed. Media folk are ambitious, persuasive, tenacious and implacable; you need to be sure of the reasons why someone is hesitant before bullying them into appearing. The ethical implications are enormous.

There may be a number of reasons for their reluctance:

- they have been in a traumatic or deeply personal situation and don't want to bring back the memory, especially in front of an audience of millions;
- they don't want to be recognised;
- they've been mistreated or misrepresented by the media in the past;
- they do not think their story is important enough;
- they're afraid of making a fool of themselves.

All the regulatory guidelines are specific about approaching the extremely distressed. Section 7.4.41 of the BBC Editorial Guidelines states: 'We should normally request interviews with people who are injured or grieving following an accident or disaster by approaching them through friends, relatives or advisers.

We should not:

- put them under pressure to provide interviews
- harass them with repeated phone calls, emails, text messages or knocks at the door

- stay on their property if asked to leave
- normally follow them if they move on.

If you persist with someone in this position, you *must* ensure your actions are justified within the remit of the guidelines.

Being mistreated or misrepresented by the media in the past is a common reason for being turned down. I know how the media operate and I've turned down programme appearances – even when offered a fee!

A rural headmaster once refused me permission to film his pupils. Apparently, a film crew had filmed there a year or two previously and because no-one had explained the filming procedure (I hesitate to use the words 'misrepresented' or 'lied'), the children had re-enacted the same shots over and over again until they were cold, hungry, in tears and hours late for school. He was understandably angry and upset. I commiserated, cajoled and sweet-talked my way, speaking to many of the parents (it was a small school) and finally persuaded him to let us film. The director and crew were warned to shoot as quickly and economically as possible. A bouquet of flowers, for what it was worth, was dispatched with the facility fee and thank-you letter.

An arrogant and mob-handed attitude can do untold damage to the general perception of film making, especially if there is little prior information on the processes involved. Filming takes a long time, and for those being filmed it can be boring. It always has been and it always will.

For those who turn down taking part because they don't think their story is important enough, you must rely on persuasion. The offer of a fee may sweeten it. The same applies for those who don't want to be filmed because they are afraid of making a fool of themselves. In my experience, these are the hardest to persuade and you may have to concede failure. Some producers don't take kindly to this. My attitude is pragmatic. If someone is persuaded against their will, the likely outcome is that they will be dreadful and you may as well have given up gracefully in the first place – as well as possibly contravening regulatory bodies' codes.

On the other hand, most people are only too willing to talk to the cameras or to a journalist.

Doorstepping

This is the practice of turning up unannounced with a camera or sound recorder and demanding that someone speaks to you while you record. *Cowboy Builders* on Channel 5 is a typical exponent, as are the paparazzi who stalk celebrities for a photograph or sound bite. It goes without saying that such people don't want to be recorded. Apart from current affairs programmes and the news, researchers are rarely expected to do this. The main considerations are ones of ethics (privacy) and safety. Irate victims tend to take offence. Matt Allwright, a presenter of BBC's *Watchdog,* had a protein drink poured over him whilst interviewing someone for *Rogue Traders.* The producers thought it was urine.

The BBC's Editorial Guidelines on doorstepping are in Section 7 (Privacy) and include doorstepping for news and current affairs with and without prior approach, doorstepping for comedy, entertainment, news gathering and research. The BBC includes phone calls and intercoms in doorstepping but not vox pops. Section 7.4.30 says: 'It often involves an infringement of privacy and should normally be a last resort'. It requires approval by senior management.

Anonymity

For those who do not wish to be recognised, can you justify persuading them to take part if they are putting themselves in physical danger? Should someone coming out as gay be faced later with parental ostracism and the subsequent emotional turmoil? In many countries, homosexuality is illegal. How would you feel if, by appearing on television, what you were terrified of materialised?

Many media professionals, in order to persuade someone to appear, promise anonymity by making the contributor unrecognisable. A common method is to record the person under low lights or in silhouette. This cannot be guaranteed – not necessarily because of lack of integrity from the director or cameraman's part but because someone in the transmission area adds luminance to what he sees as poor lighting. Alternatively, film the person facing away from the camera. This is still no fail-safe; hair colour and style are recognisable to anyone in the know, as is the other approach of filming extreme close-ups of mouth and eyes. Another common method is pixelation or facial blurring. This has a variable result; by half-closing my eyes, I can recognise most of the features of someone and if I knew them, I could certainly identify them. To quote Section 6.4.12 from the BBC guidelines, '*Blurring rather than pixelation, which can be reversed, is the best way of ensuring anonymity in pictures*'.

Voice disguise is an option; although people feel less vulnerable on radio, they still request anonymity and voice disguise is an added security on television too. To do this, complete co-operation with the sound and editing department is required; it must be explained on air and in the voiceover that the contributor's voice has been intentionally distorted. In extreme cases, actors' voices are used. They need to be paid.

In order to ensure anonymity, a mixture of the above strategies is usually employed, with varying success.

There are other reasons for anonymity. In *UK Border Force,* some people's identities are concealed because they have been, for instance, screened for drugs; a court case might be pending and revealing their identity could compromise the trial.

Number plates are blurred for reasons of security and confidentiality. This is the domain of the producer and video editor but the researcher needs to be aware of it as an extra safeguard in checking it happens. The BBC Editorial Guidelines say:

> We must ensure when we promise anonymity that we are in a position to honour it, taking account of the implications of any possible court order demanding the disclosure of our unbroadcast material. When anonymity is essential, no document, computer file, or other record should identify a contributor or source. This includes notebooks and administrative paperwork as well as video and audio material. (BBC Editorial Guidelines, Section 6: Fairness, Contributors and Consent, Anonymity 6.4.11)

Children

Working with children is a potential minefield. Even more so since the deficiencies of safeguarding children from such as Jimmy Savile and Stuart Hall have been exposed.

Most children love the idea of appearing in the media: television, radio and newspapers. For a one-off event, a Saturday morning children's programme or their photo in the paper, great. The child isn't taking time off school and may actually learn something about how the media works. However, there are regulations to be considered and, since Jimmy Savile's exposure as a prolific paedophile, considerably more pressure on protecting children.

- Any child under 16 interviewed for the media must have parental permission.
- The child itself must give informed consent.
- Any information disclosed about children should not put the child at risk therefore surnames are rarely revealed.
- Children under 16 must be chaperoned at all times by a responsible adult, usually a parent. The child must never be left alone. If several children are coming from the same school, depending on the number, one teacher can accompany them. Legally, however, if a child (or children) is accompanied to the studio by anyone other than a parent, parental permission must be sought in writing beforehand.

- Chaperones (other than parents) must be approved by the local education authority (LEA). Teachers are, of course, already licensed by their LEA.
- Chaperones must have a *clean* DBS check (Disclosure and Barring Service – replacing CRB, Criminal Records Bureau) or DS (Disclosure Scotland) in Scotland. Just because someone has a DBS check, it does not mean they have a clean record. A DBS check reports *any* police record even if the offence was years ago. For instance, someone convicted of shoplifting when they were 18 will have this recorded on their DBS check. Obviously, anyone with recorded violence or offences against children should not be employed. The BBC DBS checks all staff likely to work with children before employing them (at the time of writing) to ensure that events like those of Jimmy Savile never happen again. In Scotland, the BBC protects children via the Protecting Vulnerable Groups Scheme (PVG Scheme).
- For time off school, the head teacher must grant permission. Very often, a parent is prepared to approach them for you. Head teachers tend to consider a pupil appearing on television and radio as educational but in the current climate against parentally condoned truancy, the head teacher *must* give authorisation prior to recording.
- According to Equity rules, if a child actor or model is *working*, the chaperone is a professional and will be paid. This applies even to parents.
- Remember, these rules apply anywhere – not just in studio. Jimmy Savile allegedly molested children and vulnerable adults wherever he could.

Other considerations:

- check beforehand what they intend to wear and suggest they bring a change of clothes in case their choice is unsuitable. Children are more likely than adults to insist on wearing sweatshirts emblazoned with commercial logos (e.g. Nike, Adidas) and must be encouraged to wear something else, however unfashionable it might appear to their friends. This is less important for newspaper photos although obviously it depends on why the child is being interviewed or having their photo taken. In this case, remind the parent that it would be good if the child were in, say, their Brownie uniform or their sports gear;
- as a rule of thumb, children under 16 appearing as themselves on television and not acting in a drama do not require make-up. The make-up department prefers to make the final decision;
- remind them to go to the loo first.

Child employment is heavily regulated and a child performing on stage, television, film, commercials or as a model must be licensed by their LEA. The casting department usually oversees this and is well aware of the current legislation governing child actors regarding the number of hours they are allowed to work and the time off between working hours.

Some LEAs interpret the rules very strictly, insisting all children in their area are licensed even for one day off school. In my experience, this rarely happens but I have come across it. An example of a licensing problem occurred in 2013 when three boys aged under 13 were refused licences by their LEAs to perform live after 7pm in the BBC's *Last Night of the Proms* (*The Times*, 20 September 2013).

To obtain a licence, three weeks' notice should be given before the performance in question. Any less than this and it depends on the LEA as to whether it can process the licence in time. Some are more accommodating than others but it may simply come down to how stretched they are in the office.

One of the licence's requirements is that a child missing more than a certain number of days from school has to have a tutor but, apart from appearances in soaps or feature films, this is rare. The casting department can recommend one. As with the chaperone, the tutor must be approved by the LEA and be in possession of a clean DBS check. Both chaperones and tutors need somewhere to wait whilst the pupil is on set. This may be as simple as a chair at the back of the studio or even next to them in the audience. For children with a tutor, a suitable room must be supplied for schoolwork when the child is not required on set. This can be a dressing room or the green room.

Although it appears that Jimmy Savile wasn't afraid to touch children inappropriately on set, it was in the dressing rooms that he was at his most dangerous. It is impossible to totally prevent child molestation should someone be determined enough but stringent systems must be in place to give children as much protection as possible. Obviously, children must never be left on their own and should be accompanied everywhere in the television and radio studios.

For further guidance on working with children, contact the LEA, Equity and the casting department. The regulatory bodies' guidelines, Ofcom and the BBC, are useful and updated whenever issues come to light. The BBC's Child Protection Policy can be found online.

Audiences

Tickets for television recordings are free. The length of time it takes to record a show, the constant repositioning of cameras, the restrictions on audience sight lines and the fact that, if mistakes are made, certain takes and links may be recorded many times mean that, at the time of writing, no television company would dare charge. Also, as the audience is often an integral part of the show, it could be argued (although no-one ever does) that perhaps the audience should be paid to be there.

The BBC and larger television companies have dedicated departments to fill audience seats.

It is increasingly rare for researchers to be called upon to find an audience although they may occasionally be asked to find specific people with specific stories to sit in the audience. *Surprise Surprise* and *The Jeremy Kyle Show* are examples. In this situation, an accurate list of where everyone is sitting is essential for the director, floor manager, cameramen and sound recordist (so that people can be miked up). It is usually up to the researcher to provide this.

For radio shows such as BBC's *Gardener's Question Time*, the audience will have an interest in gardening and the show is recorded live at venues around the country. For this reason, gardening clubs and horticultural societies contact the production offices offering themselves as hosts. The host society is responsible for allocating the tickets and may charge for spares.

Finals of programmes like *The X Factor* and *Britain's Got Talent* where friends and supporters of the finalists sit in the audience may have tickets allocated by the production staff.

The audience for *University Challenge* consists of student supporters organised via the university and the production office. The student body may pay for the transport.

It is common for a maximum number of tickets to be allocated, the number depending on the show's popularity. Virtually all shows' audiences are filled by online application nowadays with group bookings made by telephone.

Daytime recordings create the most logistical headache for providing an audience. In the not so distant past, the local old people's home provided banks of old ladies for afternoon recordings. This is less common nowadays because production personnel prefer the aesthetically attractive, youthful audience. No comment. I will add, however, that media students often fill studio audiences . . .

Because of insurance and health and safety requirements, most studios have a lower age limit of 16. *You've Been Framed* and radio's *Counterpoint* are examples of a handful of programmes accepting younger children who must be chaperoned. Another issue is one of truancy. During one of Manchester's frequent truancy sweeps, a child was caught accompanying its parents to a recording at Granada TV – with no head teacher's permission.

It occasionally happens that contributors need to bring their children – teenage mothers taking part in a current affairs show, for instance. Check with the producer if there is money in the budget for a qualified and vetted nanny. The last thing a programme wants is a tabloid scoop about abandoned babies in the green room.

The tickets sent to the audience will state contractual details and health and safety issues like the no smoking/no eating policies. A warning clause will also be inserted if animals are likely to appear or if there are flashing lights. This covers the television company against complaints of allergies, issues with pregnancy, phobias and epilepsy.

Audience clothing is worth mentioning. For some shows, audience members wearing prominent logos may have to be moved to a less obvious position, or have their tops put on backwards or inside out. In shows where lighting is an issue, people wearing darker clothes may be moved nearer the front for the required visual effect. The tactful rearrangement of audience members around the studio may fall on the shoulders of the floor manager or an available researcher.

Studio practice

Bringing guests into studio

The guest has been booked so now they must turn up for the recording with the minimum of hassle, angst and other potential problems. Planning is required to ensure everything runs smoothly once they arrive in studio.

In the case of celebrities, although the casting department sends the contract to the agent, it is worth writing an email or faxing the agent with the following details:

- the name of the programme, date and recording time;
- the topic to be discussed or what the guest is to do;
- travel details.

It is unusual for researchers to book train tickets but as they are the contact point for the agent, celebrity guest or contestant, they often liaise. In large companies, the travel desk books the tickets and either sends them out or gives them to the researcher to do so. Frankly, I recommend sending the ticket direct to the celebrity rather than the agent as there is less possibility of snags. Make sure you note down the travel details first. For internet bookings, print several copies of the details, including one for yourself.

The guest may have certain requirements which the researcher, as point of contact, should pre-empt and either deal with personally or inform the relevant person. These include:

- dietary requirements: vegetarian, coeliac disease, etc.;
- diabetics requiring regular mealtimes;
- special considerations, e.g. reinforced chairs. Warn production designers and floor managers *in advance*;
- sensitive skin requiring a special brand of make-up which may have to be brought in specially;
- book a parking space in the car park if the guest is driving.

Depending on the programme and the treatment, the director, producer and presenter also need:

- special props such as copies of books. The agent or manager can help or point you in the right direction;
- a biography and/or background notes (see page 83).

In order to troubleshoot potential disasters, the researcher can:

- get a direct contact number (although most agents won't reveal celebrity numbers) to confirm travel arrangements in person, thus preventing misinformation and last-minute changes;
- give your mobile phone/home number to the agent/guest for out-of-hour emergencies;
- telephone the day before to confirm and check there are no unexpected hitches like illness. This leaves time to set up a replacement;
- if a guest is staying overnight at a hotel before recording, phone to confirm their safe arrival. Depending on your relationship, it may be a friendly gesture to personally check their well-being.

Should the unthinkable occur and a guest fails to materialise, the more notice there is, the better. You will get excuses, some of which are true, some not, but the result is the same – a no-show.

The production assistant (PA) is usually responsible for assigning dressing rooms and sending the list to Reception but get a copy before guests arrive. The floor manager or director devises the recording schedule (the running order) and again, check it in order to reassure guests when they arrive so they know exactly what is happening.

If a guest is squeezing in a job whilst performing on stage or working on a film, the timings are crucial and it is *essential* the celebrity leaves the studio (or your newspaper interview) on time.

The above are recommended for *all* programme contributors, although you should seriously consider whether to give out personal phone numbers to all and sundry. Some companies issue company mobiles to its staff and I recommend this number is handed out rather than your own personal phone. Keep the phone with you at all times but switched to vibrate when necessary . . .

Minding guests

I know of a young man who had a three-day interview for a six-week runner's contract in a famous post-production house. One task he was given was to get hot chocolate for the staff to see how polite he was. He got the job. On his first day, he minded a well-known presenter recording a voiceover. Why am I quoting this anecdote? Because someone in the production office takes on the role of host or hostess minding contestants, celebrities, experts and whoever is involved. This is often the runner or researcher. In the early days of television, the call-boy (a young lad or girl in their first job) accompanied actors between dressing room, make-up and wardrobe and onto the set. Nowadays, apart from an assistant stage manager (ASM) working on a large production, the researchers do it.

Together with dollops of tact for nervous guests, the researcher must be familiar with the studio set-up and the location of make-up and wardrobe departments. They must be aware of the recording schedule so no-one is late to the studio floor. If a guest has brought personal props or photographs, the researcher ensures the props are safe and the photographs sent to the correct department for recording. If in doubt about which department, the floor manager will know. As the floor manager is probably more approachable during recording day, check with them rather than the director or producer who is likely to be fraught up in the control room.

For anyone expecting travel expenses or an appearance fee, the researcher must obtain a float in advance. Payment may, however, be the responsibility of the PA or the casting department. Now that money is usually paid by bank transfer, check the company procedure beforehand. Always obtain a receipt to clear any float.

Background notes for presenters and producers

The presenter/interviewer and producer need to know what each contributor, contestant or expert is likely to say. Biographies of celebrity guests for background information may also be required. What nobody wants, and hasn't time to read, is 30 pages of closely written information or random internet searches.

- Half a side of A4 should (depending on the programme) be sufficient.
- Bullet points will do.

Information sources for background notes and what to include

- *Celebrities* – the agent or manager, publisher or IMDb (Internet Movie Database website) will provide short biographies and a list of credits. These can be précised into short notes but may already be concise enough.
- *Experts* – *Who's Who* (a directory of influential people still living) may have your guest listed alongside their date of birth, status, education, publications, hobbies and other useful information. This directory is now an online subscription service although libraries hold a hard copy. *Debrett's* online is another directory with biographies especially of the peerage and those who have received honours from the state. Speak to their professional society. Ask the expert themselves.
- *Contributors making short points on a chat/quiz show* – the initial phone call. Their name (correctly spelt) and a summary (two or three lines maximum) should suffice.
- The internet! Remember, however, that this is secondary research and may perpetuate inaccuracies.

It is worth including guidance questions to lead the presenter more quickly to the guest's anecdote.

Talk back system

Presenters and interviewers are wired up to the talk back system with an earpiece so that they can receive direct instructions from the producer and director whilst the show is being recorded. Researchers are usually wired to the same system and therefore immediately contactable.

Rarely does a researcher find themselves in the studio control room (also known as the gallery or box depending on the television station) during recording. More often, they are found on the studio floor or running (walking purposefully . . .) between the dressing rooms, make-up, wardrobe and green room (the waiting area named after theatre green rooms traditionally painted green to relieve the glare from the stage lights).

Clothing for contestants

Researchers are always asked what should be worn in studio. Unless there is a house style (colour co-ordination, for instance), the answer is simple – whatever the guest feels comfortable in. There is one caveat: clothing with large logos and trademarks is regarded as sponsorship and is not permitted. Guests will be asked to change it.

Some clothes are more televisual than others. Although cameras are better than they were, large solid blocks of primary colours can flare or wash someone out, and narrow strips or small spots are apt to strobe. Think of sofas in daytime chat shows ... Even wardrobe designers are fallible, although well aware of what *should* work. For this reason, suggest contestants bring an alternative just in case. This also helps should someone else on the same programme wish to wear the same colour which might make it hard to differentiate them.

Celebrities are generally guided by agents, managers, A & R, or themselves. Wardrobe assistants are on hand for last-minute ironing and stitching on of loose buttons.

Payment

Payment? This is a difficult question. Most people are only too willing to appear free for those 15 minutes of fame. Local newspapers never pay the general public for a contribution to a newspaper article. Radio stations don't pay people who phone in. For television news, no-one is paid. Quiz programmes don't pay – what's the point when the contestant has the chance of winning thousands of pounds? However, travel expenses are usually covered.

Some programmes include out-of-pocket and travel expenses in the budget and some don't, so confirm with the producer before mentioning it over the phone or in an email. Members of the public assume the media are oozing with money; if the issue hasn't been raised beforehand, it's embarrassing when someone asks for payment. Always explain if expenses will be paid (or not) and if there is any other reimbursement.

Fees for celebrities have been discussed earlier in the chapter.

Experts expect to be paid and should be; a typical fee, depending on the level of contribution, may be around the £100 mark. They also expect travel expenses to be reimbursed (unless the programme provides a taxi). Some stations, notably the BBC, have set (notoriously low) fees, the rate depending on the contributor's status. The expert may ask for more. Politicians and the like (spokespersons for news items) are generally unpaid. For newspapers, it is unusual for experts to be paid but, again, it depends on their contribution. Check with the editor. Other companies negotiate (the lower the better) and the amount depends on the type of show, the budget, the contribution, the length of time the guest is required and how desperate the producer is to include them!

And afterwards . . .

Thank-you letters, transmission and publication dates

It is a matter of courtesy to thank contributors both when they leave the recording session or after filming and in a follow-up thank-you letter. Contributors are desperate to know when they are 'on telly' or 'in the paper' and if you know the transmission or publication date, the follow-up letter can confirm it. If by chance, and it happens quite frequently, the TX or publication date changes, a quick phone call or email will do wonders for the credibility and goodwill of the station and newspaper.

An alternative way of letting people know TX dates is in the permission release form or letter confirming their appearance. It is not always possible to inform contributors when their programme is likely to be transmitted (and even if they will actually take part). The production office should have a vague idea. '7pm on Tuesdays from February' is far more helpful than 'sometime next year'. Because production schedules are so frantic, this removes the burden of phoning everyone up especially as, by transmission, the production team is likely to be working on different projects.

For journalists, it may be harder to guarantee the inclusion of a story or a quotation in a newspaper especially if something more newsworthy comes up. Thank the contributor when you take their quotation or story. People don't usually expect a thank-you letter for appearing in the newspaper.

Copies

Contributors often request programme copies, giving the excuse that they will be away on holiday, they forgot it was on, they live outside the transmission area, etc. Few TV stations make provision for this service, a commonly given reason being that if everyone who requested a copy got one, there'd be no time to make the programme. A more valid reason is that the cumulative cost of engineers' time is too much. A final reason, of course, is copyright. By letting people know the TX time and warning them in advance that copies cannot be made, the request is averted beforehand. With YouTube, BBC iPlayer, YouView, podcasts, VOD and similar technologies, contributors have other resources to preserve their 15 minutes of fame.

For people who have made a significant contribution to a BBC TV or radio programme, i.e. as a performer or member of the production team, if the show is held in the archives, a contributor's copy can be requested. This service is not available for people who appeared in the audience or crowd scenes. Terms and conditions can be found on the BBC's website giving information as to which programmes can be purchased. At the time of writing, a single DVD from the original broadcast master is £108. An audio CD copy of a radio programme is £60. If the contributor had been promised a free copy by the programme makers, this must be supplied by the production team.

Journalists never promise that an article can be vetted beforehand and they also never promise to send a copy of the article. Nowadays, with so many newspapers online, it is easy enough for someone to print their story up from the computer.

Personal safety

There are some strange people out there and ambitious media people want to make interesting programmes and newspaper articles. This inevitably means working on weird, bizarre, sensational, controversial and, at times, dangerous ideas. When working on programmes about crime or the abnormal, the researcher is putting themselves at risk and personal safety is a serious issue. The creative industries are increasingly concerned with risk assessment and avoiding potential problems. Taking precautions is advisable before meeting new people. Bearing in mind that the most dangerous situations are unpredictable, anyone genuine will appreciate and understand the need for such measures. They, too, are at potential risk meeting someone calling themselves a researcher or journalist.

- Always let someone in your office know where you are going and whom you are meeting.
- Leave the phone number of where you are meeting them with a colleague.
- Take a mobile phone, leave it on whilst away from the office but don't use it when driving which is illegal.
- Ensure your mobile phone is fully charged.
- Meet in a public place, although this may not be possible if you are meeting the person at their house, place of work or assessing filming on location. Refer to Chapter 8.
- Work out the route before you leave. Check the SatNav route before you go. Fastest journey time usually supplies the major routes. Shortest route might take you down narrow lanes which aren't navigable. We've all heard the stories of cars getting stuck in fords, etc.
- Ensure your car is roadworthy and there is sufficient petrol. Your car should be insured for business use.
- Leave with plenty of time so you are not stressed and flurried.

Ethics

All regulatory bodies take a serious view of how people are treated by the creative industries. Children, the sick, old and infirm are of special consideration. Examples of spurious practice are found in all aspects of the creative industries. CBBC's *Hoopla!* was investigated by Ofcom when a child involved in an eating contest was seen retching into a bucket on a programme transmitted on 2 November 2012. *The X Factor* was investigated by Ofcom for humiliating contestants at the transmitted audition stage, in particular those whose children may be bullied at school because of their treatment on the show (Alison Brunton performing a Lady Gaga routine in September 2012).

In June 2013, the Press Complaints Commission resolved an issue in which the photograph of a man who was at school with one of the men facing charges for murdering Lee Rigby in Woolwich was published in the *Sunday Mirror* without his permission. The newspaper published a retraction.

It is easier to write than to do – but think *hard* before making any decisions. Your actions affect other people as well as your career.

Summary

- There is no 'one stop' place to find contributors.
- Double-check all arrangements.
- Whenever possible, get direct line and mobile phone numbers to save going through switchboards.
- Take note of gut feelings that something is wrong. You are usually right.
- Refer to the Ofcom Broadcast Codes, Channel 4 Producers Handbook and BBC Editorial Guidelines about dealing fairly with contributors.

Further reading

Couldry, Nick, Madianou, Mirca and Pinchevski, Amit (eds) *Ethics of Media*, Palgrave Macmillan, 2013

Frost, Chris, *Journalism: Ethics and Regulation*, 3rd edn, Longman Practical Journalism, 2011

Harcup, Tony, *The Ethical Journalist*, Sage, 2006

Keeble, Richard, *Ethics for Journalists* (Media Skills), 2nd edn, Routledge, 2008

Websites

Amazon: www.amazon.co.uk

Athletics events and athletes' biographies: www.britishathletics.org.uk

BBC Editorial Guidelines: www.bbc.co.uk/guidelines/editorialguidelines

BBC College of Journalism: www.bbc.co.uk/academy/journalism

BBC College of Production: www.bbc.co.uk/academy/production

Celebrity Bulletin: www.fens.com

Celebrity Intelligence: www.celebrityintelligence.com

Channel 4 Producers Handbook guidance: www.channel4.com/producers-handbook

Debrett's, an authority on the peerage and etiquette with biographies of influential people: www.debretts.com

Drama UK, amalgamation of the Conference of Drama Schools and the National Council for Drama Training: www.dramauk.co.uk

DueDil, free online database checking company and director information: www.duedil.com

The Handbook, London venue guide and celebrity PR resource: www.thehandbook.com

IMDb, International Movie Database: www.imdb.com

IMG Worldwide, global sports, fashion and media business also representing mainly sports talent: www.img.com

Magic Circle, magicians' trade association: www.themagiccircle.co.uk

Ofcom: www.ofcom.org.uk

Personal Managers' Association represents agents for actors, writers and directors: www.thepma.com

Sport England: www.sportengland.org

Spotlight, directory of actors, choreographers, directors and presenters: www.spotlight.com

The White Book, events production directory, free to use search engine: www.whitebook.co.uk

Who's Who, online subscription directory of eminent people in the UK: www.ukwhoswho.com

5
Pictures, photographs and film clips

Imagine a world without pictures. By means of mobile phones, tablets and digital cameras, the most inaccessible places in the world and the most outrageous events can be seen anywhere with, literally, a click of a button. If only life were that simple in media terms.

At some time in their career, everyone who works in the creative industries will handle photographs, pictures or film clips. For TV it is mainly visual – archive news clips, photographs of an ageing Hollywood actress in her heyday, a family photo, a clip from a feature film. For radio, it is sound archives and film/television clips with sound tracks suitable for broadcast although the job is increasingly involved with providing visual images for websites, iPhone streams and webcams. For the journalist, newspapers require visuals and, with cross-media platforms, the website does as well.

The most important consideration is copyright. Whatever you use, the chance is that someone somewhere owns the rights to the material.

Downloading samples of material from agencies via the internet is a useful research tool but no material found on it is copyright free for broadcast use or in newspapers. Pathé News (see later) has samples on the internet intended for downloading by students on media courses. For broadcast use, however, royalties must be paid. A search on the internet may throw up a useful production still from a film and, by contacting the distribution company direct, it may be possible to use it royalty free if it is *promoting* the film but promotion is only possibly before general release and for a short period immediately afterwards. The distribution company will provide extracts and inform you of the copyright holder if it isn't them. By all means, use the internet for inspiration and ideas and for downloading samples from agencies, but the official body still needs to be contacted.

Who owns the rights? The person who provides the photographs, films and pictures often does so but do not assume that the source itself is the only owner

– or indeed *the* owner – of the rights. In some cases, you may have to pay two fees or more.

Photographs and pictures

Photographs, paintings, lithographs, drawings and other visuals add an extra dimension to every area of the media. The old cliché is true: a picture paints a thousand words.

The most uncomplicated photograph to find and use is one supplied, owned and *taken* by a contributor; the snapshot taken by mum of daughter ten years ago. The contributor took the photograph, owns the copyright and, by supplying it, tacitly gives permission to use it. These photos are increasingly printed in local newspapers, on radio show webpages and local TV news for a prize or merely the kudos – the 'see your photo on telly' approach. It's doubtful that the photographer will expect payment and everyone is happy with the arrangement.

Strictly Come Dancing used Instagram in the 2013 series to capture contestants as they stepped off-stage so viewers could see their reactions to their performances. Live events like the BBC's *The Great North Run* urge relatives to send Instagram photos of competitors. In Channel 4's *Gok Live: Stripping for Summer* the audience was encouraged to send Instagram images to be broadcast. Social media companies are keen to exploit situations which promote them. By utilising UGC, TV programmes involve the audience to add impact. A cheap content ruse?

Schools and other institutions are increasingly taking photographs and sending them to a newspaper, together with a covering press release, for an event a journalist did not attend. Again, the copyright officially belongs to the institution concerned but by supplying it to the newspaper, they are implicitly agreeing to publication. They may request an agreement with the paper for copyright ownership for future use.

It gets more complicated when someone else took the photograph, a wedding being the perfect example. Technically, the copyright is owned by the photographer even though the bride and groom understandably believe that, because they commissioned the photos in the first place, they own the copyright. It is a frustrating exercise seeking the photographer for permission, especially when short of time. Many researchers take the expedient and pragmatic approach that most photographers won't remember an individual wedding (unless it is a celebrity one). This seems reasonable but repercussions can result in an unbudgeted expense and you, the researcher, being deemed responsible.

Another presumption is that, because copyright lasts 70 years after the death of the originator of the work, paintings like Leonardo da Vinci's *Mona Lisa* are out of copyright and the picture can be reproduced on screen or in a newspaper without incurring a fee. Wrong.

Firstly, one needs a photograph of it. The photographer owns the copyright of the photograph and expects a fee. An alternative is to send a photographer or film crew to the Louvre in Paris but, not only must the photographer be paid but the Louvre will charge a facility fee as well. You could go on the internet and find a photograph – but this was taken by someone who expects to be paid. With luck, the TV, radio station or picture desk of your newspaper already has a photograph on file taken by a staff photographer . . .

Photographic verification

But what about photographs supplied by the general public to newspapers and TV companies? The citizen journalist photo received via UGC. It could be of a catastrophe like the Thai tsunami or a misdemeanour by a celebrity. In the age of social media, these photographs are increasingly common and publication without verification has been the undoing of many a media professional. Piers Morgan, the now ex editor of the *Daily Mirror,* was one such casualty when, in 2004, he published fake photographs of British soldiers abusing an Iraqi prisoner. He insisted at the time that he did not know they were faked.

In the same way that articles must be verified, so must a photograph to ensure that it is not manufactured for malicious or mischievous purposes. The exif system (Exchangeable Image File Format) supplies information as to date and time, type of camera, model and make (including smartphones and scanners), aperture, shutter speed and focal length for images and sounds. Some smart-phones have co-ordinates: longitude and latitude. Ask the person supplying the photograph about the type of camera they used, where and when they took it, etc. If this doesn't match the exif data, something fishy is going on, com-promising verification. It may be expedient *not* to use the photograph.

Google Earth can check the area the photographer says they were in; is the background the same? Is the time of the day accurate by the position of the shadows? If not, beware.

Reverse image searching is useful. The website TinEye checks if other photos are the reverse of the one supplied to you. If yes, the source of the photo is misleading you and out for a quick buck.

Examples of where newspapers have caught fraudsters include a Syrian lesbian blogger exposed as a 30-something male student in Edinburgh. Someone contacted the *Guardian* saying they were from Syria when they were in India. It is easy to disguise one's identity in internet chat rooms so why should bloggers and photographs be any different? Verify photos before publication to save later embarrassment or worse.

Unfortunately, at the time of writing, video is hard to verify as there is, as yet, no exif system for it.

Photo and picture acquisition

Getting the *perfect* photo can be difficult. Newspapers employ photographers but a local paper may have one staff photographer bookable via a diary. National newspapers have more staff photographers but also engage freelancers. When a photographer is unavailable, for instance when working on another story, it is common, especially in local newspapers, for the journalist to take the photo. Most national newspapers nowadays encourage their staff to multi-skill, expecting journalists to add photography to their repertoire. Copyright law at the time of writing is that the photographer owns the copyright for the photograph with a reciprocal arrangement with the newspaper.

When making a television programme, a stills photographer can be booked to work alongside the crew and, of course, the same for a radio outside broadcast (OB). In the age of multi-skilling, it is unlikely that anyone will prevent you from taking your own photos – if you have time! Remember, the copyright is jointly owned by yourself and the media company should the photos be used elsewhere. You may need to negotiate . . .

So where else can you access the 'perfect' photograph or picture?

First, ask the contributors or people you are working with if they can supply photos or pictures – then go to the picture library.

Photograph and picture libraries

A major source for photographs and pictures is libraries and photographic agencies.

In a large media company, first contact the in-house picture library which may provide what you want. If the company owns the copyright, there is no royalty payment. For photos and pictures they store but for which copyright is held elsewhere, the librarian or picture desk editor should have details of the copyright holders and it is a simple step to negotiate reproduction permission and the fee. For unfamiliar names or an obsolete phone number, a call to the

British Association of Picture Libraries and Agencies (BAPLA) may provide an up-to-date contact.

Unfortunately, in-house picture libraries in TV companies are often of limited value as they are restricted to production stills or material for use in programmes that have little bearing on the new topic. For BBC researchers this may not be so. The BBC photo library dates back to 1924 and is run as a commercial enterprise where everyone pays a charge for using the facility. Because it is a public service organisation, its images cannot be used to endorse or promote third parties. For those working on BBC productions, there is a nominal internal costing charge.

Commercial libraries and agencies exist to make money from the photographs held in their databanks and the largest contain hundreds of thousands of images taken by a wide range of freelance photographers who own the rights to their own work. Both the agency and the photographer earn money when photographs are reproduced in books, magazines, newspapers, television or the internet. The agency supplies photographs and pays the photographer a certain percentage from the commission, usually 50% but this varies between agencies.

Libraries specialise. One holds collections on geography, another sport, action shots, people, natural history and so on. *The Kobal Collection* specialises in cinema and television, and holds paraphernalia such as film posters and fan magazines. *The Press Association* library specialises in photos printed in newspapers from the 1890s to today. *Rex Features* is renowned for its collection of show business and celebrities. Some specialise in archive material and here you will find lithographs and prints from books instead of photos although they might house a few of these by default. This is useful for visual material before the advent of photography. The *Mary Evans Picture Library* is perhaps the most famous.

For account holders, it is common for a library to allocate a dedicated account manager with a direct phone number and email address.

The governing body for picture libraries and agencies is BAPLA which publishes a list of its members. The website, www.bapla.org.uk, has a search facility where, by typing in the image you want in the category search, it will list the agencies supplying them. Specific images can be requested and the names of relevant agencies emailed back to you.

Agencies can be contacted by phone or email. Most agencies catalogue their photos online so that you can select photos from your computer. They cannot be downloaded without permission and many agencies use 'watermarks' (their name digitally embossed on the online photos) as a security measure. Visits to libraries (such as *Mary Evans* for archive prints) are strictly by appointment.

Once you have negotiated with the agency, photos and pictures can be down-loaded electronically. Images are mostly supplied as JPEG but sometimes there are special requirements so check you have the correct format.

There are other sources, including Flickr, Pinterest, Instagram, Creative Commons, etc., but just because they are on the internet, usage is not necessarily copyright free. In fact, it's best to assume that the pictures are under copyright and seek permission accordingly from the site or profile owner.

Flash fees

A sad indictment of modern life is that photographers find it harder than ever to make a living at photography; citizen journalism, ever smaller cameras, smartphones and low-price, royalty-free images have seen to that. However, in *specialist* areas where access is difficult (e.g. North Korea) or where quality really matters, prices have held up. There are so many images 'out there' that a photographer must showcase their pictures with multiple agencies in the hope that their work may be used.

The usual payment for reproducing photographs and other copyright pictures is the licence. In TV, it's the 'flash fee' (a reproduction or licence fee for the use of the images). The overall cost of the licence depends on how long the photograph is 'flashed' on screen and how many times the programme is likely to be repeated. The standard payment is a set fee for the first flash lasting a stipulated period of time, usually 30 seconds. A repeat flash within the same episode is normally a percentage of the first fee, commonly 50%. The cost itself depends on the source.

Because of the sheer volume of images on the internet nowadays, the price of the flash fee has remained constant or slightly diminished over the years as has the general cost of using photographs in newspapers or magazines unless it is a specialist market. There is no standard fee although most agencies charge around £70 for the first flash for one transmission in the United Kingdom but may charge more. Of course, for worldwide rights with more than one transmission and for a licence of up to ten years, the cost may be much higher. If you want to use the image in the opening titles, the licence is considerably more expensive. Deals can be struck if a photograph is used several times in a series or if the agency supplies a large amount of pictures.

For newspapers and magazines, the licence fee depends on the circulation figures and the type of newspaper. The picture agency *Alamy* has an online up-to-date pricing calculator and, at the time of writing, a 1/8-page photo for a national newspaper with a print run of up to a million copies and placed on an inside page but also online worldwide for one day could cost £210. For a provincial or free newspaper with a print run of 100,000 and printing the same photo inside with no website appearance, the cost could fall to £115. Of course, for regular clients, the pricing varies from the online calculator. In effect, deals are struck for the right client.

It is common practice for the agency to demand a credit printed next to the photograph; a notification of copyright, if you like.

Clearing copyright

The method by which permission is sought for the use of photographs (and music, see Chapter 7) is called 'clearing copyright'.

For pictures and photos, it is a simple procedure. The agency providing the photos sends or emails a form (effectively the licence) that is either completed by the PA (picture desk editor in newspapers) or anyone else taking the responsibility. It includes how long each picture was featured on screen. With account holders, a lot of the clearance is done online.

Fees are usually paid after transmission or publication although permission must be sought prior to reproduction (i.e. recording) or publication. Many agencies insist on fees being paid within three months of supplying the pictures.

Agencies pay the photographers who supplied the photos. With everything online nowadays, it should be simple for agencies to keep track of what photographs have been supplied and therefore automatically pay the right photographer but it is good sense for the journalist or researcher to log the photos used so that, when the invoice arrives, it can be checked against the photographs, thus ensuring you only pay for what was used. If you say to the agency 'We used ten of your photos', the agency won't know who to pay. *Alamy*, for instance, needs a specific list of images to raise an invoice.

Pictures and video on Twitter, Flickr, YouTube, Facebook, Instagram, etc. are, of course, still protected by copyright. In April 2012, Facebook bought Instagram for an estimated $1 billion. Shortly afterwards they provoked fury from its users by changing its policy to permit the buying and selling of photographs on their site to any third party (commercial, marketing and advertisers) without notification. A threat of boycott – and the policy changed. By all means, use the internet for inspiration and ideas but be aware that copyright must be established and the actual copyright holder may be difficult to ascertain.

Releases are required for any image or clip used for commercial use, i.e. to sell a product, promote something or raise money for a cause. For anyone working on a news programme or in newspapers where images are used for editorial purposes, releases are generally not required. If the images do *not* include people, buildings, trademarks, brands, works of art, etc. or if the people and buildings are not recognisable then, again, you do not need a release for commercial use. However, for images still in copyright such as works of art, you might still need additional third-party permission and therefore specialist legal advice. In these cases, speak to either the agency supplying the images or to the company lawyer.

Credits

It is not a legal requirement to credit individual photographers on-screen. However, for newspapers, books and magazines, especially when the photograph is of high aesthetic and technical quality and for reasons of copyright, it is common for both the photographer and the agency to have a picture credit.

It is also common for picture agencies to be credited at the end of television programmes when a large amount of their material is used within the series. A clause in the licence may insist on this.

It is usually stipulated that archive material (e.g. cinema and television clips) has a full on-screen credit displayed at the end of the programme. For feature film and television clips, the convention is to reveal the on-screen credit whilst the clip is playing. For sporting and other events governed by exclusive television rights, screen credits are also usually displayed during the broadcast of the clip itself. Double-check with the providers where the credits should be screened.

Photographers have the right to object to their photos being distorted or mutilated if they consider that it would damage their reputation.

It goes without saying that all captions, whether in the newspaper or on screen, must be spelt correctly.

Film and television clips

It is a common assumption that a documentary consisting almost entirely of archive footage is cheap to produce. After all, it's 'only a load of old films'. Unfortunately, nothing could be further from the truth and compilation programmes using a large amount of old footage can be extremely expensive – depending on who owns the copyright. The reason? Finding unique or hitherto little seen material is expensive in research time and royalty fees do not come cheap. Clips from feature films do not make cheap programmes either unless the company making the programme already owns the copyright.

When programmes use large amounts of library footage, it is common to hire specialist film researchers, often on a freelance basis. A few large companies employ specialist film researchers to be consulted in-house by anyone needing expert help.

A word of warning: unless the brief is relatively simple, a few shots of Paris, say, or a clip from a recent feature film for a celebrity interview, money and stress may be saved in the long term by employing a film research company. Check their charges and consult your producer. Simple briefs should be easy because this is how film libraries make their profits.

Where you start depends on what you want. Remember the curse: 'It'll only take an hour' always takes a lot longer!

Locating film clips/stock-shots and sound and video archive footage

There was considerable press coverage in May 2013 about the failure of the BBC's Digital Media Initiative (DMI), the intention of which was that all BBC archived material would be accessible from any BBC staff desktop from Salford, Bristol to London. It cost the BBC a reputed £91.4m. The DMI's Fabric Archive Database launched in 2012 is still available at the time of writing to help BBC staff search and request access to footage. BBC Scotland has a different system based on off-the-shelf tools so that staff in BBC Scotland can easily access BBC Scottish footage. It remains to be seen whether the BBC will replace the DMI.

For anyone working for a large company, the first stop is always the in-house film, video and sound library. There is no problem with access or copyright unless the material contains footage brought in from elsewhere and the librarians and notes on the logging sheets will forewarn you of this. Internal costing systems, however, are common and the budget may incur the same incidental costs as you would have to pay elsewhere. The information sheets will tell you what you can and can't use. Drama can be difficult and this is covered later.

Stock-shots are generalised film clips such as a beach scene, woods, Blackpool Tower and so on. They are too short and insignificant to warrant employing a video crew for a whole day. For stock-shots, again, it is worth going to the in-house video or film library first and asking if they have anything suitable. Everything is currently being digitised with catalogues generally available to everyone meaning that it is increasingly common to look for stock-shots yourself and check suitability. In my experience, in-house library stock-shots are often disappointing and there is a compromise between cost and quality. With the sheer volume of digital material nowadays, better-quality stock-shots are out there although it takes time to find them. Cost and time often win! If the stock-shots are not good enough, the next stop is the commercial stock-shot library, similar to an in-house library except that you pay commercial rates for the footage. The rates are still considerably cheaper than employing a video crew. The internet lists a huge variety of stock-shot libraries, although the quality of their material is variable. Of course, organisations such as the BBC, ITN, NBC, Channel 4, etc. all supply their footage at a commercial cost to other media companies.

Like photo libraries, stock-shot libraries specialise in their content from sports to geography. Beware the royalty-free claims; this is usually not applicable to commercial media companies.

A useful source is the British Universities Film and Video Council at www.bufvc.ac.uk. Its Researcher's Guide to Screen Heritage is a comprehensive directory of publicly accessible film and video collections, including sound. It has links to online resources such as radio archives, regional sound archives and specialist collections such as the National Motor Museum Film and Video Library, the Scottish Screen Archive at the National Library of Scotland and the National Media Museum, to list a few. As usual, copyright clearance is an issue for broadcast material.

The British Library's sound archive listening service is at the British Library in London with over a million discs and tens of thousands of tapes stored, including oral history and BBC broadcasts. The catalogue for the millions of recordings held in the archive is updated daily. The British Library online sound archive at http://sounds.bl.uk provides free online access for UK universities and further education institutions to 50,000 rare recordings of music, spoken word and others. The British Library runs a specialist reference team which can locate specific sound and video archives. This is generally free of charge but if you wanted to use any of the archives in a programme, you pay for the copy of the sound archive (the dubbing fee) plus the licence fee. The web addresses for other useful sound resources can be found at the end of the chapter. Again, copyright for media use must be checked first and you may have to pay.

News archives

News footage comes from a variety of sources. Before the advent of television, the main news source was the press and the wireless (radio) but an important visual source was the cinema newsreel, an important element of cinema-going until the late 1960s.

British Pathé News is perhaps the most famous of the cinema newsreels. Its footage dates from 1895 until 1970 when newsreels were superseded by television. British Movietone News has material from 1929 to 1979.

For other sources of news footage, ITN (which also manages footage from Reuters, ITN, Visnews, ITV Production, Fox News and Fox Movietone plus other collections) and the BBC are the most obvious. ITN at www.itnsource.com has footage from 1896 (archive film) and the material can be searched, viewed, ordered, licensed and downloaded online in a variety of formats. Check the format required for the programme before ordering to ensure the correct format.

The BBC library is at www.bbcmotiongallery.com and includes more than two million hours of footage from collections from the BBC, BBC News, CBS News, sport, CCTV (China), NHK (Japan) and ABC (Australia), among others. Much of the material is rights managed although there is some royalty-free footage but, as usual, 'royalty free' usually means for members of the general public and not media organisations. Licence agreements are online and you can price the clip as you view.

All sources have an online search facility whereby you merely type in a subject, e.g. Bluebird, and a list of associated stories will appear, often with running times. View the clip from your computer and negotiate the royalty payments. There will be a different charge for the general public downloading footage onto their PC than for media use – and the cost for the PC will be considerably less. If your company has an account with a news library, it is merely a matter of logging in with the password and sorting out your order and payment. Remember to inform the producer or editor of all costs – preferably *before* you order anything. It is easy to overspend. Most footage can be downloaded to a computer which makes it extremely easy for editing.

The main problem with *foreign footage* is the copyright issue. Both the BBC and ITN have stringers working abroad and their archives contain foreign filmed footage and details on the rights holders. NBC Universal Archives (mainly American footage) has a video library dating back to the late 1940s. This archive also includes the NBC Radio collection dating from 1935, some earlier rarer recordings, some film clips from Universal Film Studios and a photo agency. You must register to use this service. For other foreign news sources, it would be expedient to use a specialist film researcher.

ITN Source displays a warning on its website about third-party clearances – in other words, any material not owned or controlled outright by ITN but which is on its website. Effectively, if you want to use this type of material, you must still get written permission in the form of a licence from the third-party copyright holder.

The rights to the footage you have used will remain with the original rights holder, depending on the terms of the licence. It is also worth mentioning that, in the ITN terms and conditions, any material supplied by ITN cannot be edited to change the meaning or to bring ITN into disrepute. Nor can you use footage in which a news reporter or presenter appears or can be heard. If you want to use such footage, you must contact the ITN sales team directly.

Royalties for news footage

Footage is paid by the amount used and there is a minimum charge. Generally, the minimum is 30 seconds (or part of) although for ITN, it is a minute (or part of). It is possible nowadays to buy per clip regardless of how short it is.

Whichever source the news footage came from, the total royalty levied depends on how much is used, what it is used for (i.e. television, the internet – which has different rates for streaming, download-to-rent/own, etc. – adverts, corporate videos, feature films), the transmission area, the number of transmissions and the length of the licence (five/ten years and 'in perpetuity' is common).

On a sliding scale, feature films are the most expensive. British Pathé News at the time of writing charges £81 per second (minimum charge 10 seconds) for footage to be included in a feature film 'in perpetuity'. There are lower charges for museum displays, CD-Roms, the internet, pop promos and advertising. For television rights, there is another scale, with a minimum charge of £10 for 60 seconds for one country, unlimited transmission and one specified programme. The more countries the programme is sold to, the higher the rate. Licences apply for a fixed term, say five or ten years, and should the programme be repeated outside this time scale, the rights must be renegotiated.

For digital delivery with a 5 MB broadcast quality, mpeg2 files, same-day delivery, British Pathé (at the time of writing), charges:

1–3 clips	4–6	7–9	10–12	13–18
£50	£70	£90	£104	£122

For Quicktime (next-day delivery), charges are:

1–3 clips	4–6	7–9	10–12	13–18
£58	£111	£164	£216	£290

Using the online pricing calculator at the time of writing, a 15-second mute clip of King George VI's funeral in 1952 from BBC Motion Gallery for a national TV documentary for up to five years on broadcast-quality PAL would cost £209. Using the same clip for advertising nationally in all media with a five-year licence and broadcast-quality PAL costs £2,839. Download the licence. Easy.

As with picture libraries, deals can be struck if a large amount of footage is to be used.

Many film libraries will conduct film research for free as part of their service although you must register first.

Television programmes

Until 1957, British television consisted of one channel, the BBC (equivalent to BBC1). In the early days of television, many of the programmes were transmitted live and the only way to record copies was via a system called telerecording whereby a camera literally filmed what was being transmitted via the cathode ray tube. Not only are these copies of extremely poor quality compared to what we expect today (if copies exist at all) but they are, of course, in black and white. The first colour transmission on British TV was in 1967, although some programmes after this time were still made in monochrome.

There are no copies in existence for many well-loved BBC favourites because they were wiped by overzealous librarians clearing shelf space or by accident – the policy at the time was *not* to keep copies. The occasional episode turns up such as those found in the archive of the comedian Bob Monkhouse after his death in 2003. This archive is now held by Kaleidoscope (www.kaleidoscope. org.uk). Kaleidoscope also publishes books on various programme genres such as light entertainment, comedy and music programmes such as *Top of the Pops*. Several of these books are only published digitally. See www.kaleidoscope publishing.co.uk.

Although one imagines that the rights to television programmes belong to the company who made them, this depends on whether the television company is still in existence and whether the company has been taken over or merged into another. ITV companies from the early days of independent television, Rediffusion and ATV for instance, have disappeared. The original stations which made up ITV, such as Yorkshire, LWT and Granada, have been incorporated into ITV. There are myriad independent producers, some huge and part of a global conglomerate and other much smaller ones, all providing programmes for the BBC, ITV, Channel 4 and 5 and Sky.

Anything that was transmitted by ITV franchise holders (Carlton, Border, Granada, LWT, etc.) is held at ITN Source as well as the Carry On, ITC, Korda and Rank films. Refer to the section on news above.

For BBC programmes, as for news, contact BBC's Motion Gallery at www.bbc motiongallery.com. At the time of writing, the archive was being set up and once the item required is located in the catalogue, an email using BBC Archive's Workbook must be sent to the sales team who will explain licensing terms and arrange delivery of the footage.

Drama is more complicated.

Television drama

Acting is a notoriously precarious and impecunious profession – a household name this year may never be heard of again. Those few actors earning a living wage today may work in a burger restaurant tomorrow.

Actors' contracts state how many times the programme may be repeated within a set time limit and after this has expired, any repeat fees paid depend on the initial agreement. Using extracts from television drama can be complicated and the payment depends on the original agreement. The Equity Television Agreement 2013 outlines all fees negotiated with the BBC. There is also a need, in certain cases, for the performer to consent before the extract can be broadcast, especially, for instance, any extract criticising or ridiculing an artist's performance or which is of an explicitly sexual nature. For BBC compilation programmes, everyone except walk-ons has to be paid based on the highest fee they received from the original recording. Walk-ons receive a new fee at the current recording day rate. Chorus singers are also paid (Equity Television Agreement 2013, Section 8, 806e). ITV programmes work under the Producers Alliance for Cinema and Television (PACT) agreements negotiated with Equity and they, too, have deals for repeat fees in compilation programmes.

At the time of writing, the fee for a BBC programme for an extract not exceeding one minute was £21.50 per artist. For an extract longer than one minute but not exceeding four minutes (five for schools' programmes), the walk-on would receive £42.85 (Equity Television Agreement 2013, paragraph 1210). The fee for a main artist depends on their initial fee.

Although BBC programmes using BBC excerpts do not have to pay royalty fees (similarly ITV programmes using ITV clips), when ITV programmes use BBC extracts in their programmes and vice versa, royalty fees must be paid for the use of the clip *as well as* extract rates to the actors – a 'double whammy' in effect. Depending on the station and the production company, there is a minimum charge of either 30 seconds or one minute or part of thereof just as there is in using news or sporting clips. Of course, if the production company owns the rights (a Granada programme using clips from *Coronation Street*, which it makes) there are no royalty payments. However, in this example, the actors still have to be paid an extract fee.

Sporting events

Sport is big business and companies around the world negotiate for the rights to own, screen and sponsor sporting events which makes broadcast clearance extremely complicated. The rights to broadcast Wimbledon and the Olympics (but not the Paralympics in 2012 which went to Channel 4) were all the domain of the BBC which also holds the UK broadcasting rights to the Olympics until 2020 and the live Wimbledon rights until 2017. The rights to the FIFA World Cup Finals in 2014 and 2018, however, will be live on the BBC or ITV. This is because certain events are governed by Ofcom's Code on Sports and Other Listed and Designated Events and *must* be transmitted live and free-to-air on terrestrial television in the UK, effectively meaning ITV, BBC, Channel 4 or Channel 5. Premier League football games could be on BT, Sky Sports or ESPN with the highlights on BBC until 2016. Athletics could be on any number of platforms, depending on the event and which TV station bid the most, and range from BBC Scotland (the Great Scottish Run) to Eurosport, Sky Sports, Channel 4, Channel 5 and the BBC. As you can see, finding the rights holder is extremely complicated and the rights may be different for television and radio! To justify the billions that the exclusive rights cost, the broadcast companies must recoup their investment *and* make a profit.

The result is that, once you have located the footage, you may have to pay twice: once to the copyright holder and also to the holder of the event. To make it more complicated, depending on the event and where the item is to be transmitted, there may be more than one rights holder.

A simple example is the Olympics. A payment is required to the owner of the clip you want to use (e.g. the BBC for the 2012 Olympics and Channel 4 for the 2012 Paralympics) and a second payment is made to the International Olympics Committee.

The good news? Because of digitisation, once you have located the required footage, information should be supplied on where to go to clear the rights. However, it is the responsibility of the company requesting the footage to ensure all clearance is carried out correctly. That may be you. If the clip has not yet been digitalised or is of a certain age, clearance may not be straightforward.

The cost of using clips from sporting events can mount up and, for programmes with limited budgets, be prohibitive.

Notwithstanding the problems of locating and paying for the reproduction rights, there may be other reasons why the footage cannot be used. For instance, events sponsored by a tobacco company must be checked against the editorial policy before it can be shown on the BBC (Editorial Guidelines).

Feature films

The contact for *recent* feature films is their distribution company. For older feature films, the use of extracts can be extremely complicated because it may be almost impossible to work out who owns the rights simply because the rights of many films have been bought and resold many times. Unless you want to use an extract from a new film and the rights are relatively easy to negotiate, I recommend the use of a specialist film researcher.

When using newly released or pre-general release clips for a radio or television programme, it may be possible to use the material free of charge. This is usually the case in programmes like *Film 2014* when film critics review the feature. Chat shows such as *Graham Norton* and *This Morning* occasionally use the same premise. The trick is to use a different extract from the other shows. The distributor will offer you a limited choice of extracts and they will demand an on-screen or verbal credit.

Film ratings

Feature films and television programmes of a more adult nature are given age ratings below which the film is not suitable to be viewed. Trailers and the use of excerpts from films must also abide by the ratings so that, for instance, the use of a clip from a British Board of Film Classification (BBFC) 15-rated film may not be suitable for a daytime television programme. The Ofcom broadcast code, Section 1, Protecting the Under 18s states categorically that BBFC 18-rated films cannot be transmitted before 21.00 (except pay-per-view services), may still be unsuitable at that time and R-rated films should not be broadcast at all.

In August 2012, Ofcom received complaints about *Wolverine* shown on Channel 4 before the watershed and concluded that there were six instances of violence in the film which were unsuitable for children. Channel 4 had already edited the film to remove some of the violence but this was not enough for Ofcom's codes. The film had originally been classified as a 12A.

Attitudes change and films classified more than 15 years ago may now be regarded as suitable for transmission earlier than their original rating might imply. Many films have been reclassified by the BBFC. Clips should still be vetted for their suitability.

Service charges, handling costs and dubbing fees

Film and stock libraries usually charge administration fees to cover staffing costs; British Pathé News's charges are stated earlier in this chapter. Some companies may charge for their librarian's time finding clips and pictures (although others offer free research) and other costs may include downloading material to you.

Formats

As footage has been digitised over the past few years, it is unlikely that material you request will be in an outmoded format such as film (35 mm, 16 mm and even 8 mm) or the old video tape formats of 2 inch, 1 inch, BETA or VHS, etc. Rare and archive footage, however, may still be in these or other formats. It is unlikely but . . . Documentary researchers still encounter these and, should you wish to use the footage, it must be transferred via a speciality post-production company into a currently broadcastable format. Radio researchers and journalists might, depending on their current project, also come across archaic formats.

Copyright

Copyright laws change regularly and it is such a complicated issue that some law firms specialise in it. This, therefore, is a brief guideline to point you away from simple but expensive mistakes. If in doubt, talk to your rights department for advice.

In the Duration of Copyright and Rights in Performance Regulations 1995, the copyright protection afforded by the Copyright, Designs and Patents Act 1988 was extended to 'life plus 70 years'.

The copyright for sound recordings, however, only lasts for 50 years from the year of making or release. Groups like the Beatles and Rolling Stones are contesting this and it may be that the duration of sound recording copyright is extended in the future.

For photographers employed full time by a commercial company (for instance, a local newspaper), the copyright to their photographs belongs to the company and the photographer's salary and any costs are met by them. The copyright of photos shot for use in specific television programmes and for promotional purposes (such as radio, internet, etc.), if taken by staff employees, belongs to the production company and the images are ostensibly free of copyright for use by that company. This rule does not apply to photographs taken by freelancers and it is in the interest of the freelancer to ensure that copyright matters are dealt with in their contract or their photos may be used indiscriminately and for which they receive no payment.

Creative commons

This is an organisation allowing creative materials to be used by anyone within certain boundaries, for instance, as long as it isn't used for commercial purposes; a sort of public domain with limitations working alongside the laws of copyright. Unfortunately, for anyone working within the media, this does mean that you would have to negotiate fees for using anything within creative commons should it be for newspapers, television or radio. I have seen credits for creative commons' work in newspapers. It is useful for personal blogs. The site can be found at www.creativecommons.org.

Pirate copies

This is a big problem, especially for film companies where it is estimated that $6.1 billion were lost to the industry in 2005 (Motion Picture Association Survey). Technically, any reproduction without permission of a work still in copyright is a pirate copy. Legitimate creatives have no justification whatever for using a pirate copy of a film or music CD. In the extremely unlikely event that you are offered one, theoretically you could be prosecuted for merely handling it.

Working in the media, there may be occasions when you have access to a legitimate music track or copy of a film on general release in the US but not in the UK. Just taking a 'quick copy' for your own use or downloading it to the internet (!) without prior permission from the copyright holders is illegal and, if caught, you risk a hefty fine, imprisonment and, of course, the loss of your job. As for making copies for profit, courts deal very harshly with people convicted of this and you will never work in a creative industry again. Film distributors are so scared of pirate copies of unreleased films being circulated that often only one master is kept, held in a secure vault. The fear of piracy is why many films have simultaneous opening dates in both the US and UK.

YouTube and other social media sites can proliferate piracy so be aware of this. Downloading film, television and audio clips from YouTube and transmitting them in the media could be infringing all copyright rules. Those who uploaded the clips in the first case are effectively putting pirate copies on the net.

Legal and ethical considerations

A short note on the ethical use of identifying children in photographs. Many celebrities forbid the photographing of their children or identifying them in the media and there are many reasons why *any* child cannot be identified. Children in court cases are the obvious example. For general use, permission should be sought from parents. Schools often forbid photographs of their pupils to be taken in case the pictures are used by paedophiles. Surnames are never revealed.

The issue of disturbing images must be considered. Before publishing such images, get an executive decision first. Remember that different cultures have different sensibilities and in certain situations, photographs of women are culturally sensitive.

It is worth remembering that the people who in February 2013 tweeted alleged photos of the child killer Jon Venables as an adult were charged with contempt of court. Media professionals need to be aware of more than just copyright law. See Chapter 10.

Because of the risk of epilepsy, attention must be drawn to flash photography before transmission.

When in doubt, check first.

Summary

- All pictures and films are subject to copyright and should be cleared beforehand.
- The copyright of some films and photographs can take a long time to clear as copyright holders may be difficult to locate.

Further reading

Coward, Simon, Down, Richard, and Perry, Christopher, *British Television Comedy Research Guide, 1936–2011*, Kaleidoscope Publishing 2011
Coward, Simon, Down, Richard, and Perry, Christopher, *British Television, Music and Light Entertainment Research Guide, 1936–2012*, online edn, Kaleidoscope, 2012
Writers' and Artists' Yearbook has useful chapters on copyright. A & C Black, published annually: www.writersandartists.co.uk

Websites

Archive.org, non-profit internet archive of internet digital library sites: www.archive.org

British Association of Picture Libraries and Agencies: www.bapla.org.uk

BBC College of Journalism, guide to copyright: www.bbc.co.uk/academy/journalism

BBC Motion Gallery: www.bbcmotiongallery.com

BBC Photo Library: http://bbcphotosales.co.uk

British Library: www.bl.uk

British Library sound archive: http://sounds.bl.uk

British Pathé News: www.britishpathe.com

British Universities Film and Video Council: www.bufvc.ac.uk. Guide to Screen Heritage is at www.bufvc.ac.uk/archives

Creative Commons, non-profit organisation sharing creativity and copyright-free materials: www.creativecommons.org

Imperial War Museum, 33,000+ sound recordings related to war since 1914: www.iwm.org.uk

Intellectual Property Office UK, information, guidance notes and legislation on copyright: www.ipo.gov.uk

ITN news library: www.itnsource.com

Kobal Collection and Art Archive: www.picture-desk.com

London Sound Survey, Creative Commons-licensed sound recordings of London: www.soundsurvey.org.uk

Mary Evans Picture Library, Researchers' Handbook published 2006: www.maryevans.com

Movietone digital news archive: www.movietone.com

NBC Universal Archives: www.nbcuniversalarchives.com

Oral History Society: www.ohs.org.uk

Pinterest: www.pinterest.com

Sound Cloud, 'YouTube' of sound: www.soundcloud.com

TinEye, reverse image search: www.tineye.com

World Intellectual Property Organisation: www.wipo.int

6
Props, sets, prizes, question setting and teleshopping

Procuring props – 'properties' in full – is the official responsibility of the props buyer and the props department in television via their line manager. The set designer (also known as the production designer) eponymously designs the set, oversees the manufacture (usually off-site) and its construction in studio. So why should this chapter be included?

For television researchers working in LE, quizzes, children's programmes and magazines, the producer may request an unusual prop or a specific prize. The person sitting nearest is assigned the job and this is usually the researcher. For those working in radio and journalism, the marketing and promotions department is largely involved in organising prizes for competitions but just occasionally, it may fall under your jurisdiction to provide or organise something loosely associated with this chapter.

A producer devising an off-beat programme wanted a futuristic set made from *objets trouvés*. His heart was set on aircraft wreckage. The production designer hadn't a clue where to find it but knew I had contacts in the RAF and was in touch with several aircraft museums. Enough aircraft flotsam and jetsam was found for him to be spoilt for choice. I even suggested a sculptor specialising in *objets trouvés* who was contracted as assistant designer. The icing on the cake, as far as the producer was concerned, was that the aircraft wreckage was free; only the transportation came out of his budget.

The magic word is *free*. One of the reasons a producer asks the researcher to find props for the set or prizes, apart from the researcher being in the production office, is because the props department tends to pay for them, either by hiring or buying them outright.

Alternatively, there is 'prop placement' where companies provide their product for free to TV shows so that it can be placed on the set. There is no guarantee that it will be seen – but it might be! This is now acceptable whereas 20 years ago officially it was not.

Prizes

The rules on the cash value of quiz prizes have changed over the years and when ITV was regulated by the IBA (since replaced by the ITC and now Ofcom), the value of prizes was limited. Now there is virtually no limit; a million pounds is up for grabs (literally) on *The Million Pound Drop* and, at the time of writing, five winners in the UK had won a million pounds on *Who Wants to be a Millionaire?*

The rules governing the BBC mean that they cannot be influenced by any third party which affects their policy on prizes for quizzes and game shows. As the BBC is funded by and accountable to licence payers, BBC prizes are generally cheaper than those on commercial channels because the BBC must 'provide the very best value to the licence fee payer' (BBC Editorial Guidelines, Appendix 4: Framework for Funding Prizes and Awards). The BBC now accepts 'modest donated prizes from a third party' (BBC Editorial Guidelines). Prizes stipulated in the guidelines include concert or theatre tickets (a popular radio show prize), books and DVDs. The BBC is expected to pay the travel and accommodation costs for the winners and a researcher might find themselves responsible for co-ordinating this. If there is a range of prizes, the production team should ensure there is a range of donors. A local radio station with several football teams in its vicinity should offer tickets to games for all teams and not just one. However, the programme cannot permit the prize to influence the BBC's 'editorial integrity, objectivity or independence'. In other words, the programme cannot accept a free gift as a prize and then publicise the donor. The BBC cannot offer *cash* prizes for viewers, listeners or online competitions and must not accept cash to pay for prizes (BBC Editorial Guidelines, Appendix 4: Framework for Funding Prizes and Awards; Donated Prizes.) This explains why *The Million Pound Drop Live* is on ITV and not the BBC. BBC game shows are expected to pay for their prizes and they should be 'original rather than expensive'. The BBC, like Ofcom, stipulates that prizes for children should be age appropriate and of the 'money can't buy' variety. Cash prizes are prohibited for children (BBC Editorial Guidelines, Section 17: Interacting with Our Audiences; Prizes). This explains why the BBC offers exclusive sweatshirts, CDs and trips to the studio as prizes. You might be the person co-ordinating it all.

There are a lot of rules to consider about fairness and ensuring the prizes are described accurately during the programme. When in doubt, refer to Ofcom and the BBC Editorial Guidelines. Many rules are stipulated in the Lotteries and Amusements Act 1976.

Question setting

In order to win those prizes, there has to be a competition and, for legal reasons, there is a difference between a lottery – winning prizes by luck – and using 'skill, knowledge or judgement' (BBC Editorial Guidance, Audience Interactivity [Competitions, Votes and Awards] summary). In other words, broadly speaking, for a radio listener to win a trip to the studio, they can't be the first person to phone in but they can be the first person to phone in and answer a question correctly. However, the rules on running competitions are complicated and you may need to seek advice. As also stated in the BBC Guidelines, 'Competitions should *always* have a clear editorial purpose'.

Quizzes often commission specialists to set the question and their names are credited at the end of the show. However, a handful of quiz shows specifically employ researchers or question setters to write them.

Question writing is a particular skill requiring high attention to detail; a question can't be repeated in the same series and the answers must be correct. Either way, verification is extremely important, both to check the answers are correct and to ensure there is no ambiguity or the possibility of two or more correct answers. For this reason, many quiz programmes contract separate question verifiers to double-check accuracy. If a contestant queries an answer on camera, it is common procedure to refer to the verification source; the name of the book and page number, the Wikipedia reference plus a third proof to the correct answer, be it an internet source or printed literature.

Greg Hughes, a producer at Capital Radio, writes the questions for his own shows, and verifies the answers himself. He often ensures that word answers are spelt in a particular way by saying it on air and spelling out the words.

Compliance is important. Terms and conditions must be explained and full terms and conditions are always included on the internet and repeated on air according to all broadcast regulators' rules.

Programmes like *Pointless* (where the answer depends on how many people out of 100 know the answer) employ a market research company to survey the general public so the production team is largely not responsible for validating answers. However, there is still a need for transparency should results be queried.

Who Wants to be a Millionaire? has, literally, a million pounds on offer. Naturally, contestants are desperate to win and even in less high-profile competitions, the stakes are high. It is not just the ignominy of losing; nobody wants to appear a fool. Nowadays, several programmes are recorded back-to-back in the same afternoon in front of a studio audience with other contestants awaiting their turn in the green room and watching proceedings on a monitor. The director in the control room concentrates on getting the best pictures and the most exciting programme; they do not want and haven't time for a semantic discussion as to whether or not an answer is correct. Even less if it is on radio and the contestant is arguing – live on air – that they are right.

Accuracy of both the phrasing of the question and confirmation of the correct answer is crucial and the yea or nay is a split-second decision. 'I think it's right' isn't good enough.

The use of premium phone lines is highly regulated. Many programmes partly pay for their high-value prizes through the cost of the premium phone lines used to enter the competition itself (*Report of an inquiry into television broad-casters' use of premium rate telephone services in programmes* by Richard Ayre published 18.7.07 on Ofcom's website). The BBC is not permitted to run competitions in order to make a profit (Editorial Guidelines, Appendix 2: Code of Conduct for Competitions and Voting).

The cost of calls is expensive but regulators insist on a cheaper (or free) method of entering a competition, usually via the internet. All rules, terms and conditions, including the cost of the call and the time when the competition ends, must be stipulated. This is for all competitions run in the media whether television, radio or in the press. There are restrictions as to when you can use premium lines and, as Greg Hughes at Capital points out, there may be occasions when the producer must ensure that listeners can only make a certain number of calls so that they don't spend too much on the premium phone line. PhonepayPlus (formerly ICSTIS) is the independent regulatory body supervising premium rate telephone competitions and it issues a code of practice.

In *Who Wants to be a Millionaire?* a valuable prize was awarded to a contestant who gave an incorrect answer, as pointed out by the *Daily Mirror* in March 1999. This is marginally less offensive to the audience that invalidating a correct answer so that the contestant loses when they should have won. The tabloids love it, the programme is discredited and the taint of scandal affects not only the audience rating but the programme continuance. Any whiff of unfairness accorded to any competition will discredit the programme or media company – possibly irreparably.

Product placement

The impartiality of programmes where one product cannot be endorsed over another is an integral part of UK broadcast regulations. Effectively, products cannot be 'plugged'.

Product placement (PP) is when a product such as a branded soft drink or a specific holiday group is mentioned or shown on television, in a radio programme or film. An example is James Bond driving a specific car in a film.

The BBC, upholding its rules of editorial integrity and independence, generally prohibits this in all but strictly enforced occasions as stipulated in its Editorial Guidelines. However, for BBC *commercial* television channels it may occasionally take product placement if this does not undermine editorial independence. The BBC also has a strict policy about featuring logos and credits online. Effectively, they should not be used unless editorially justified (BBC Editorial Guidelines, Section 14: Editorial Integrity and Independence from External Interests; Logos and Credits Online 14.4.21). The guidelines also insist that no credits can be given in return for free or reduced cost services.

Product placement in commercial television is strictly governed by Ofcom because, of course, commercial TV and radio are financed by advertisers and sponsorship. From February 2011 Ofcom rules changed, permitting product placement in series made for television, sports programmes and light entertainment programmes but under no circumstances may product placement be used in news, religious, current affairs or children's programmes. Certain products are banned, including tobacco and tobacco products (e.g. cigarettes and electronic cigarettes), alcohol, food or drinks high in salt, fat or sugar, gambling, infant formula and medicinal products.

The first product placement, Nestlé's Dolce Gusto coffee machine, appeared on the set of *This Morning* for 13 weeks at a reputed cost of £100,000. In November 2011, *Coronation Street* featured a Nationwide cash machine in the shop. One of the advantages given for PP by research agency BDRC Continental is that it makes programmes more realistic – supermarkets, such as those found in *Coronation Street*, would stock real brand names rather than invented brands – and it suggests that viewers will believe in a product if they see it on a show they trust. At the moment, PP is nowhere as prolific as in the USA although it is expected that its use will expand.

All shows where product placement is featured must have the P symbol at the beginning of each show. However, to quote from Section Seven of Ofcom's Broadcasting Code, a programme should not 'give undue prominence to the products, services or trademarks concerned'.

ITV's *Lorraine* broke the rules in November 2012 when Danni Minogue promoted a milk product. According to Ofcom's ruling, 'although the discussion was brief, the overall effect was to "promote and endorse" the product'. In 2011, Amanda Holden overemphasised a group of law firms on ITV's *This Morning*. Ofcom rapped *The X Factor* for unduly promoting the Corinthia Hotel during pre-recorded inserts in 2013.

The most common programmes which could be accused of undue product placement are chat shows and daytime programmes like *This Morning*. Anyone working in this field must be aware of what is and isn't permitted and check with the programme producer, Ofcom Broadcast Codes and BBC Editorial Guidelines.

Sponsorship

Not only does *Coronation Street* use product placement in its shows but it is also, like many independent television programmes, sponsored – at the time of writing by www.comparethemeerkat.com. Viking River Cruises sponsors drama. Nivea sponsors *This Morning*.

Sponsorship is when a brand pays for a series of short sequences around a programme featuring the product logo and message. There are strict Ofcom limits on how many seconds the sequences can last at the programme's beginning, end and during the commercial break.

Under no circumstances, however, can the sponsorship company influence editorial policy or programme content. At a basic level, when *Coronation Street* was sponsored by Cadbury, the characters could not be seen eating Cadbury chocolate.

This is not a debate on the sponsorship issue but merely an explanation of the difference between sponsorship and product endorsement.

The BBC charter, in order to retain its editorial independence, does not permit advertising or sponsored programming for any service funded by the licence fee.

Props

Although obtaining props is the brief of the props buyer and props department, small productions may not have the budget to use what is now generally a freelance service. Also, there are times when a researcher gets involved simply because of the nature of the prop required. I once had to find a six-inch replica of Nelson (as in Nelson's Column, London). This eventually involved commissioning a sculptor to make a plaster cast mould which was turned into six resin models by a specialist props maker.

There is something called, helpfully, *researcher's props*, dating from when the media industry was heavily controlled by ACTT (the former film and TV union now amalgamated with other entertainment unions to become BECTU), which consist of one or two items taken for filming and for which the researcher takes responsibility: a towel for a presenter likely to get wet or a fun gizmo to be referred to in a link. The researcher's props avoid taking a separate props person on location.

The main reason why a media professional gets involved with props is when contributors bring them to studio (television or radio) or location or a newspaper journalist wants to use a prop in a photograph. *Prop (or product) placement* (see above) is generally the domain of prop placement companies and largely not under the day-to-day researcher's remit.

Action props and standby props

Action props are used as part of the action and can be as insignificant as a newspaper for an actor to read or as large as a lorry driven down the road – an *action vehicle* in this case. On a large production, the props people are assigned to either action or standby props.

Standby props are set dressing: ornaments on a mantelpiece, food in a fridge, books on a shelf.

Action vehicles

Researchers are not expected to organise action vehicles but it occasionally happens that the action vehicle finds them. A taxidermist who collects classic cars becomes an LE item and the researcher who suggested the story in the first place co-ordinates the recording.

For recording in studio, the set designer needs to be informed so that space can be allocated for the car. The researcher, as the taxidermist's main contact, will co-ordinate the arrival and departure of the car but may need to liaise with the props department if specialist transport is required. The car, of course, may be driven to the studio. The set designer informs the stagehands where the car is to go. The floor manager must be warned as they are responsible for health and safety.

It is helpful to have the car's dimensions (a) so the designer knows how much space to allocate and (b) to check the car can get through the dock doors (the entrance to the studio). Studios are designed for large sets but these are constructed to be assembled and pulled apart like jigsaws. The external and internal access must be clear on the recording day. There is also the question of where to keep large 'props' like this when not being recorded. This one is too big to be kept in the cage – literally, a large metal lattice work cupboard in which props are stored outside the studio.

For filming on location and filming from vehicles, refer to Chapter 8.

Animals

A friend of mine once set up a maggot grand national in studio. The set designer built a two-foot racecourse identical in every way and maggots were let loose (if that's the word) to squirm their way around. Afterwards, the macho Geordie stagehands refused to touch them, resulting in a plague of bluebottles the following week. Does this contravene the television health and safety manifesto about ensuring animals can't escape?

Studios have guidelines for working with animals (including maggots?) both in studio and on location. The guidelines are basic common sense. It is worth noting that *The Dangerous Wild Animals Act 1976* (enforced by local authorities) requires the licensing and using of specific wild animals, therefore expert advice is mandatory. Animal handlers experienced in television and film work are expensive but may save hours of angst and insurance claims.

The health and safety issues are designed to cover both animals and people. For reference, see the Health and Safety Executive (HSE) directive *Working with Animals in Entertainment* which can be downloaded from the web. The sort of things to be aware of include the following.

- *Phobias*. I have known floor managers refuse to work on shows with spiders and snakes. Members of the audience may have the same fears. Reptiles and birds are other common phobias. The reverse of audience tickets should mention whether there is a possibility of animals being in the show.
- *Allergies* are common. Asthmatic attacks may be brought on by cats or birds. Warn the audience and the crew via the tickets or the crew office.
- *Pregnant women* are advised not to go near certain animals. Pregnant women may be in the audience, or involved as contributors or crew.
- Inform people with as much notice as possible so that if they have an allergy or a phobia, there is time to replace them. Floor managers work shifts and their rota can be swapped.
- Organise food, water and somewhere for the animal to be kept away from noise and strange surroundings. Rehearse the item with animals last and film them first.
- Straw or hay in the studio must be fire retardant but as this is toxic to animals, ask the owner or handler for practical alternatives.
- Salmonella and *E. coli* bacteria can be spread by farm animals and pets so the basic hygiene rules of washing hands after touching animals must be stressed.
- Provide protective clothing for all relevant personnel if required.
- All studios should have qualified first aiders present. Any accidents or bites that occur must be reported in the accident book.

- It is unlikely that poisonous snakes or spiders will be free in studio, but the handler should be aware of antidotes and it is recommended that the relevant animal is confined in some way.

This may sound alarmist but the unexpected always happens during recording. This is why working in the media is so exciting. Animals are notoriously unreliable and, as usual, warn everyone of your intentions in order to minimise the chance of untoward events.

Producers and directors conveniently forget that animals and children do not perform to order. A parrot that dances to music at home invariably won't in the *Britain's Got Talent* audition. The pressure on its owner, who may never have been in a television studio let alone one with an audience, is immense. Make huge allowances for both of them and be extremely sympathetic to the owner. My own attitude is, by all means bring the parrot into studio on the off chance it will perform, but chances are – it won't. Most producers won't thank you for telling you this. In the case of auditions for *Britain's Got Talent*, whatever the ethics, this is part of the audience appeal.

Journalists also come into contact with animals; writing an article about a local community farm, visiting a house where there are pets are common examples. It is advisable to take common-sense approaches here.

Armourers

Somebody suggests that the presenter swings a pirate's sword on location. Great – except . . .

If weapons such as swords, rifles and guns are to be used, stringent health and safety rules must be met. For this reason, it is usual to employ an armourer who knows the current regulations, will supply safe weapons and equipment and keep strict control over them whilst filming. Names of armourers can be found in the trade directories and through Equity, and the props department can recommend reputable and licensed armourers used in the past.

Returning to the pirate's sword – use a plastic one.

The use of *replica guns* (and real ones) in a public place is illegal unless the police have been informed and given prior permission. They will not sanction the use of real firearms.

Nor is it permissible to use imitation police uniforms or police cars in public; the charge is *impersonating a police officer*. Drama productions and location managers are well aware of this and the procedure for filming legally but a researcher must not be beguiled into dressing up a children's presenter in a facsimile uniform and filming in Trafalgar Square. The excuse 'I didn't know' is unacceptable.

Magicians

The director of an LE show will have had wide experience of working with magicians but for daytime magazine, cable and satellite or children's programmes, it often falls to the researcher to liaise between the guest (in this case, the magician) and their personal requirements. Magicians often make their own props or have them made especially for them, but occasionally (far be it from me to divulge any magician's tricks) in order to camouflage, for instance, the sound of machinery, the conjuror will request music crescendos at the crucial point. The sound department and the director must be fully aware of such requests.

Trampolines, gymnastics and aerial work

Children's programmes often feature dramatic and visual activities like trampolining and gymnastics in studio. Trampolines are large structures and, in a specially constructed gym, often set into the floor to minimise accidents. In the studio, as a health and safety issue, both the trampoline frame and the height of the studio ceiling have to be considered. The director can tussle with flare from the studio lights and the unsightly gantry shots but if there isn't enough height, there is a serious problem. Safety aspects must also be considered for gymnastics and other aerial stunts such as high-wire circus acts. Check with the company health and safety officer. It may be better to film on location. In the 2013 season of *Britain's Got Talent* the judges went outside to watch an aerial gymnastics act which is a good example of gymnastic troupes' requirements being taken into serious consideration.

Teleshopping

The number of teleshopping channels has proliferated over the past few years and they often fill the late night/early morning schedules on mainstream channels rather than, as in the past, going to a black screen. There are minimal opportunities for researchers as such working in these stations although there are producer roles and, of course, studio jobs such as floor managers and camera crews.

The product research – buying, product specification and special features – is supplied by the buyers who mainly come from the retail industry. It is their job to research the product and write briefs for the presenter – often described as 'host' in this genre. The product brief is also supplied to the producer. Any further information to be explained on air, such as special features, the current price of the product and the amount of time left for a sale, can be conveyed by the producer to the host via the earpiece.

Most teleshopping channel studios are based in industrial estates, basically in warehouses. It is all done 'on the cheap' and, rather than ratings, the success criterion for a teleshopping channel is how much money is made per minute on product sale. This information is highly confidential and zealously controlled.

Insurance

The producer has overall responsibility for health and safety on a television or radio programme; the editor in a newspaper. Legally, all media companies must have employee and public liability insurance but anything hazardous or unusual should be checked with the underwriter or broker so that, should anything go wrong, the underwriters will pay. Large media organisations get their cover from several insurance companies depending on the issues involved.

However, insurance issues are often overlooked because of ignorance or lack of time.

Does the props' owner or animal handler have adequate insurance? Is it valid when they are away from home? Check what cover they have; the programme's insurance company may want details. Extra insurance cover is cheaper than claims. For a journalist merely reporting a story, insurance is less of an issue unless, of course, they are inadvertently involved in something untoward.

In certain cases, the insurance company may request the services of security staff to ensure irreplaceable or expensive props are protected: a valuable dog collar collection, the million pounds in *The Million Pound Drop Live*, a celebrity guest wearing a priceless tiara. Make a special feature of it on camera. The more mean-looking the security guard, the better the television.

It is occasionally necessary to have fire officers in studio, for instance if pyrotechnics (including lit candles) are involved. The health and safety office can advise on this.

Whenever there is a studio audience, it is a legal health and safety requirement to have security personnel trained in both fire and first aid, and many studio security personnel are ex-firefighters. However, if there is no audience, this may be overlooked. Should a fire-eater be taking part in a programme, it makes sense to warn the floor manager and the insurance underwriter and have a fire officer present whilst the item is recorded. The researcher must also warn the set designer who will in turn check the lighting rig (where the studio lights are situated). A sensible question for the researcher to ask is 'How high do the flames go?'. Media personnel learn the tricks of many strange trades . . .

Risk assessment

The key to minimising the hazard during dangerous activities is, of course, risk assessment and media companies are far more aware of this than they were. All BBC production staff are required to undertake risk assessment training as part of their induction. Most companies insist that risk assessment forms are completed prior to filming or recording. For more details, see Chapter 8. The risk assessment in working with sets and props is perhaps minimal but there are hazards to be aware of, especially when dealing with members of the public.

You cannot be too careful where insurance and health and safety are concerned.

Websites

BBC College of Production: www.bbc.co.uk/academy/production
BBC College of Journalism: www.bbc.co.uk/academy/journalism
BBC Editorial Guidelines: www.bbc.co.uk/guidelines/editorialguidelines
eBay, for finding props: www.ebay.com
Gumtree, for finding props: www.gumtree.com
Health and Safety Executive: www.hse.gov.uk, and working with animals in entertainment worksheet: www.hse.gov.uk/pubns/etis4.pdf
Ofcom: www.ofcom.org.uk
PhonepayPlus, regulatory body for premium phone lines: www.phonepayplus.org.uk

7
Music

The lion stalks a zebra to the crashing sound of the orchestra in a natural history documentary. The jukebox plays in the Queen Vic in *EastEnders*. Revisit a favourite moment from *The X Factor* on YouTube. Imagine modern life without music! Music is a luxury product, why should it come cheap?

Everyone who works in the media deals with music at some time in their career, whether interviewing an opera singer about their latest performance for a newspaper, chatting informally to a pop star, organising a performance for the *Jonathan Ross Show* or finding atmospheric music to cover a short sequence on *This Morning*. For radio producers on a music station, it *is* their job. All are common occasions where you might deal with music; all incur copyright implications and other practical issues.

It goes without saying that a specialist music researcher, a magazine music journalist or a radio producer on XFM is interested in music – but it isn't enough to be fanatical about today's popular music; there are thousands if not millions of people with the same interest and all of them after your job. You need an encyclopaedic passion for the history of pop, today's, yesterday's and tomorrow's, embracing the whole gamut of the industry. A music producer on Classic FM must know about jazz, country and today's music – perhaps next year's classic. The music of James Horner (*Titanic*, *Avatar* and the 2013 *Romeo and Juliet* amongst others) and John Williams (the *Harry Potter* theme plus dozens of film scores) both regularly feature on Classic FM. You will devour the music press, make friends with the record companies, especially A&R, and attend gigs, concerts and festivals as often as a busy media schedule will allow.

For a radio producer working on a chart show – or indeed any music show – the music played depends on the playlist and what's currently in the charts. The copyright issue is dealt with automatically on a day-to-day basis; the tracks are chosen according to a formula and very often in consultation with the record companies.

One of the perks of working in the media is that you may be sent tickets to concerts and festivals and given access to lots of music. You may have to 'pay for this in kind' by writing an article for your newspaper or including it as an item in a programme. There's no such thing as a free lunch but this is a pretty tasty one!

There are other issues which may occasionally crop up. Capital Radio uses a playout system for its music. Secure digital downloads are watermarked for extra security. There are occasional streams whereby the producer can listen to the music three times before it is deleted – good for ensuring embargoes if a track is released on a specific day. If a producer wants to give out the top 40 albums for, say, a prize for a Christmas special, they must contact the record companies because all music is supplied digitally and digitally stored at the radio station.

An important legal issue should be mentioned here. If you are working on a radio station, Ofcom sets a music-to-speech ratio with which your station must comply. Capital Radio in London has a ratio of 70% music to 30% speech. A radio station's output must, by law, be monitored and be available for checking by Ofcom at a moment's notice. This is done digitally and is generally of no worry to employees in a radio station but, as has happened in the past, should a radio station transmit more music than the ratio permits, Ofcom can fine the station. In 1999 the then governing body, the Radio Authority, fined Oxygen FM (Oxford) £20,000 and shortened its eight-year licence by two years for not keeping the tapes to prove its music-to-speech ratio. The station went off air. In extreme cases, Ofcom can revoke the radio station licence and the station will close.

Copyright

As in all creative products, someone owns the rights and using music on a television or radio programme or online, whether live or recorded, must be paid for. Music is relatively complicated in copyright terms; because there is rarely a sole owner, it may have to be cleared with various parties or agencies.

The main agencies clearing rights for music on behalf of rights holders are:

- the Musicians' Union (the MU), acting on behalf of musicians;
- PRS for Music, formerly the Performing Rights Society, which administers the copyright in songs or compositions on behalf of its members: music publishers, songwriters and composers (see later in chapter);
- Mechanical-Copyright Protection Society (MCPS) now part of PRS for Music, collects royalties for songwriters, composers and music publishers.

The MCPS looks after mechanical copyright and mainly licenses the physical copying of recorded music onto CD, DVD and digital copies;

- Phonographic Performance Ltd (PPL) represents the owners of recordings, usually record labels, and the performers on sound recordings whether featured artists or non-featured (e.g. session musicians);
- British Phonographic Industry (BPI) – the association of the major UK record companies;
- Association of Independent Music (AIM) – the umbrella body for independent labels in the UK.

There are other agencies to be aware of: Equity (the actors' union which also represents singers), Video Performance Ltd (VPL), part of PPL and dealing with the licensing of music videos when played in public or broadcast on TV, Incorporated Society of Musicians (ISM) representing conductors, amongst others, and British Academy of Songwriters, Composers and Authors (BASCA).

The Copyright, Designs and Patents Act 1988 (continuously amended since) covers the *copying* of music for use in TV and radio programmes, feature films, TV and radio commercials, videos (retail, corporate and educational), retail multimedia (computer games, for instance), the internet and products such as a free CD with a children's comic. For the rights to copy, a royalty fee is normally paid. The right to make a copy, whether physical or digital, is granted by a rights holder or their representative in exchange for a licence fee or royalty.

In order to simplify the process of clearing basic uses, rights holders can join a collection society (e.g. PRS for Music) who can administer certain licences and grant rights on their behalf. PRS for Music and MCPS grant annual licences to the users of music, e.g. broadcasters and live venues, and distribute the royalties to the songwriters, composers and music publishers whose music they use. Any production company can be heavily penalised for using music without a licence. Merely downloading music from iTunes for a media programme can land you in a copyright quagmire.

Who owns music copyright?

This can be a variety of people: the record label, the publisher and the composer(s), or whoever paid for the recording, the artist or producer. However, other people are also paid for the reproduction of their work: the artist performing a cover version of a song written by someone else, the musicians performing the backing track, the arranger, and the copyright holder who may be none of these.

For CDs and records, the place to look for the copyright information is on the sleeve, jacket or CD cover. It may be on the insert, printed on the CD itself or on the label on the vinyl disc. The information is often hard to spot and, because of the small print, even harder to read. For digital music, any recording should have metadata embedded that includes the name of the label (or whoever owns the rights) generally indicated by the Phonogram symbol ℗, the year of recording and other crucial information. Wikipedia is another source and often includes the label, year and performers. www.allmusic.com is useful and PRS for Music, PPL and the MU can all help. The MU has a database of recordings and broadcasts made under its trade agreements from the last 50 years or more.

Although large independent production companies, radio stations and the BBC often have blanket licence agreements (see PRS for Music), not all music is covered in the agreement – foreign music, for example. In this instance, copyright must be cleared with the copyright holders directly or through a collection society overseas. See later in this chapter.

PRS for Music (and MPCS)

PRS for Music is an organisation representing the interest of songwriters, composers and music publishers and grants licences on behalf of its 100,000 members to anyone playing or performing music in public, e.g. TV and radio stations, theatres and music venues, public houses, restaurants, shops, etc. The organisation distributes the royalties, promotes the value of music and champions copyright protection. PPL licences are also required in these venues when recorded music is played.

All television and radio stations therefore have a PRS for Music licence permitting them to play both live and recorded music. For radio stations and the BBC, the blanket licence agreement with the PRS for Music means that a yearly fee allows any PRS for Music-managed music to be played without obtaining a licence for each individual piece. This includes jingles to symphonies. Effectively, for radio stations, they can usually play what they like – cost is not an issue. The tracks played are detailed on the playlist cue sheets and digitally sent to PRS for Music which automatically distributes the royalties.

The Musicians' Union

According to a major research project by DHA Communications commissioned by the Musicians' Union, in 2012, 56% of musicians surveyed earned less than £20k per year and 60% of musicians reported working for free in the previous year. The MU works on behalf of its 30,000 plus highly skilled members to improve their working conditions, negotiating with employers on contractual terms: rates of pay, health and safety, and copyright protection amongst other issues. The MU sets minimum rates for, amongst others:

- live events on TV, radio and online;
- recording sessions for commercial audio release, TV, film, adverts and video games;
- live performance;
- miming;
- backing track use;
- the use of audiovisual extracts in new programmes;
- synchronisation of existing recorded music featuring musicians into TV programmes, adverts and films.

In other words, the MU will be involved in any live and recorded music event for radio or TV. All complicated music dealings should be negotiated by the producer and/or the music or legal departments in the media organisation. For advice on rates of pay for musicians, contact the MU's recording and broadcasting department.

Live music

There are few things more exciting than a band playing live. However, OBs and live events are very expensive and, in the case of commercial radio stations such as Capital, often connected to a commercial client sponsoring the event in order to defray costs.

Bands in studio or on an OB

A lot of organisation is involved – egos and costumes and instruments and performance paraphernalia combined with the pervasive hangers-on who appear to have no apparent purpose but getting in the way.

A programme researcher might be responsible for co-ordinating the downloading of any digital music from the record company although this could also be the responsibility of the sound department. The researcher may be responsible for obtaining the band's lyrics for typing into the script, assigning the dressing rooms (often the PA's responsibility), liaising between the A&R department of the record company, listing the band members, session players and their instruments together with the people accompanying them, issuing call times for the groups and writing links for the presenter. If there are several bands in a programme or at the OB, this could be a full-time job.

On a programme where a music item could consist of the current chart topper doubling as a celebrity guest, the researcher may well work on the normal show items as well as co-ordinating the band's contribution.

What does the researcher do during a recording day? Mainly crisis management. A lot of the planning and organisation should already have been done. The beginning of the day is frantic with writing links (if not done previously), ensuring the presenter and everyone else know what is going on as well as fielding the phone and dealing with various problems as the bands make their way to the studios or OB location. Once the rehearsals and recording are under way, the researcher's job is to troubleshoot and check that everybody knows what is happening and where they should be. If the job has been done properly beforehand and no untoward events occur (acts of war and God that nobody can predict or anticipate), the researcher may hover between studio or stages, control room and production office for referral in case of queries and problems. As for copyright, if a band or orchestra is transmitted live, the composer's and publisher's rights should be covered by the PRS for Music agreement – but this is worth checking. There may be a problem if session players are not signed to the label and they may need an MU contract if they are to be paid the correct fees. For budgeting, the producer should be made aware of all fees.

The following is a checklist of what a media professional needs to be aware of or find for an OB and television/radio show:

- how many are in the group;
- the names of the group members;
- who plays which instruments;
- the band's line-up and where they stand/sit/perform;
- if they intend to mime, sing live vocals or perform entirely live;
- if they are singing live vocals or miming, a backing track may be required. This should be cleared for backing track use – generally the case when a track has been released but worth checking with the label;
- the lyrics of the songs and, in a group, who sings what (for the director);
- a list of the equipment they are bringing;
- names of the roadies setting up the equipment and anyone else coming along with them (e.g. their manager or the A&R representative).

In return, the band must know:

- when and where they are arriving;
- where to park their vehicles;
- how long they are called for;
- how much of their performance will be recorded and/or broadcast;
- what time they are free to go (they may be on tour and squeezing the TV or radio programme into a busy schedule);

- what time they are rehearsing/the sound check/performing/recording and in what order (handing out a running order when they arrive should suffice).

If the band is from America (or anywhere outside the UK), there may be discrepancies between their equipment and the UK electrical supply and transformers, and suitable power supply systems should be ordered. It is not unknown for a band's equipment to be in a dangerous condition and time should be allocated to check this before the sound check or recording takes place. All artists should have their equipment Portable Appliance Testing (PAT) tested regularly and compliance is indicated by a sticker on each piece of electronic equipment.

For a programme with several bands performing, it is common for each to be given an area in which to perform where their roadies set up the equipment. The stage manager, floor manager or set designer may be responsible for the stage plan. Because the TV researcher (the producer in radio) is often the first point of contact for the record company, it often falls to them to provide the details by which the stage plan is drawn up.

On large productions, getting the bands into wardrobe and make-up is often the job of the floor assistant or runner. On other occasions, the researcher ensures that, after the sound check, artists are taken to wardrobe and make-up. As some make-up is elaborate (think Lady Gaga), make-up assistants prefer to start with the most ambitious requirements.

A recording schedule may bear no relationship to the actual running order as most shows are edited into the transmission reel. In chart shows, it is common to record more bands than there is room for in the programme. The reason? A band may hit the Top 10 next week but be unavailable to record because of touring commitments.

Live music and miming

It is commonly assumed that all acts performing on TV are mimed. Some producers prefer live performances because they believe it is televisually more exciting although it may incur additional costs – hiring extra musicians, for instance. Many groups perform live vocals to a pre-recorded backing track and others, usually with an energetic dance routine, might mime the vocals whilst dancing. This final option would be regarded as 'cheating' on talent shows such as *The X Factor*.

Sound checks are only done for bands performing live. These balance sound levels and ensure equipment is working properly. The studio sound department works with the roadies for the sound check.

The backing track is relayed into studio so that everyone can hear it. The musicians play alongside and 'record to play back'. The instruments are often left unplugged and it is common practice to use a dummy drum kit. The backing track is transmitted alongside the pictures recorded in studio. As a point of interest, for miming to his own performance, a musician is paid a minimum fee of £22 per hour for a minimum 4-hour call (PACT/MU Agreement 2010).

At the time of writing, *The X Factor* has dropped the big band and is using pre-recorded backing tracks instead. These are recorded in different keys because each could be sung by any competitor at, for instance, the sing-off at the end of the show. The backing track is provided by the label that also, therefore, provides the names of the musicians for fees and royalty payments. Incidentally, the commercial release fee for iTunes is under the BPI/MU Agreement. When *The X Factor* is on iTunes, a session fee is paid per player.

On a show such as *Strictly Come Dancing*, the band might be there at 6am to set up their instruments (with the help of the floor manager, ASM and researchers) and clock off at 10pm after the show. The researcher must check who each musician is so that they can be paid the correct session fee. It is crucial to note who performed on which programme as extracts may be used in the future. Those players will be paid a secondary use fee.

Session players

Session players are freelance musicians earning a living by playing an instrument at a recording session. They are generally booked by contractors known as *fixers* who choose from a pool of reliable, talented freelance musicians who are required to sight read without rehearsal and record up to 20 minutes of music in a three-hour session with a minimum of takes. The contractor usually takes care of all the paperwork, pays the musician at least the minimum MU rate and takes a fee (around 10%) from the broadcaster or producer for their service.

Recorded music

Music for sequences

One of the more enjoyable (and frustrating) jobs in television and radio is choosing music to liven up an otherwise lacklustre sequence and enhance its atmosphere. The only way to ensure that the music fits the topic, the mood and style of the editing is trial and error and by playing the music alongside the relevant pictures. This involves selecting a number of tracks, all of which have been heard beforehand, and taking the shortlist into the edit suite. It can be a lengthy process.

You will know by the *tingle factor* if the track works even though the sequence needs trimming and tweaking for the cuts to fit the music. In other words, if the hairs on the back of your neck stand up, that's the right one.

The producer, editor and director will have suggestions of their own, in which case the editor might become, with the aid of the production assistant or the music department, the person in charge of clearing the copyright.

In-house music department or music library

The in-house music department or music library is becoming a rare beast except in very large organisations such as the BBC. If one exists where you are working, draw on its expertise. The library staff can be helpful in several ways. First, they are experts on a wide range of music and are constantly asked to help with music requests, which, together with running the music library, is their role. Like a bookshop, they order up music, online or, for older, rarer music, via vinyls and CDs, chargeable to the programme budget, lending out music from their enormous stock.

Music librarians are experts on copyright and the royalty costs of using music and, should you have a burning desire to use a piece of music which will create clearance complications or cost a huge amount, the music department will forewarn you.

The amount of royalties payable to use music is variable and what you can and can't use depends on the music agreements and your budget. For dubbing commercial audio into independently made TV programmes in the UK, the MU currently takes a fee for the performers of £20 per 30 seconds or part of thereof. The BBC and ITV have blanket licences with the MU for dubbing so no further clearance is necessary in terms of the performers' rights. The rights of the label will be covered by the BBC's PPL blanket licence and the PRS for Music licence should cover the rights of the song itself. If in doubt, check that all rights are cleared.

Library music (production music)

The cheapest music of all is library music: music specifically composed for the media industry and intended for inclusion in audio and audiovisual productions. Each 'tune' is written to set lengths: typically 2–3 minutes, 59 seconds,

30 seconds and 5–10-second stings. Every track has a short description that tends to be a little different from what you expect when you listen to it. Nowadays, the vast majority of library music is catalogued and accessible online although many companies send out CDs on demand. The CDs are generally free because the music library makes its money from the royalties paid on transmission.

Well-known music libraries include Warner/Chappell Production Music (formerly Non-Stop Music) with over 200,000 music tracks in the UK (www.warnerchappellpm.com); AKM Music Library (copyright-free music) (www.akmmusic.co.uk); De Wolfe Music (www.dewolfemusic.co.uk); EMI (www.emiproductionmusic.com); West One Music (www.westone.music.com); and Universal Publishing Production Music (www.unippm.co.uk) which incorporates former music libraries such as Bruton. Audio Network (www.audio network.com) may be useful with its online catalogue specifying genre, mood, instrument and production genre. It is a PRS for Music member but not MCPS. For music and sound effects, www.soundrangers.com might be useful. A list of libraries can be found in the Broadcast Production Guide published by *Broadcast* magazine.

In the broadcast television and radio industry, there used to be considerable snobbery and disdain for library music but the quality has been improving. Music libraries go out of their way to help you pick their music instead of commercial material. They are, of course, much cheaper to use and, through the Independent Production Company Licence packages, PRS for Music and MCPS provide a blanket licence agreement for all libraries registered with them. At the time of writing, a blanket deal with a music library costs £4–5000.

Each music library has, literally, thousands of tracks to choose from with a bewildering range of choice, making the prospect of finding a track that works with the pictures exasperatingly time consuming. With such a huge array of choice, music libraries employ various strategies to help you find the appropriate track. The Cutting Edge Group (www.cuttingedgegroup.com) has a sonic search function which means that an iTunes track can be dragged and dropped for a similar (cheaper) Cutting Edge track to be found. This company (as do several others) produced music for feature films such as *Atonement*, *Eragon*, *The King's Speech* and *Lord of the Rings*. In most libraries, consultants help find the appropriate track. Phone the library, describe the sequence for which you are seeking music – 'I want something with a science fiction feel to cover shots of a production line at a biscuit factory' – and the consultant will suggest a suitable selection. As the library makes its profits from the royalties, you will hear the music online for free. The copyright information for this type of music is easily accessible; as the music is played online, the metadata appears alongside the music itself.

Recorded commercial music

Commercial music is more expensive than library material. It has the advantage of being instantly recognisable – what *is* that tune? For well-known classical pieces there is no alternative to the 'real thing'. Carl Orff's *Carmina Burana*, for instance, is featured in *Only Fools and Horses, Britain's Got Talent*, the 2003 film *Cheaper by the Dozen* and the *Old Spice* advert, amongst others. For lyrics appropriate to your sequence, you may have to use commercial tracks.

The wider the transmission area, the more expensive the royalties. The cheapest is for a single transmission in the UK and the most expensive is world rights in perpetuity. Online only is the cheapest of all. For audiovisuals such as those used in museums, the rates are lower.

Because of the symbiotic relationship between music and radio (they cannot exist without each other), there are few potential problems in the use of commercial music for *radio*. Most commercial recording agreements allow almost unconditional use of music on radio and the only issue that may arise is that of moral rights which is unlikely to be invoked.

For television, however, the use of music can be problematic and mistakes extremely costly. If a production team checks first and discovers the music they want will cost £20,000, they will go about it in a different – and cheaper – way. If the team doesn't check till afterwards, it is too late; it's another £20,000 on the budget.

A warning about *Happy Birthday to You*. The music was written by two Kentucky sisters, Mildred and Patty Hill, in the 1890s. So why is it still in copyright? Because the current owner, Warner/Chappell Music, bought a claim to it in 1988. This is the biggest grossing music of all time, reputedly earning £30 million over the years and about $2 million each year; even a tinkly jingle on Casio must pay the licence. Beware using the music in *anything*; a simple *Happy Birthday* sung at a children's birthday party could cost a lot of money. The copyright is scheduled to go into the public domain in 2030.

There are several reasons why tracks cannot be used, for example:

- the *cost* of world rights and especially for artists from the United States;
- the issue of *moral rights*; in other words creative work must be treated with integrity.

The cost of the music is obvious and is explained throughout this chapter.

Some composers, publishers and copyright holders *must* be contacted beforehand for express permission to use their music as they have asserted their moral rights although this is usually for advertisements. There may be a number of reasons why they turn the request down. They simply might not like how it will be used. For instance, a vegetarian band might refuse a request to play their music on an advert promoting lamb. Another example; in January 2013 Thom Yorke from *Radiohead* threatened Prime Minister David Cameron with legal action should any of *Radiohead's* songs be used in a Conservative campaign in a future election campaign.

Parodies: Irving Berlin (*White Christmas, There's No business Like Show Business, Anything You Can Do, God Bless America*, inter alia) took exception to his work being parodied and in 1964, took *Mad* magazine to court for rewriting lyrics to some of his songs. Eventually he lost the case but several songwriters are strict about such parodying and you must be careful about doing this in any broadcast programme or newspaper.

Cutting music: when editing a film or compiling a sound montage for radio or the internet, many editors want to cut the music to fit the pictures, edit out bars or repeat choruses. This is done all the time, although, officially, editing music in this way is not permissible without prior consent from the copyright holders.

Film scores: generally a film score is recorded under a 'combined use fee' which is a buy-out clause under an MU agreement – but it is only bought out for that particular film. That music, therefore, cannot be used in another film without additional fees being paid to the musicians and other rights holders. Cutting Edge Music has an agreement with the MU at the time of writing so that it can clear the use of the scores and pay MU members a royalty. If the score has been released on CD, follow the procedure for commercially recorded music.

Signature tunes: the use of signature tunes within other programmes needs consent from the copyright holders and it may be wise to contact the MU and PRS for Music. The *Mastermind* theme tune came from a music library and therefore is an exception to this although it has been re-recorded.

Extracts: it used to be the case that using several solo instrument bars from a full orchestral work meant the whole orchestra had to be paid. Nowadays, the MU will only collect fees for those musicians in the clip. The extract fee may be as low as £165 for extracts no longer than two minutes each with a total of six minutes for a 30-minute programme. A clip show, however, may charge a higher fee per extract as it constitutes 'high content use'.

Always check beforehand if you can use the music the way you want to.

Foreign music

You are working on a documentary about Greece or writing an online travel article about Portugal and suggest adding national music for local colour. On your last holiday you picked up a CD of Portuguese or Greek music. Can you use it?

The answer is probably yes (for a price) but, as always, the copyright needs to be cleared. Because the music is Greek/Portuguese, it is unlikely that PRS for Music has licensed it and it might be virtually impossible to find the copyright holder unless you speak the language fluently. PRS for Music works in 150 territories globally and has reciprocal agreements with equivalent societies so by contacting PRS for Music in London, you will be given a contact in the relevant country who may be able to arrange a licence for you. Whether or not you can afford the royalties depends on the budget.

For music from all countries, go through the same procedure. If there is an in-house music department (at the BBC, for instance), it is suggested you contact it prior to going down the PRS for Music route as it may feel you are usurping its professional status.

PRS for Music does not cover the rights of the musicians abroad although it should be able to point you in the right direction. If not, speak to the MU and involve your music department.

Pop videos

Pop videos are a popular item in programmes simply because they are cheaper (and easier) than performance. Nowadays, the agreement for broadcasting pop videos without incurring extra payments to the musicians or band is contracted when the videos are made. Check with the record company.

For tracks recorded since June 2011, the label pays a fee to the VPL when the music video is made which is paid out by the MU to its members on that track. For tracks recorded prior to June 2011 (when the new BPI/MU Agreement came into force), the label must pay a buy-out to each individual musician. If in doubt, the label can confirm when the music video was made and if it's cleared for broadcast.

A note of warning; in 2011, Ofcom issued a reminder that explicit music videos should not be transmitted before the watershed. This followed the transmission of a video by 50 Cent at 9am on *Greatest Hits TV*. Rihanna's video for 'S&M' containing scenes of bondage was screened on WTF TV during the day and was also ruled unacceptable.

Drama

Only the BBC (and independent production companies commissioned by the BBC) tends to make radio drama. PRS for Music has a blanket agreement with the BBC making it very easy to use music in any radio drama.

Most incidental music for TV drama is specially composed and recorded. The composer may be contracted to deliver a recording in which case they may be responsible for booking the musicians and will be paid a 'package fee' covering their time and recording costs. Alternatively, the production company will hire the players or book a contractor to do so.

At the time of writing, the BBC session rate per musician was £210 for three hours during which time up to 30 minutes of music can be recorded (BBC/MU Agreement).

Music clearance

Music clearance is the term used for sorting out the payment paperwork and/or the licences.

Any TV programme commissioned by the BBC, ITV or Sky has a blanket licence with PRS for Music which includes commercial, library music and synchronisation rights. However, any *independents* working for them must clear the music directly with the MU. Not all music is represented by PRS for Music and therefore music must be cleared beforehand with the copyright holders.

At the BBC and the major ITV companies, the clearance usually falls to the production assistant and in radio, the broadcast assistant, researcher or producer. The PRS for Music blanket agreement means that all that usually needs to be completed once the programme has been made or broadcast is the 'P as Bs' form (Programme as Broadcast), or cue sheets. Due to playlists, this is increasingly sent automatically electronically.

However, on a show where a researcher has been instrumental in choosing the music, they need to pass on the relevant information. The last thing a PA wants to do is chase up a freelance researcher now working in another company and ask for details long since forgotten.

Because it is in everyone's interest, PRS for Music has made the clearing process as simple as possible. It requires:

- name of production;
- production type (e.g. TV broadcast, radio advertising, online webpage);

- transmission area (e.g. regional, UK, Europe, Europe and the USA, world-wide);
- number of transmissions;
- the label;
- the artist;
- record/CD or reference number;
- track number;
- title of track;
- publisher;
- composer or arranger;
- copyright owner.

You should keep notes of the last seven bullet points.

For an independent production company making a programme for Channel 4, Channel 5 or any other UK broadcaster that doesn't have their own blanket licence to cover the mechanical rights, the music *must* be licensed under the IPC blanket licence offered by PRS for Music. The responsibility for clearing the music lies with the production company and not the broadcaster. Also, as a rule of thumb, for worldwide rights and for USA and Canada, you will need the publisher's prior approval. For Channels 4 and 5, there is a rate card for both commercial and library music. Additional rights for all media, series deals and annual deals are also available for library music only.

Standard exclusions apply under the IPC blanket licence and there is an excluded works list. As an example, the use of any commercial music for title music requires prior approval and the fee is at the discretion of the rights owner. Clearance for worldwide rights can be approved or denied depending on the context of use, specific work being used and the terms required.

PRS for Music encourages media professionals to speak to it before embarking on any programme.

Fees and royalties

It is interesting to see the amount charged for the use of music. The PRS for Music rates are reviewed from time to time.

- Channel 4 – £118 per 30 seconds (two transmissions and 30 day +/– VOD).
- Channel 5 – £90 per 30 seconds (two transmissions and 30 day +/– VOD).
- S4C – £48 per 30 seconds (five transmissions and 35 day +/– VOD).
- Worldwide – all media per programme rate for library music, any length of programme and in perpetuity for producers clearing rights for third-party independents, £774 (February 2013).

- Worldwide – rights per episode not including UK TV, £413. The rate can be topped up to the higher rate if there is interest from abroad and the UK.
- News content is not licensed under the IPC blanket licence.

Summary

The key is to determine:

- what is the music for, e.g. internet, radio, film, television, advertising, audiovisual products?
- where is the product going to, e.g. UK, worldwide, USA, Europe?
- how long will it be there, e.g. in perpetuity, five minutes, over two transmissions?

Further reading

Rutter, Paul, *The Music Industry Handbook* (Media Practice), Routledge, 2011

Websites

All Music, music resource on albums, bands, musicians and songs, reviews, sound samples and discographies: www.allmusic.com

Association of Independent Music (AIM): www.musicindie.com

BBC College of Production online resource has an item on music copyright at: www.bbc.co.uk/academy/production

British Academy of Songwriters, Composers and Authors (BASCA): www.basca.org.uk

British Recorded Music Industry Ltd (formerly British Phonographic Industry): www.bpi.co.uk

Broadcast Production Guide, subscription: www.theproductionguide.co.uk

The Knowledge, database for events management and TV, etc.: www.theknowledgeonline.com

Musicians' Union: www.musiciansunion.org.uk

Phonographic Performance Ltd (PPL) and Video Performance Ltd (VPL): www.ppluk.com.

Producers Alliance for Cinema and Television (PACT): www.pact.co.uk

PRS for Music and MCPS: www.prsformusic.com

Spotify, Swedish music streaming company: www.spotify.com

8
Locations

By location, I mean away from the office; for journalists, that's a lot of the time. For people working in radio, there may be times when you are on an outside broadcast (OB) or recording items on locations. For those working in film and television, you are 'on location' when you are filming outside the studio.

Once a researcher has set up filming, they usually go on location with the crew. They are responsible for ensuring everything goes well, acting in a variety of roles from gopher through to ensuring that anyone they brought on location knows what is happening and feels well cared for. They may pay expenses to contributors and ensure they sign the release (permission) forms although both of these responsibilities will be carried out by the PA if there is one on the crew. With a small crew, the researcher minds props and special requirements such as towels and clothing. Organising the location and equipment involved is part of the pre-production schedule. On very small productions, the researcher may even direct the shoot.

A small production hasn't the budget for a location or production manager and therefore the researcher, together with the PA, may book hotels, transport and any other administrative details. They may even organise the shooting schedule which, for a drama, is the role of the first assistant director (shortened to 1st AD; the floor manager does this in studio) but the producer may prefer to organise it themselves.

Before anyone leaves the office or goes on location, some sort of risk assessment should be carried out. For the local journalist who knows their own area, this is as simple as taking safety precautions outlined later in this chapter. For recording an OB or filming, a recce should be carried out. This can be combined with meeting possible contributors when you must ask yourself – do I want to include them as a contributor? Is their story relevant and good enough?

The recce – reconnaissance

One of my most memorable experiences in television was a day spent with the RAF in Yorkshire setting up an item on fast jet training. It revealed a stack of issues. The time it took to measure me up (and therefore the crew) for the ejector seat. Would the cameraman fit? Would the camera? If the camera dimensions were too big, I needed to order another that would fit. Could the cameraman and director fly in the same plane? No – so how many planes could be supplied for filming? Did the crew require special clothing? Would the RAF kit them out? Did they need the cameraman's measurements? Which ones? Could we film on the runway? Where was I to obtain earmuffs and to what specification?

This particular assignment drew to my attention the little detail of dress in the officers' mess. If we were to lunch there, the men had to wear jacket and tie, not jeans. For women (the PA and myself), it was 'smart casual' – but not trousers. Plenty more issues were raised during the day and filming would have been pretty stressful without such a detailed recce. The organisation on the RAF's part was, as usual, supremely professional.

Today's programmes like *24 Hours in A&E*, *Brit Cops* and *Lights, Camera, Action!* all have issues plus the health and safety aspects of film crew and general public, some of whom are part of the 'cast', if you like, and others are encountered during the filming itself. OBs need to cover the same general considerations.

Effectively, a recce should tell you everything, including the following.

- Is the location suitable?
- What special equipment is required to record there?
- Are there any sound or camera problems?
- What risks are taken to record there?

And:

- how to get there and how long it takes;
- how easy it is to find the location;
- where to go for lunch.

Napoleon said that an army marches on its stomach but he hadn't met a film crew.

Now let's look at the essential points to consider in a recce or when you leave the office. Much of this is relevant to both journalists and broadcast media.

Take lots of photos to show directors or producers when you get back to the office. For journalists, these photos can illustrate the article.

Contacts

- Who are you meeting? Their name, designation, address, phone number. Is there a direct line, must you go through the switchboard, have you got their mobile number?
- Whenever possible, get the mobile or direct number even if it's ex-directory. A lot of time is wasted going through an automated system before speaking to the person you want, especially when away from the office.
- What story do they have to tell, if any? How articulate are they? Is their story coaxed out of them or are they natural talkers? This is less relevant for journalists but crucial for radio and TV. Their appearance shouldn't be an issue but is (refer to Chapter 4) unless it's for radio.
- Can they grant filming or interview permission or must they refer up? How long will this take?

Events

- What happens? If possible, recce the event at the same time it is scheduled to take place. In other words, if you are recording on a Wednesday, recce on a Wednesday. This reveals snags like flight paths, e.g. sound problems.
- If possible, see the event first. Take still photos. If it's a one-off, it is essential to see the location before recording.
- How many people are there? How many take part? How many watch? What do they wear? How noisy are they?

Directions

- How do you get there? I was once given instructions to go to the second house on the right after the phone box. Seven miles down the road and five cattle grids later, I found the phone box. The house was a mile and a half further on. Maps are helpful, verbal instructions are (usually) better. The postcode for SatNav with a little verbal clarification is perfect.
- Directions need to be relayed to the crew or anyone else travelling to the same location at a later date. Write down helpful hints for the crew when you arrive at your destination to go with the SatNav postcode. Remember, SatNav sometimes takes you down cul-de-sacs and if this is the case, warn everyone. Electronic device apps are available but only work where there is a signal. Printed maps are useful on remote locations without a satellite signal. Maps are copyrighted so photocopying them is illegal but everyone does it.

- On large drama shoots and OBs, it is common for the production manager to erect signs on the road indicating the correct direction ensuring no-one gets lost or overclaims travel expenses.

Printed literature, pre-publicity, maps

- Pick up all printed literature publicising the event and anything which may be helpful. This can be used in the article (watch copyright), for voiceovers or commentary points. Of course, they are probably online but this saves searching for them.
- If there are maps of the hospital, shopping centre, factory, government building, etc., collect them too.

Parking

- Where does the crew park? Do they need money for meters and pay and display? Can parking be arranged? The police and local authority cannot officially arrange parking for filming but for large drama shoots and OBs, they usually sort something out.
- The parking for the crew and OB vans must be as secure and as physically close to where recording takes place as possible. There is a lot of expensive and heavy kit to carry. *Shameless* originally shot in the streets of Gorton, Manchester, but after too many break-ins and problems with security from bystanders, changed location. It may be expedient to hire a security firm to help with cordoning off the road with cones, etc. Yellow high-visibility jackets may be required for any crew working in or near roads.

Ease of access

- Is it easy to get to and easy to record in?
- Does someone have to find a key to let you in?
- Are there places the crew or journalists cannot go? Golf clubs in particular forbid women in certain rooms. You may be female or there may be women on the crew.
- Are there lots of stairs to climb? Is there a lift? Is it in the middle of nowhere and how far from the road? Are there steep slopes? Near water?
- Will you need security passes? If you are recording on Ministry of Defence land, government property or somewhere equally politically sensitive, it is common for crew names to be emailed a few days beforehand for security clearance. Under these circumstances, security passes are occasionally

pre-issued and sent to the office to be handed out to the crew before recording.

- Check if any other information, such as full names, date and place of birth and photographs, is required for security checks. Proof of DBS checks may also be required.

Lighting

- What is the lighting like? Will a basic lighting kit (two red-heads and a blonde plus sun gun, gels and filters) be enough or do you need more? For a large area, the film crew or film office needs to be informed beforehand. For radio or newspaper journalists, this is not an issue.

Power supplies

- How far is the nearest electricity supply? Must you order extra cables? Is there an electricity supply or do you need a genny (generator)? This is only necessary for very large shoots or OBs and it is unlikely you would be doing the recce on your own. In very large establishments, especially factories, you need to check the voltage in case an adaptor is required. This is even more important if you are recording abroad where 240 volts is not standard.
- Because of health and safety requirements, some television companies insist on sending extra 'sparks' (nickname for an electrician), particularly when filming in schools and hospitals. They stand by the lights ensuring nobody accidentally walks into them. Also, should there be a mains disruption, there will be at least two people to work on the reconnection.

Noise

- Schools, hospitals, factories and airports are very noisy. Music in shopping centres is a hindrance to recording and will need copyright clearance.
- If the location is dangerously noisy (e.g. an airport or factory) earmuffs might be obligatory.

Most sound engineers insist that ambient noise (especially music and background hum of machinery) is turned off whenever possible. They are excellent at locating both the source and people responsible for turning it off. Some noisy machinery, life-saving medical equipment for instance, cannot be turned off.

Filming directly under a flight path creates difficulties for the editor who cannot cut from a noisy 'plane overhead' shot to a quiet shot without it being pretty obvious. If a plane flies overhead, the take is usually reshot. The same applies in a shopping arcade where one shot in a sequence has 'Blue Suede Shoes' in the background and the next 'Yesterday'.

Under such circumstances, either find a quieter location or warn the director/ sound recordist beforehand and be prepared for a long day's shoot with plenty of retakes.

Catering

• Where is the nearest suitable restaurant? How long does it take to drive from the location? What time does it open/shut? Can you pre-book? How expensive is it? There is usually a budget limit. Is there a variety of meals to cater for vegetarians? How secure is car parking?

On large drama shoots, a location catering company is contracted to feed crew and cast. The responsibility for booking them falls to the location manager.

If you are working long hours out of the office, it is important to eat. Often, you are so short of time and in such a rush that you may forget. For the sake of your health, pick up a sandwich if nothing else.

Toilets

• If interviewing or recording at someone's house or an office block, this is not a problem. It is a concern in the middle of nowhere but less so for men who can utilise the nearest bush. Don't ignore the laws of indecent exposure . . .
• If filming in a shopping centre, check where the nearest public lavatories are.

My advice is to use the loo whenever you see one even if you don't want it at the time.

Health and safety when alone

There are several basic precautions to take when you make an unaccompanied trip and are effectively the same as when meeting a programme contributor (Chapter 4).

• Tell someone where you are going and when you are due back.
• If you are meeting someone for the first time, meet in a public place if possible.

- Take a mobile phone with you, leave it switched on but don't use it whilst driving. Ensure it is fully charged.
- Park in a well-lit area.
- Ensure you have enough petrol in the car.

Joanna Geary of the *Guardian* suggested the use of the Glympse app. This app shares your location with a specified person so that if you are not back within a stated time, they can put emergency measures into motion. Both parties must have compatible phones.

Risk assessment

In this litigious age, health and safety for yourself, crew, general public and equipment is paramount. It is essential nowadays to complete a risk assessment form after a recce and before recording and most productions will not be sanctioned without signatures from various line managers, including the producer. In many companies, some sort of risk assessment is required before a recce. The BBC College of Production has useful online advice for journalists and broadcasters.

Some large events may already have their own media arrangements and risk assessments in place. A copy of these is useful and may offer a glimpse of what you need to be aware of when filming. Add their risk assessment to your own to avoid repetition. If anything changes on the day of recording, amend the risk assessments in your notes so that, should the unthinkable happen, you have been seen to update the risk assessment. This evidences good safety management.

The HSE publishes a useful checklist covering and expanding on risk assessment, including crowd management. Start at www.hse.gov.uk/event-safety/index.htm or www.hse.gov.uk/entertainment/theatre-tv/index.htm.

Recce notes

On your return to the office, write down all your impressions together with phone numbers, contacts and directions. Include any relevant photos to jog your memory.

If you didn't like the location but the people were good, consider importing them somewhere else but carefully consider the ethical and political implications. There is a diplomatic problem with liking the location but not the people, especially if they are integral to the location. Under these circumstances, the judicious way is to start again with a new set of people at a different location.

Call sheets

On a small production (or a relatively large one on a tight schedule), you may be the only person who knows what and where you are recording.

For those who need to know, the information is communicated on a call sheet. On large productions, especially dramas, the call sheet is devised, written and updated by the 1st AD and distributed to all crew members, actors and walk-ons; in short, to everyone involved. Individual companies and production teams have their own house style but the required information is standard.

Call sheets include:

- title of production;
- the production company, its address and contact numbers;
- date of recording;
- date of transmission (written as 'tx') if known;
- personnel and their designations, e.g. cameraman;
- crew mobile phone numbers, e.g. the director's, yours, the PA's;
- the location, address, contact names and numbers. The crew like to know who they are meeting and address them by name;
- time of filming – include whatever is relevant:
  - crew call times,
  - leaving time from base (time is needed to load equipment into the car),
  - travel time,
  - estimated arrival on location,
  - set-up time,
  - rehearsal time, if any,
  - wrap time,
  - location departure time (time is needed to load the equipment),
  - arrival back at base,
  - off-clock time (after equipment has been stored away),
  - important times such as when an event is scheduled to start and finish. The crew sets up beforehand so that they start shooting as soon as events get under way;
- the base address, especially if you are travelling, e.g. hotel name and phone numbers;
- transport arrangements, for example who is travelling with whom, train and plane times and numbers;

- meeting place before you leave to film – crew room, hotel lobby;
- directions – always include both maps and written instructions. Highlight the destination in red. Give distance and time estimates. Are you crossing toll bridges? Is cash required? Give postcodes for SatNav;
- car parking arrangements. Include maps if possible. Is cash required for parking?
- is there a long walk, difficult route from the car park to the location?
- is special equipment required? Clothing? Lighting? Other equipment?
- health and safety requirements;
- brief synopsis. The crew always ask what they are filming but it is helpful to give a two- or three-line synopsis at the end of the call sheet. In a drama call sheet, this is essential.

This looks an awful lot but it is possible to get most of it on one side although call sheets for dramas can run to several pages. If it gets everyone to the right place at the right time, the call sheet has done its job.

Finding locations

For journalists, this is not a problem. You go where the story is. Interview someone in their home, office or hospital. The consideration of *recording* in a public place is discussed elsewhere. However, there are times when the location is not immediately obvious and you need to find somewhere suitable.

The immediate and easiest answer is to ask the person if they can suggest somewhere. Get them to describe it fully before accompanying them on the recce. If, when you get there, the location isn't suitable or you can't get filming permission, find somewhere else. Your contributor may be able to help. If they say, unhelpfully, 'This is where I always go', either change the contributor or find somewhere else and tactfully persuade them to be recorded there instead.

Finding somewhere from scratch involves ingenuity. Colleagues, especially production and location managers, may make helpful suggestions. The local film or tourist office can help. The governing association is worth a try as are clubs or other people involved in the same pursuit. Follow up all suggestions and recce each one until you find what you want or the time runs out and you must compromise. The British Film Commission may be helpful; it has suggestions and fact sheets on its webpage.

Historical and technical accuracy is occasionally a consideration although location filming is notorious for taking liberties. The Virginia scenes in Granada's *Moll Flanders* were shot in the West Country. *Captain America* (2011) filmed their New York scenes in Manchester. Who said the camera never lies?

For films and commercials, it is common to use specialist location-finding companies. It is unlikely that you will have the budget.

Facility fees

If you record in a location owned by the National Trust or other such organisations, be prepared to pay a facility fee. Some locations are only too pleased to have the extra publicity, merely charging a token fee to cover extra staff and electricity, whereas others charge on a sliding scale depending on the time you take, the type of programme and the amount of trouble you put them to. Unless it's a drama or an OB – when the location manager will negotiate fees – you are unlikely to be asked for an exorbitant fee. Remember to check first. Producers and editors take the presentation of an unexpected invoice extremely badly.

When filming in someone's house, it is courtesy to offer a token payment for their electricity and time, especially when energy bills are so expensive. This depends, of course, on the budget but a few pounds should suffice. The poorer the contributor, the more likely they are to need the money and contributing towards their electricity bill may mean the difference between filming or not. Again, check with the producer.

Reporters rarely pay facility fees.

Location files

It might be a good idea to keep a location file. Whenever an interesting potential location is encountered, on the way to work or in the papers, note it down or cut out the relevant article and stick it in the file. To a certain extent, the file is out of date quickly as locations change; building sites do not remain building sites for long. When a specific location is needed, rummage through the file to turn up something useful. Location managers also keep location files.

Recording permission

Organising permission to record can be done when you return to the office but is worth bearing in mind whilst conducting the recce.

If you intend to record on private land, permission *must* be obtained from the owner. Shopping precincts such as Bluewater, Lakeside, the Metro Centre and the Trafford Centre are all private enterprises requiring prior permission. Open-air precincts may also be private land.

The precinct manager can give permission for recording in the public areas but should you wish to record inside individual shops, separate permission is required from the shop manager. They may need to refer to head office and it is common to be asked what you intend to film and why.

Merely filming shop fronts without permission can cause awkward moments although most crews do it, especially in the local high street and for local news. The best practice is to obtain authority to film a shop frontage before taking out a crew. Pop inside and ask the manager. For filming outside their shop, they usually say yes instantly. Keep a note of the person who gave permission in case they have a holiday on the day concerned. Some managers are more cautious and if the shop is one of a chain, it may involve a phone call to the head office; the number can be found on the internet.

Ask in the first instance to be put through to the public affairs department or press office and see how you fare. In some cases, the PR is handled by an outside agency and you may find that obtaining permission is neither straightforward nor quick, with everyone enquiring about the programme, the content and how the item will be used.

Recording in the street also officially requires permission. The police should be informed but if there is a local film office, they may do this for you. Please note that film offices are not a replacement for general research and are too busy to answer questions such as 'What is the phone number for the local taxi rank?'.

Take the name of the police officer granting permission. Should an officer stop you in the street, you can refer back. In busy areas, especially central London, permission is not guaranteed and there may be stipulations such as hand-held filming only (i.e. no tripods) and moving on if the police consider you are causing an obstruction. The police have the power of arrest for causing a breach of the peace or a disturbance. This is especially relevant in London and other cities.

It is commonplace for film crews to record in the street without police per-mission – especially news crews. On the whole, the police ignore them unless they are causing an obstruction. Do remember that the police have a duty of care towards the general public, including film crews themselves. The presence of cameras may be the catalyst for upheaval when filming marches and demonstrations where people do not want to be filmed. If the police see crews putting themselves at risk, they may ask them to move to a place of safety. This is common in civil unrest. The HSE guidance is useful and online. The British Film Commission website is another useful resource.

Release forms

Release forms are signed by contributors to prove they have given permission to be recorded and for the footage to be edited and transmitted. Often the release forms are used as a receipt for payment. The responsibility for getting release forms signed is usually taken by the PA although the researcher, who has a rapport with the contributor, may do it instead. On shoots where there is no PA, it is the researcher's (or reporter's) responsibility to ensure they have been signed.

The actual nature of the release form depends on the production company. In some, the rights of the contributor would appear to be non-existent and I have known people refuse to sign, especially if there are clauses giving the company the right to include the footage in any programme, edited in any format and without the contributor seeing or vetting the cut footage before transmission. The words of a release form from one TV company alarmed contributors so much that the PAs nicknamed it 'the blood chitty'.

Although it is by no means common to let people see their contributions before transmission, editing their contribution any which way is technically against Ofcom guidelines. As it says in the Ofcom guidelines (Fairness 7.6), 'When a programme is edited, contributions should be represented fairly'. In the same section, paragraph 8, broadcasters are warned that material filmed for one purpose and used in another should not create unfairness there either.

Should a contributor refuse to sign a release form, technically you cannot use them in a programme even if it has already been recorded. However, if they stipulate that the content can be used in the programme for which they have been filmed but no other, then the footage can be used for just that. Many companies want the option of using all recordings in, for instance, promotional material and trailers and it is unusual for people to refuse although some celebrities' agents are occasionally uncomfortable about this for contractual reasons.

Journalists rarely use release forms. They verbally check that people are willing to be interviewed which is generally sufficient. If a member of the public disagrees with the way they have been portrayed, they can complain to the newspaper and, if they receive insufficient satisfaction, apply to the Press Complaints Commission (PCC). Following the hacking scandals, the Leveson Inquiry demanded the replacement of the PCC. The press have proposed a self-regulated Independent Press Standards Organisation (IPSO) whereas the government wants a Royal Charter. At the time of writing, this is still under rancorous discussion. See Chapter 10.

Filming in a school involves the administrative headache of having parental or guardian permission for every child likely to be involved, which can mean the entire school. Children whose parents/guardians refuse (or forget) to sign cannot be included. The head teacher gives authority to film in a school.

There are ethical considerations when recording children. In a film about child abuse, the viewer may construe that the featured children have been abused which contravenes several broadcasting codes. It is common for programmes on sensitive topics to use general views (GVs) below the neck of children playing or filming them slightly out of focus. Refer to the codes.

The hospital administrator or chief executive gives permission for filming in a hospital; think of all the current reality programmes set around A&E. There are issues of filming people in potentially sensitive places such as hospitals and ambulances. The Ofcom codes stipulate (Section 8.8, Privacy):

> Separate consent should normally be obtained before filming or recording and for broadcast from those in sensitive situations (unless not obtaining consent is warranted). If the individual will not be identifiable in the programme then separate consent for broadcast will not be required.
> http://stakeholders.ofcom.org.uk/broadcasting/
> broadcast-codes/broadcast-code/privacy

Channel 4's *24 Hours in A&E* gets the floor producer to talk to the people in A&E at King's Hospital, London, to ask if they are interested in being filmed. There are two times when people can refuse: when they first arrive at the hospital or when the programme is being edited. The production staff will again contact the people involved to double-check if they are still happy to be included in the programme. Obviously, the reasons for refusal or acceptance are down to the people concerned and the circumstances; some people regard the transmission as a thank you to the staff who treated them so successfully or as a eulogy to the loved one who died. The senior clinicians at the hospital clear consent from the hospital staff but anyone unwilling to take part will not be filmed or, if they are unavoidably in shot, have their faces blurred.

People in such programmes are often too ill to sign a form and here the next of kin can sign it. Section 7.5 of Ofcom's broadcast code states:

> In the case of persons over sixteen who are not in a position to give consent, a person of eighteen or over with primary responsibility for their care should normally give it on their behalf.

Considerations in public and sensitive places

Filming people in public places

If they are not central figures in the item, one doesn't need permission from everyone who 'just happens to be there at the time'. The same applies for people filmed in hospitals (see previous pages), factories and department stores. As the British Film Commission says on its website, 'You do not need to ask passers-by for permission to feature their faces in a film'. However, Section 8.7, Privacy, in the Ofcom codes states:

> If an individual or organisation's privacy is being infringed, and they ask that the filming, recording or live broadcast be stopped, the broadcaster should do so, unless it is warranted to continue.

Obviously, should someone come up to you and object, as happens in, for instance, *Brit Cops* and *Police, Camera, Action*, the footage containing them either cannot be used or, as usually happens, is pixelated so the people cannot be identified. Most people on the whole don't mind, unless they are performing something illegal or unsociable as in *Brit Cops*.

There are ways and means of avoiding disputes. Where members of the public gather, for instance in a pub (private property and filming permission should be obtained beforehand) or shopping centre (also usually private property), a large notice informing customers that filming is taking place inside means that, should they enter, they are assumed to have given their consent to be filmed.

However, people may resent being filmed for a variety of reasons, e.g. in *Brit Cops* and the like, especially in politically or socially sensitive places. Being filmed in Manchester's gay village may be one of them, especially if viewers assume (wrongly) that everyone in Manchester's gay village *is* gay. Your risk assessment prior to filming will reflect this.

For radio recording where faces are not seen, there are usually few problems and for journalists asking permission without a camera in sight it is generally unproblematic.

Filming from bicycles and motorbikes

Let's get filming from bicycles out of the way first. This is the biggest no-no ever. It is both dangerous and illegal. And yes, ambitious researchers working on satellite television programmes wanting to make a 'mark for themselves' have attempted what they think will be a spectacular shot. There are serious repercussions; it will get you fired, arrested and maybe killed. Not necessarily in that order. And don't think you can sneak the shot in. Once it is transmitted, the HSE will demand to know how you got such an interesting effect – and then you'll be fired.

Filming from the back of motorbikes is another taboo. Cameramen filming the London Marathon are specially trained, their bikes adapted and the cameras fitted to mounts specifically for that purpose. They also have a driver. When directing a cameraman filming from the back of a motorbike, the researcher must be sure the cameraman is fully insured to do so, is trained and has taken the appropriate health and safety measures, including the wearing of appropriate protective clothing and having the camera fixed to a camera mount.

There are plenty of specialist small cameras nowadays that can be fitted to helmets and to cars which can be operated by remote control. Use one of these instead. One company providing miniature cameras for filming in extreme conditions such as skating, snowboarding, surfing, etc. is GoPro.

Filming from cars

Filming from a car is far less problematic although, again, certain measures must be taken to protect the crew and general public. The BBC Academy has a short film on loading a crew car which can be found under self-shooting.

The car must be driven according to the Highway Code and the driver must obey all legal requirements. The HSE guidelines offer general filming guidelines (including off-road) when filming on the roadside and from vehicles (including motorbikes) and the following sums up its points for specifically filming from a car (www.hse.gov.uk/pubns/etis22.pdf):

- a risk assessment must be conducted beforehand;
- a driver cannot film and record (see below);
- a seat belt must always be worn;
- shooting through a sunroof is too dangerous and not allowed;
- when shooting through a side window (with seat belt on), don't lean out and don't let the camera lens protrude beyond the plane of the car;
- tracking should not be done from the boot of a saloon car or from any open doors;
- tracking from car to car should only be done on private roads unless you have police and local authority permission; the cars should be specially modified;

- if filming up and bys (when a car drives up and past the camera) from the roadside, the camera and tripod must be a safe distance from the edge of the road and on the inside of any bends;
- it is illegal to race on public highways.

This sums up the more obvious points but basically means that filming point of view (POV) shots through a car window is perfectly permissible as long as the relevant precautions mentioned above are taken. Your employer must, by law, have issued its own local guidelines and you should be knowledgeable about them before filming. If you don't comply and an accident happens, not knowing the rules does not act in your defence.

As a general rule, let the cameraperson do the difficult shots. If you are filming on your own, filming from a vehicle is unsafe unless the camera does not require an operator, is switched on before driving away and switched off after the shot is finished when the car is parked in a safe position. As it says in the HSE guidelines, 'A person at the wheel should not be distracted from driving, for example by being in sole charge of recording equipment' (www.hse.gov.uk/pubns/etis22.pdf). An example of a self-operated camera is one mounted on the front of a racing car or in a police car during a chase as seen in programmes like *Police, Camera, Action*.

To film something elaborate such as five vintage cars driving down the road, it is expedient from a health and safety angle (as well as legal) to film on private land. There is more control and the added dimension of a scenic background.

Using police cars in dramas is illegal, as is dressing up as a police officer where the offence is 'impersonating a police officer'. You will need complete police co-operation for this.

Railways and trains

Railways and stations are other public places where you may wish to film – such as Michael Portillo's *Great British Railway Journeys*. These take time to set up; I mean days rather than hours unless you already have good contacts. If it is a request for TV and radio news, it may be arranged quite quickly via the Network Rail media management team.

Network Rail owns the track, bridges, tunnels, level crossings, viaducts and 17 key stations (including the main London stations, Birmingham New Street, Manchester Piccadilly, Liverpool Lime Street and Glasgow Central). Although it owns all other stations, these are *operated* by train operating companies. Stockport, for instance, is operated by Virgin and the station is used as a stop-off for railway companies, e.g. Northern Rail and CrossCountry, which operate trains using that route.

For filming on a Network Rail-managed station, the first contact is Network Rail which can be contacted by phone and email. You will never be permitted to film on the track. Expect to pay a facility fee.

Network Rail has a number of specialised media contacts listed on its webpage: filming and photography; national, trade and specialist journalists and regional journalists. The five regional offices can be contacted by phone and the numbers are published on the web. All can be contacted by email as a link from the website.

For the stations managed by other companies, find out who manages the station and contact them. This may take some time . . .

When recording on stations, remember that the general public are rushing to catch trains and not looking for tripods. Some companies may not permit you to film on platforms just on the concourse. The crew should consist of enough people to keep both personnel and equipment safe. Don't place the camera close to the edge of the platform, especially if high-speed trains go through the station; in other words, if a yellow line has been painted on the platform don't cross it to film. The voltage on the railway system is considerably more than the wiring at home and electricity can 'jump' gaps of up to nine feet. It's common safety practice for a railway official to accompany you when you are recording. Heed their advice.

Airports

As ever, you can't just turn up and record! *Inside Gatwick* took months to set up. Prior permission is required and security issues are paramount. It's harder to get permission to film beyond customs and immigration although *Border Control UK* did just that. These areas are technically 'out of the country' and, just as in a railway station, an airport official will accompany the crew and journalist. Phone numbers can be found on the internet. Smaller regional airports may be more amenable to filming. If you get to film on the runway, earmuffs will be required and health and safety issues are vital.

Others

Filming in *court during a trial* has been illegal in England since 1925 under the sub-judice laws which is why news programmes and newspapers use illustrations by court artists. However, filming in court has been permitted in Scotland since 1992 but only if all parties consent. In cases where Scottish trials have been filmed, it is usual for the courts to insist on vetting the footage before transmission. There is some movement to permit filming in English courts; for instance, from October 2013, TV cameras will be allowed into a *court of appeal* but judges are warning the government that, if access is extended to criminal trials, it might open up the judicial system to disruption and deter witnesses from giving evidence. At the time of writing, the government is insisting that witnesses, defendants and counsel will not be filmed.

It is notoriously difficult and time-consuming to obtain permission (if given at all) to film in *prisons and juvenile institutions*. The governor is the person to approach for visiting and filming permission. They may need to consult a higher authority and approval takes a long time. If the subject matter is trivial, expect to be turned down although recently there has been more sympathy towards filming in prisons. A list of all crew members will be required prior to setting foot on the premises. Once in, prison routine takes precedence over filming and the crew must work around it. They will be accompanied at all times and locked in and out through a succession of doors, all of which takes up valuable filming time so the film schedule must take account of this. The security is two-way; many prisoners are dangerous and the crew's safety is paramount. If you intend to film prisoners, prior permission from the prisoners themselves is mandatory. Because of the nature of their crimes, this is often difficult to get. The feelings of their victims must be taken into account and you may cause offence to both the victim and the viewer.

Churches and places of worship are far simpler to set up. The vicar, priest, minister or dean is the person to approach in the first instance. However, the final authority for the Church of England lies with the chapter of the cathedral or the parochial church council. If you are filming a service, remember that the words are covered by copyright. Also, remember that for many people, their place of worship is sacred and to be treated with respect.

Theatres and concert halls have their own pitfalls – the people. Filming in a theatre and concert hall *per se* is not a problem unless you want to film actors or musicians. The Musicians' Union and Equity exist to counteract the appalling employment records and level of pay for their members and there are minimum union rates for filming their members. This usually involves an official contract via the casting department. The theatre management may also insist that their staff (cleaners, electricians, security) get paid for their time. As usual for dramas, the location or production manager together with the casting department will organise everything but these points should be borne in mind should you suggest a 'quickie' shot backstage at the local rep. The Equity TV

Agreement 2013 which deals with contracts between the BBC and Equity members states, for instance, that theatre extracts will not include the denouement of a play. There is no fee for a news item with a transmission time of under two minutes; above this, the minimum is £33.40. For magazine programmes, any extract under three minutes has a minimum fee of £50. Per actor of course! All recordings require the prior consent of all actors involved. For ITV productions, refer to the PACT agreement.

For reporters, many of these problems do not arise because they are not recording anybody in sound or pictures. They still need to gain entrance and permission for many of these places although a quick phone call should suffice.

Hazardous activities

All activities are risky, even crossing the road if the correct precautions aren't taken but in media terms, some are regarded as more hazardous than others.

Filming from helicopters requires a considerable amount of setting up, not only because of Civil Aviation rules but also because of the high risk involved. In January 2013, a helicopter crashed in central London, killing the pilot and a man on the ground. The pilot was extremely experienced, having been a stunt pilot in films such as James Bond's *Die Another Day*. At the time of writing, the UK Air Accident Investigation Branch had not finalised its report as to the circumstances. The following month, three people were killed in a helicopter crash in Los Angeles filming for a reality show. For insurance purposes, flying in helicopters is regarded as a hazardous activity even though many documentaries feature them, e.g. BBC's *Helicopter Heroes*.

The quickest way of finding a company to charter a helicopter is via the Civil Aviation Authority (CAA) website where a list of Air Operator's Certificate (AOC) holders is found, the local airfield or a trusted source. The CAA or local airfield will inform you of the current regulations.

You *must* use a licensed operator, one holding a CAA AOC and preferably one with filming experience.

A reputable firm will insist on a camera mount but often the camera operator prefers hand held. The most common camera mount nowadays is a Tyler mount. Some remote control devices are also used. Harnesses may also be required for the operator's safety. If the mount has to be bolted to the helicopter's fabric, documentation is required to prove airworthiness.

Except for larger, very expensive helicopters, there is usually little room for anyone other than the cameraman and perhaps the director. It is also a question of weight; the heavier the aircraft, the less manoeuvrable in certain situations which may affect safety. It is common nowadays for the director to double as cameraman.

Hiring a helicopter is expensive. They charge by the flying hour which includes the flying time to and from the location and any waiting time. Helicopter companies expect to be chartered for at least two hours. Charges are upwards of £600 to £1300 per hour at the time of writing depending on the size of the chopper and the current cost of aviation fuel.

If you persuade a helicopter pilot to take you up as part of their day-to-day activities, and this could include journalists writing a feature article on, say, rescue missions, you would not be expected to pay. Of course, you may not go where you want to because, if there is an emergency, it takes precedence and you may be dropped off.

Insurance is a major issue for passengers and equipment. Helicopters with an AOC must have insurance covering aviation-specific liability in respect of passengers, baggage, cargo and third parties. Insurance for third parties should cover death, personal injury and damage to property caused by accidents. Check with the helicopter company but inform your company's underwriters of the crew who will be flying. Because of the chopper's status, both personnel and equipment need to be specifically covered.

There are rules as to where chartered helicopters can fly. In the London crash in January 2013, the pilot was taking a specific and authorised route in low visibility and it had been suggested he should not fly. The helicopter's operator's advice should be heeded.

If you get the chance to fly in a helicopter, take it. It is an amazing experience and one of the perks of working in the media.

Light aeroplanes are less versatile for filming although cheaper than helicopters. The main criteria for commissioning helicopters also apply to light aircraft and the insurance underwriters must be informed.

The alternative is to commission specialist companies who supply model planes with cameras. No risk to the crew at all!

Dangerous locations

What constitutes a dangerous location? Sticking a camera and yourself at the top of a cliff is obvious but everything is relative. The hard shoulder of a motorway is lethal. Media companies nowadays are extremely conscious of health and safety issues and in most cases you cannot do anything without completing a risk assessment form first. Crews are excellent at taking care of themselves but tragedies still happen – usually on location. If in doubt, check with the safety officer where you are working. A change of location may be required.

When filming or reporting a particularly dangerous event, check the insurance cover especially if you, as a journalist, want to have a go yourself. It is also essential to check public liability insurance.

Stuntmen and stunt arrangers

The producer, the location or production manager usually hires stuntmen and arrangers but it is useful to be aware of who they are and what they do. Most stunts are choreographed by stunt arrangers, often ex-stuntmen too old to perform the stunts themselves but with enough expertise and knowledge to set them up safely and dramatically. There are a few stuntwomen in the industry but it still occasionally happens that women's stunts are provided by thin men in wigs. Stuntmen and arrangers tend to be specialists in pyrotechnics, cars, fight scenes and so on. The trick is the editing together of the video to make the action seamless and fluid. Action sequences, like all films, are shot in sections.

Although the general researcher is rarely involved in dramas on this scale, they may well find themselves involved in a documentary about *The Making of* . . . such and such and a reporter might write an article about it. It is useful, therefore, to have an idea of the questions to ask the stunt arranger before sending out the crew or turning up for the interview.

Television drama involves filming sequences from many different angles but in stunt work it is understandable if the first take is the *only* take. Be prepared.

A simple sequence might be where an out-of-control lorry overturns and the people inside are trapped. The stunt arranger might set it up like this. A lorry is driven down a road in the first shot. For the second shot, it goes up a ramp fitted with what is effectively a cannon. The exploding cannon (unseen by the viewer) flips the lorry over. The camera cuts and the stunt driver climbs out. Cue smoke and fire for the next shot through the broken window to a shot of dummies burning inside. Nowadays, with computer-generated imagery (CGI), the audience would see the burning actors. In extreme stunts, of course, the entire sequence may be produced via CGI.

It is illegal to use weapons – including replica ones – in public places. Location managers and 1st ADs are aware of this but do not be tempted to shoot a 'fun' item in a Bristol street involving a pretend gun and a children's presenter.

An armourer might be required. See Chapter 6. Equity has a list of licensed armourers. It is also illegal to impersonate police officers so the children's presenter cannot wear a facsimile police uniform. Other rules for filming in public places are found on the British Film Commission's website and for further guidance on all issues mentioned in this chapter, consult the regulatory bodies' guidelines.

Personal practicalities

Clothing

Standing around in freezing weather is tantamount to torture. And if it is raining as well . . . I knew a PA whose hair froze into icicles under a rain machine during a night shoot.

Be prepared. Forget looking attractive during an OB or film shoot or out on a news mission. Being cold is a bigger turn-off. A thick impermeable jacket with hood and removable lining is essential. Ensure it is rainproof. Five hours in the rain penetrates most clothing. Eight hours leaves you wet and numbingly cold. For anyone who needs to look respectable for the camera or to interview someone, wear a smart jacket under the practical waterproof one.

Remember the anatomy below the waist. Lorry drivers often wear tights under their trousers. So do film and radio crews. I've been known to wear two pairs of tights with two pairs of socks under thermal long johns and jeans – and still been perishingly cold.

Even with a hood, a woolly hat is recommended; most heat loss is through the head. Not wearing a hat can lead to hypothermia.

Umbrellas are supplied for the camera and equipment. PAs often carry a spare umbrella. Researchers and reporters are advised to carry one in the car. If nothing else, it keeps the clipboard or notebook dry. Under such conditions, a pencil is more useful than biro. Keep wellingtons permanently in the boot.

Summer has its own drawbacks. Shorts are great. So are t-shirts (ensure your clothing is commensurate with the formality of the job) and take and use plenty of sunscreen. *Always* wear a sun hat or baseball cap, especially for those who are thinning on top. Drink lots of water.

Because you get so engrossed in recording or interviewing, it is easy to forget to slap on the suncream and forget the water intake. This is the road to sunstroke.

Whenever you see a lavatory, use it. You never know when the next one will turn up. This is not so important for men but vital for women.

Many situations require the use of high-visibility yellow jackets. Don't be too proud to wear them.

Relationship warning

Working on location and/or away from home means long hours under high pressure. People get close within an extremely short period of time and sex is a temptation. When you get home, the frisson evaporates.

Be warned, most location relationships do not last but often cause the break-up of previous relationships. No wonder marriages are notoriously short-lived in the media industry.

Summary

- Always leave a location tidier than when you arrived.
- Keep noise and disruption to a minimum. Respect the general public and the local residents.
- You cannot do too much preparation.
- Prioritise health, safety and insurance.

Further reading

Broadcast Production Guide, published annually in association with *Broadcast* magazine, MBI (formerly EMAP)
Gates, Richard, *Production Management for Film and Video*, 3rd edn, Focal Press, 1999
Mitchell, Leslie, *Production Management for Television* (Media Skills), Routledge, 2009
Stradling, Linda, *Production Management for TV and Film: The Professional's Guide* (Professional Media Practice), Methuen Drama, 2010

Websites

BBC College of Journalism: www.bbc.co.uk/academy/journalism
BBC College of Production – useful podcasts and other resources on filming and location work: www.bbc.co.uk/academy/production
British Film Commission re filming in the UK: www.britishfilmcommission.org.uk
British Tourist Office: www.visitbritain.com
Broadcast Production Guide: www.theproductionguide.co.uk
Civil Aviation Authority: www.caa.co.uk
Creative England, agency supporting film and production: www.creativeengland.co.uk

Equity, actors' union: www.equity.org.uk

Health and Safety Executive, filming, crowd management, recording from vehicles and event management, etc.: www.hse.gov.uk

The Knowledge, production suppliers' directory: www.theknowledgeonline.com

Press Complaints Commission: www.pcc.org.uk

Producers Alliance for Cinema and Television (PACT), represents independent film and TV producers: www.pact.co.uk

Scotland Screen Commission for filming in Scotland: www.creativescotlandlocations.com

The White Book, events management directory: www.whitebook.co.uk

9
Working abroad

Filming, recording and researching abroad are theoretically exciting and seen as a perk of working in media but . . . journalists especially might find themselves, literally, under fire. At best, it is a chance to see new places and meet interesting people while someone else – hopefully – foots the bill. The downside is that you are working and not a tourist. You might see an awful lot of hotels, routes to and from the airport and not much else. If filming, the rest of the crew might finish and be in the bar whilst you are bashing a red-hot phone checking that tomorrow's schedule is flawless. For a journalist, the evening might involve making new contacts, writing up notes and/or the article itself and zapping it back to base.

In a large television company for a prestigious programme or on a national newspaper, your flights, hotel and transport and shipment of equipment will be done for you by the location/production manager or the travel desk. Bear in mind that *you* are the one abroad and you are the one sorting out problems when you get there. Keep a tag on all arrangements for your own peace of mind. Unfortunately, due to the ever shrinking budget, you might find yourself in charge of the logistics. For freelance journalists, you might be sorting out your own arrangements.

I am assuming in this chapter that you are not working under especially difficult conditions such as civil unrest or war. There are many dangers and health and safety issues for foreign correspondents and other books specialise in this subject. However, it is worth mentioning that a private club, the Frontline Club, exists for people such as photographers, journalists, diplomats and film crews working in danger zones and its function is to give safety advice.

The following information will help you know what you are up against even when you are not personally responsible for the organisation. For those working in radio, for a cable and satellite station or in journalism, it is increasingly common to work alone whilst abroad. The reason? The budget.

Before you go

Local customs, holidays, religious festivals and weather

Before you embark on travelling abroad, check when local holidays, customs and religious festivals take place. Not all parts of the world celebrate Christmas or Easter and countries celebrate festivals unique to themselves. The country's tourist office can offer guidance on local customs but their motivation, of course, is attracting tourists and they cannot be expected to give a detrimental view of their country.

Of course, those regional festivals may be the reason you are going – to film/record or write about them. If not, remember transport arrangements, car hire, and the functioning of a hotel can be cancelled, curtailed and seriously impaired with repercussions on the schedule and, more importantly, the budget.

Climate can also cause complications. Are you going during the monsoon or rainy season? If you are working during extremes of weather or a festival, expect problems and explore contingencies.

Logistics

It's no good intending to be in Istanbul on 3 May if the travel agency hasn't been told. Also, logistically speaking, planes may not fly direct to the next location in, say, Stockholm, making it unfeasible to plan to work there a day later. The production manager and the travel agent will work alongside each other to organise the logistics but they need the information first and the production or editorial office may have to compromise. Health and safety concerns (and union rules) often insist that rest days are scheduled although in these times of straitened budgets, these may go hang. Accidents are statistically more likely when people are exhausted and constant travelling is as tiring as a long working day. Unfortunately, now that budgets are not just tight but still shrinking, you may not win this one.

Visas

For countries that require visas, leave enough time to process them, especially if you require a journalist or crew visa. It is not uncommon for it to take a week and more. Most travel agencies have a visa service which can acquire visas in person. It is not free and it is not cheap but is considerably quicker, more reliable and more secure than applying for a visa by post. For some countries, Nigeria for instance, getting a visa is notoriously difficult and time consuming.

Although the USA has a visa waiver scheme, all British travellers must have the Electronic System for Travel Authorization (ESTA) before travel. Application is online and you supply personal information such as name, date of birth, passport number, flight information and information as to where you will be staying. There is a fee for the ESTA. It is also worth noting that if you have a criminal record or intend to work, the ESTA will not suffice. Neither is it a replacement for a visa if you are travelling as 'foreign media, press or radio', in which case you need an 'I' visa.

To apply for a visa, a letter from the employer on headed paper, a photograph, the passport and fee must accompany the relevant form. For further information, visit the US Customs and Border Protection websites. The London US Embassy is virtually impossible to contact by phone.

I'd like to point out that my USA 'I' visa caused problems when travelling abroad on holiday. Some immigration officers questioned me rather ruthlessly about my intentions and it was occasionally difficult to explain that I was a tourist with no desire to write rude comments about their country. For journalists working on sensitive issues, immigration under these circumstances requires a cool head.

With modern lightweight cameras small enough to look like home movie camcorders, more and more media workers are sent abroad masquerading as tourists and without the relevant visa. Freelance travel journalists often travel as themselves, for instance. However, some writers have their *nom de plume* written in the back of their passports so that they can travel under both names. Without a journalist's visa, this may incur problems.

It is common for journalists and film crews to have two passports in order to travel to countries sensitive to each other; the obvious example is Israel in the Middle East where one country will not admit someone with an 'enemy' immigration stamp in their passport.

Admission Temporaire (ATA) carnets

An ATA carnet is an international transit certificate, a passport if you like. It is a document which can be used in different countries to cover the temporary use of goods without having to pay customs charges. In effect, it proves that cameras and equipment came from the country of origin and weren't bought abroad. The international carnet system works between the listed countries ensuring that equipment can pass smoothly, efficiently and quickly between them and also ensures that crews don't have to pay excise duty. You may also need a carnet to *travel through* any of the countries in the system even if you do not intend to film there. The EU does not require a carnet because goods are free to travel between countries.

ATA carnets are issued through the London Chamber of Commerce and Industry or one of the various regional chambers of commerce in, inter alia, Belfast, Bristol, Edinburgh, Liverpool, Manchester, Durham, Northampton and Southampton. A carnet is valid for a year from the date of issue. It takes a minimum of 24 hours to process but a rush job has an express charge added to the initial cost.

Effectively, all the relevant counterfoils in the carnet must be completed correctly and certified by the foreign customs officers when the vouchers are extracted and it is the responsibility of the film crew or carnet holder to check that details are correct because the various customs officials will not admit liability for any errors on their part. Some countries are more rigorous in imposing the conditions than others and all equipment is searched, itemised and ticked off with a veritable slanging match should it appear that the equipment does not correspond. Another time, you may be merely waved through the customs department without a second glance.

Warning: when filming with a carnet, it is inadvisable for a member of the production team returning early to base to take hard drives back with them as this might later cause the crew problems with an officious customs official.

For up-to-date information, there is a really good explanation on the Customs and Excise website under 'ATA carnets': http://customs.hmrc.gov.uk.

Insurance

Many countries, notably the USA, insist on public liability insurance and cover must be proved before a film permit is granted. The amount to which liability must be proved may be up to one million dollars. (This is another reason why some companies dispense with visas.) You may be expected to show the insurance cover (faxing or emailing a copy often suffices) but officials may ask for original proof. It is easier to organise this before flying out.

Personal insurance for a production team, film crew and equipment will be organised by the production manager who, should you be asked for public liability insurance, will help with the corroboration.

For journalists travelling on their own for a radio programme or investigative journalism, the NUJ suggests insurance covering medical bills and the cost of repatriation in the event of injury or illness. The NUJ doesn't provide insurance although it can recommend a company that will. It has a checklist of health and safety precautions. It also recommends that NUJ members check with the International Federation of Journalists before travelling for an IFJ press card.

Travel

Planes

Whenever possible, ensure you are booked on a reputable airline but, because of logistical problems, you may occasionally find yourself on Oddjob Airlines. Some carriers (I can't mention them for legal reasons) have worse than average safety records. There is not much you can do about this except travel as light as possible (some planes crash due to overloaded luggage), take your own food and water and cross your fingers. Your union and the Frontline Club can offer suggestions.

Airport security

The same security systems are in place for travelling as a journalist or with a film crew as for going on holiday – only on a larger scale. All major airports insist on X-raying all goods whether they are travelling by freight or accompanied by passengers.

Several programmes highlight issues at airports throughout the world, including *Border Patrol* and *Nothing to Declare*. Notwithstanding these, everyone is aware of the restricted articles list (fireworks including party poppers and crackers, knives, guns including toy guns, paint and chemicals) and there are also certain personal luggage articles that, because of the pressurised cabins, should not be taken on board as hand baggage. These include all aerosols, including shaving foam and hair spray. As security measures are amended according to the current security level, check the government website.

Since 9/11, only amounts of liquid under 100 ml are allowed in the cabin and must be taken through security control in a sealable, regulation, clear, plastic bag purchased at the airport. A useful tip is to carry spare bags in that little plastic bag, making life easier in a foreign airport if you don't have change in the correct foreign currency. I keep two of these bags in my hand baggage.

Mobile phones, laptops, iPads, tablets and other electronic gadgets are safer taken on board as hand baggage. Rules about using them on the plane depend on the airline itself but until recently, no electronic devices could be used on take-off or landing as they interfered with airplanes' navigation or communications systems, although this is now being relaxed. E-cigarettes, electronic games without remote control, cordless computer mice and GPS systems currently cannot be used on board. However, airlines are again expected to relax rules as to which gadgets can be used whilst flying. Airline safety announcements before take-off include turning gadgets to flight mode. It is common nowadays for the use of certain appliances to be permitted during the flight once you have taken off. Check with the airline.

If, like me, you watch the documentaries on customs and excise, you will know that certain countries have strict importation laws, especially for food, seeds and plants. Australia and New Zealand are particularly zealous. If you take food on board in the UK, remember to leave it on the plane, especially if entering New Zealand or Australia. Fines are heavy for illegal imports although you might escape with an official warning if it was a genuine mistake or oversight.

Advice for flights, especially long haul

- Restrict your alcohol intake. Don't be tempted by the free alcohol; it reacts with your body in pressurised conditions. Troublemakers are often arrested on landing.
- Film crews are notoriously boisterous. If you are travelling with the crew, respect the other passengers as much as you would if you were travelling alone.
- Carry a bottle of mineral water in your hand baggage and drink it. Buy it *after* going through security and yes, the cost *is* higher airside but more convenient than having to keep bothering the cabin crew.
- Prevent deep vein thrombosis. Certain passengers are at more risk than others, including pregnant women, women on the contraceptive pill or HRT. Airlines offer advice on exercises to do in the cabin to prevent this potentially fatal condition. Follow them. Some frequent travellers wear compression stockings – not particularly sexy but sexier than being ill or dead!

Trains

Nowadays, on the few occasions when it is necessary to travel by train, it is unlikely the budget will permit first class. This is generally fine on European trains, but in developing countries it is essential to travel first class if only for hygiene and safety's sake where there may be little apparent difference between our standard and their first class. The myriad travel websites and blogs will suggest what home comforts are sensible to take with you.

Hire cars/chauffeur services

Hire cars give you flexibility. They are a mobile and convenient base for luggage and equipment and reach places inaccessible by other means of transport. Considerations include the following.

- Who's going to drive? Most hire car agreements insist on a driver over 25 years old. Don't drive the car if you are nervous or inexperienced. If you know that someone in your team has lots of points on their UK licence, it might be expedient to suggest someone else as, clearly, they have the potential to be reckless. In some countries, for instance Saudi Arabia, women (including foreign women) are forbidden to drive.
- Ensure you have a valid driving licence for the country. Some countries allow you to drive on a foreign driving licence for a few months after which you must have a driving licence specific to that country. Some countries demand an international driving permit as well as a valid licence from your own country. Check before you go.
- Research the driving laws. Knowing the driving speed is crucial! For France and other European countries, you must have a warning triangle and reflective jacket in the boot and France introduced a law in 2013 whereby a car must also have a breathalyser in it. Some countries (EU especially) insist on documents being held in the car. Others require car headlights to be on at all times, including during daylight.
- On-the-spot fines for road and traffic infringements are common in many countries and corrupt police officers supplement their wages by fining unclued-up tourists – you may be seen as one.
- Safety issues. The Foreign Office website, AA and RAC have invaluable advice. Blogs and travel websites offer information but apply caution as not everything on the internet is accurate or up to date.

Chauffeur-driven cars are useful in countries like Japan or China where you can't read street names and signs. Drivers generally know the way and you can work in the car – writing, setting up contacts before you arrive and no worries about the rules of the road. The downside – the expense.

Hotels

Once upon a time, media personnel stayed in good hotels. When you are working hard for long hours, you don't want to sleep in a fleapit and you need to be contactable. Having said this, the urban myths are legendary (dead bodies in a New York hotel bed). However, should you be working on an off-the-beaten-track programme *à la* Michael Palin, creature comforts will, of necessity, be few. When slumming it with the jet set, remember to take suitable clothing for the restaurant – jacket and tie for the men and smart casual for the women. No jeans here . . .

There are several reasons why media personnel prefer to stay in good hotels: a reliable communications system, phones in rooms (less important now with satellite communication) and computer access, wi-fi, safes, early and late catering facilities (hopefully hygienic), laundry facilities, en-suite bathrooms and comfortable lodgings. However, the squeezing of budgets has forced many media companies to lodge their employees in lower starred accommodation.

Luggage

This is my personal advice. If you are a frequent traveller you may disagree and have your own essential items to add.

- Travel as light as you can. Use hotel laundry services.
- Pack a *rigid* suitcase with wheels attached. A rigid case dissuades petty theft and slashing. Don't buy a black case; there are thousands of black cases on the baggage carousel and, with jet lag, yours is hard to find. A suitcase with a Transportation Security Administration (TSA)-approved lock will prevent US customs from breaking your padlock (as has happened to me) or forcibly opening your suitcase. TSA-approved locks (whilst not cheap) have a universal key held by US customs.
- Attention is drawn to designer luggage. Don't use it.
- Don't take anything valuable or sentimental which cannot be replaced.

Essentials:

- passport;
- photocopy of passport details kept separately. In some countries you must carry identification details with you at all times or risk arrest. Photocopies are an alternative to the passport getting tatty. Some countries refuse entry to a person holding a shabby passport;
- spare passport-sized photos;
- insurance details and emergency numbers, including home and mobile phone numbers of colleagues back at base;
- copies of inoculation certificates (kept with passport);
- European Health Insurance Card (EHIC). This is not a replacement for travel insurance;

- credit cards (one or two only). Not all countries are as credit card mad as we are. Large parts of Europe and swathes of the Far East prefer cash. Pre-paid currency cards are an option and can be in sterling, US dollars and euros. When using a money card, pay in the local currency; don't use it as a deposit on a hotel or hire car and don't lose it! Also, if it gets swallowed in an ATM you will have to phone the bank in the country where it was issued. Travellers cheques, although still available, are losing popularity. If possible, get your employer to issue you with a company card to which all expenses are charged;
- money. In foreign currency. Small change is useful for luggage trolleys and other incidentals when you first arrive. Don't exchange money at the airport; the exchange rate and commission are appalling. Some countries give a better exchange rate abroad but check on the internet;
- tickets. Many airlines are now ticketless, issuing e-tickets and boarding passes when submitting your passport to a machine in the departure lounge. If you check in online before arriving at the airport, you still need to check in baggage. If you are flying with a non-EU passport, you may still need to check in at the desk *even* without baggage *even* having checked in online. An airline itinerary print-out is useful for back-up, flight times and flight numbers, etc.;
- body belt to keep the above safe;
- travel alarm clock (or alarm on your mobile). However, a travel clock can remain at blighty time (see next point);
- frequent travellers swear by two watches, one set at local time and one at Greenwich Mean Time. Very useful if you are constantly crossing time zones;
- personal medical kit for countries with high AIDS figures or poor emergency services;
- personal medical supplies (i.e. condoms, contraceptive pills, prescribed drugs – remember to take the prescription for proof it is yours), anti-diarrhoea preparation (see notes on diarrhoea);
- localised medical supplies such as malarial prophylactics;
- toilet rolls/travel tissues for noses/bottoms/drying hands – flat boxes are convenient;
- bottled water bought airside;
- mobile phone, iPad, iPhone, tablet, etc. and charger;
- worldwide travel plug;
- small inflatable travel pillow;
- eye mask and ear plugs if susceptible to light and noise.

I store most of the above permanently in a suitcase so that they don't get mislaid between trips. Passports and documents are kept separately.

Film crew tips

These are invaluable for any traveller whether travelling in a group or alone:

- go to the airport gate at *final* final call. I don't recommend this at all. The crew's *raison d'être* is that the plane won't go without you, especially as (since 9/11) they have to unload the luggage first and a film crew has lots of luggage. You won't make any friends and they may still fly without you!
- at immigration/port of entry, join a queue with families in it. Immigration officers deal with several people at once and the queue moves much quicker. At Washington DC airports, *run* from plane to passport control because, if several large planes arrive at once, you might queue for two hours. I have tested both of these and they work;
- do not cross the white line when queuing at immigration. This makes security personnel nervous and many are armed with automatic weapons;
- travel as light as possible.

While you are there

Bribes

Some countries are notorious for bribery. Although supposedly outlawed, it is still very much in existence. Do not initiate bribery yourself. When you come home and fill in your expenses form, bribery payments are listed as *incidentals* or whatever the accounts department recommend you to put down. You won't, of course, have a receipt and the UK tax office may query your expenses and refuse them.

Facilitators

When working in an unfamiliar country, it helps to have on-the-ground help. The US and the UK (to aid foreign crews working here) have film offices. These agencies may also help journalists and the contacts and insider information is priceless. Many services are free but check first.

The justification of film offices is to provide local income and employment by encouraging film companies to shoot in their region. Not only do hotels and restaurants benefit by the patronisation of the crew and actors during filming but the increase in tourism to film locations can boost an area's income by millions of dollars. In journalism, a favourable newspaper article lures the tourists.

Virtually every US state has a film office (some states also have regional offices) and the service offered may include (depending on the state): recommending hotels and restaurants, suggesting and shortlisting locations, finding production personnel, accompanying production personnel on recces or taking the production crew around the various governmental departments to arrange film licences. In other words, an extremely helpful and time-saving service. They are generally connected to the state tourist office and their services are usually free. Search for the film office online and you will see their facilities, locations, labour laws, explanation of permits, etc.

The Las Vegas office negotiated for me filming in casinos (many are reluctant to admit film crews), stretch limos and a couple prepared to be filmed getting married in a wedding chapel. We paid for the hire of the limo, the cost of the wedding (a goodwill gesture) and the film licence. In their terms, ours was a relatively small production.

In a country where $175 billion is contributed annually by the film industry to the US economy (figures from the Motion Picture Association of America, 2013), everyone is used to film crews on the streets, the closing of entire streets and a large police security presence. But it costs. And it can cost a bomb depending where you are and what you intend to do. The cost of one policeman in Nevada will set you back $70 per hour – imagine how many you need to close off Las Vegas Boulevard. A facilitator is invaluable when organising all this but the production covers the cost of the road closure, insurance, security presence, et al.

The cost of a permit to film in the US is on a sliding scale depending on how much disruption is caused but this varies from state to state. In Nevada the film permit is currently $45. In Las Vegas, different areas have different permit requirements and parts of Las Vegas Boulevard (the Strip) fall into different jurisdictions – and much is privately owned. In Maine, you only pay permit fees to film in Portland and the state parks. The minimum fee is very low.

Filming in cities is more expensive; New York, for instance, is very expensive. Check before filming to prevent nasty surprises.

A point to consider: film offices are manned by a minimum number of people so treat them with courtesy and respect – they have homes to go to.

For countries less organised than the States, it is a good idea to find a similar facilitator who will smooth your passage through the minefield of different laws and customs. Contacts for foreign facilitators can be found in, amongst others, KFTV (Formerly Kemps Guide) and at www.mandy.com. Translation and interpretation companies may also offer help abroad. Professional facilitators are paid for their assistance.

For journalists and travel writers, there is the choice of facilitators and fixers, travel agencies expecting a promotion for their products, and tourist offices.

Tourist offices can be useful for film crews. They are very obliging but looking after the media is a sideline to their job. By their nature, they are usually free. They are, however, less *au fait* with the specific demands and problems of media professionals and more relaxed about schedules than film crews and journalists. A travel writer I spoke to whilst researching this book effectively said that, for her purposes, tourist offices are worthless. She added that PR companies organising trips for travel writers tend to know what the writers' requirements are and are more efficient.

Embassies may be approached but treat these cautiously. They are, after all, extensions of governments and thereby politics.

Stringers are freelance journalists or cameramen/sound recordists working in their own countries earning their daily bread by submitting stories to news agencies such as Reuters, the BBC, CNN, Sky, etc. Their extensive local knowledge and language skills combined with the benefit of understanding problems associated with journalism and filming are invaluable. They are paid for their assistance.

Taking photos abroad

Generally speaking, taking a photograph of a tourist attraction is fine in any country in the world although be aware that people at such places (especially, for instance, Muslim countries) may not want their photos taken.

In the United Arab Emirates, for instance, don't photograph people without their permission, especially women on beaches, as you will be arrested. As importing magazines with pictures of scantily clad women into Saudi Arabia is illegal, think how they regard taking photos of them.

In many locations, including tourist attractions, taking photographs for *commercial* activity (e.g. publishing in a newspaper) needs a permit and proof of insurance. Sudan requires photography permits for everyone – even using a mobile phone camera.

Taking photos can be a sensitive issue. Be careful when taking photographs of government buildings, military installations such as air and army bases and the police. In many countries, bird watching and plane spotting are misunderstood, especially near the aforementioned military installations. In November 2001, 14 airplane spotters were arrested at Kalamata air force base, Greece, for espionage and were held in prison for six weeks before being released on bail.

Eventually they were found guilty although exonerated on appeal. In two words: be cautious.

Health and safety

Some US citizens have the preconceived idea that life in the UK is significantly more dangerous than in the States. To us, it's completely the opposite. Blame the media for that!

The Foreign Office issues constantly updated advice on the risks each country offers and what those risks are. The website includes countries where they advise against all travel. As expected, these countries are filling the news reports. If the Foreign Office warns against visiting a country, consider your decision carefully, especially if travelling alone.

Rape is an increasing risk for women in many countries, including Europe, and a woman accompanied by a man can be as much at risk as a woman on her own. The events in India in late 2012 are an example.

Certain countries have dress expectations. In Muslim countries, women (even those working for the media) are expected to dress modestly, especially when going into religious sites. Be aware that you will have fewer problems if you wear a shalwar kameez (or similar clothing worn by the local women) and that wearing shorts is often regarded as insensitive and provocative.

Dietary laws should be respected. Alcohol, for instance, is forbidden in certain countries. Although it might be available to westerners in hotels, being drunk in public can have serious repercussions, especially in Muslim countries. What appear to us as peculiar regulations relating to the purchase and drinking of alcohol apply locally in the USA.

Journalists are largely expected to take their own photos whilst working on an assignment. In some cultures, taking photos of people is a cultural minefield so check beforehand (see above). Film crews have more back-up but everyone must use their common sense; it's not worth risking the appalling conditions of a Third-World jail.

A short and very serious note on the use of SatNav phones and similar devices. The number of journalists, film crews and medical staff being targeted in war zones has increased exponentially. The use of such devices has been instrumental in making targeting more accurate so, whenever possible, avoid their use in dangerous situations. It might save your life.

Illness

It's bad enough being ill on holiday let alone when you are away from home and working. Diarrhoea and food poisoning are potentially your worst enemies. It can happen anywhere; my worst case of food poisoning was from a popular casino in Las Vegas.

Tips on how to avoid and treat diarrhoea and food poisoning include the following.

- Eat what the locals eat, i.e. fresh food cooked fast. When in a vegetarian country, don't eat meat as they are unused to storing or cooking it.
- Avoid shellfish.
- Eating yoghurt and banana every morning works well in preventing diarrhoea according to several film crews I have worked with.
- Avoid salads unless you are sure of the source and peel fruit before eating.
- Drink bottled water and watch the cap being removed. It is not uncommon for bottles to be refilled and resold. In high-risk areas (including St Petersburg in Russia), use bottled water to clean your teeth.
- Avoid ice in drinks. The water might be contaminated.
- Avoid antidiarrhoea remedies unless absolutely necessary – if affected, rehydrate with a proprietary brand of sugar and salts (take your own supply from the UK) and drink plenty of bottled water.

This is not a failsafe guide but should stave off the worst.

Malaria and hepatitis, etc.

These are endemic in many parts of the world. Your local health centre and travel clinic will advise you of the nasty bugs you are letting yourself in for. Take a trip there for the relevant jabs, pills and potions and ensure you follow the instructions exactly. Note – some vaccinations take a month before you are fully inoculated.

Some potentially fatal illnesses like malaria can manifest themselves weeks after your return home and it is essential to continue taking the prophylactics for the prescribed amount of time. The malaria parasite is becoming resistant to certain prophylactics so take advice on which drugs work in which area. Even Cheryl Cole succumbed!

Many countries have illnesses which we do not encounter in the UK: rabies, polio, tick-borne encephalitis, for instance. Check before you fly out, leaving enough time for any inoculations to become effective. Ensure you know how to prevent them and what to do in the unfortunate event that you are affected.

Sexual health

Everyone is aware of the risk of AIDS, hepatitis and sexually transmitted diseases so it is in your interest to either refrain from sex or ensure you have adequate protection. Take your own condoms. In some cultures, sexual activity outside marriage is prohibited (even an unmarried couple sharing a hotel is illegal in some countries) and not only may it incur disapprobation but it may be difficult to secure contraceptives locally. On all counts, the best protection is celibacy.

Relationship warning

Whenever I get home after a long spell of hotel food, I tuck in to egg and chips. Friends of mine enjoy beans on toast. This may appear a trivial reason for relationship breakdowns but, after several weeks away when the left-at-home partner has dealt with faulty washing machines and sick children, they may wish to celebrate your return with a meal out when all you want is nursery food. Add the stress and strain of filming or reporting from abroad, the close relationships forged on location and you can understand that holding onto a relationship can be difficult to achieve without tact, humour and compromise.

Finally

- Never be persuaded to carry packages for someone else.
- Don't make jokes at check-in about having a bomb or not packing your own case.
- Have the airline email or text you a day before your flights to confirm times, etc.
- Reconfirm your return flight and any others if the airline recommends it.
- Keep all your receipts.
- Enjoy the experience.

Websites

AA, for driving abroad, etc.: www.theaa.com
Airport hand luggage restrictions: www.gov.uk/hand-luggage-restrictions/overview
ATA carnets: www.hmrc.gov.uk, search 'ATA carnets' for the relevant info
ATA carnets, London Chamber of Commerce and Industry: www.londonchamber. co.uk

BBC College of Production has podcasts, films and articles on safety when filming abroad, etc.: www.bbc.co.uk/academyproduction

Benn's Media Guide World: www.wlrstore.com

British Guild of Travel Writers, yearbook includes specialist PR companies, broadcast media and travel operators: www.bgtw.org

EHIC: www.ehic.org.uk

ESTA information and application: https://esta.cbp.dhs.gov/esta

Foreign Office: www.fco.gov.uk

Frontline Club: www.frontlineclub.com

International Federation of Journalists, safety handbook and IFJ press cards: www.ifj.org

KFTV, formerly Kemps guide, film and TV production services: www.kftv.com

The Knowledge online directory: www.theknowledgeonline.com

Mandy, international film and TV production services: www.mandy.com

RAC for driving abroad, licences and regulations, etc.: www.rac.co.uk

10
Summary of legal issues

For ease of reference, I have put this chapter's contents in alphabetical order. As the law may change after publication, it is recommended that you keep up to date with current legislation. The various guidelines (Ofcom, BBC, etc.) are revised from time to time and, if in doubt, refer directly to them. The main legal issues to worry about are those of copyright, defamation and filming permission.

Accuracy

The BBC Editorial Guidelines, Accuracy 3.1 state:

> The BBC is committed to achieving due accuracy. This commitment is fundamental to our reputation and the trust of audiences, which is the foundation of the BBC.

In effect, the BBC regards accuracy as the heart of its existence.

The newspapers' *Editors' Code of Practice* (2013) has accuracy as its first point, thus emphasising its importance. A revised code came into effect from 2014 where, again, accuracy will be at its heart.

Although you cannot be taken to court for 'getting it wrong', it implies a lack of professionalism reflecting badly on you. However, a lack of accuracy or substantial proof of it (e.g. it was entirely made up or misrepresentational) *can* lead to litigation, defamation being an example.

At the time of writing, newspaper publishers were proposing the Independent Press Standards Organisation (IPSO) to oversee the way the press performs; accuracy will be a crucial objective. The government, however, was demanding a Royal Charter. See *Privacy*.

BBC Editorial Guidelines and Ofcom Broadcast Codes

These guidelines are the bibles of working practice. For anyone working in broadcast media, they are fundamental to issues of professionalism and ethics. Not adhering to them can have serious implications. As issues occur, they are updated. Both the BBC guidelines and Ofcom's codes have clear specific guidance on current law and the relevant Acts of Parliament.

Blasphemy

The blasphemy laws were abolished in the Criminal Justice and Immigration Act 2008. However, many people are still upset by slurs (perceived and real) against their religion so comments in our multinational society criticising a religion might have repercussions on the author. DM Digital transmitted a live lecture show on October 2011 in which Rehmatul Lil Alameen said that Muslims had a 'duty to kill' anyone insulting the Prophet Muhammad. The TV channel was fined £85,000 and the programme could not be repeated. This example (a) underlines how criticising religions may be perceived and (b) how Ofcom regards actions 'likely to encourage or incite the commission of crime'.

Cheque book journalism

Cheque book journalism is paying people for their story, often for exclusives. It is generally regarded as unacceptable news-gathering practice. Payment to the police and prison warders by journalists is corruption – journalists, police and wardens can be prosecuted. In August 2013, six tabloid journalists were accused of paying money to prison officers for stories and taken to court. In February 2013, Detective Chief Inspector April Casburn was convicted and jailed for 15 months for offering to sell information to the *News of the World*. Closed after being wracked by scandal (particularly phone hacking), the *News of the World* was replaced by a Sunday edition of the *Sun*. The tail end of the mobile phone hacking scandal led to the Leveson Inquiry. See *Hacking* and *Privacy*.

Children – appearing in programmes

It is a legal requirement that children under 16 do not take time out of school. From 2015, the school-leaving age increases to 18 and young people must be in education or training/apprenticeships until then. However, they will be allowed to perform from 16 without a licence. For children appearing in programmes during school hours, see Chapter 4.

Legislation governs the number of hours and type of employment that children can take. In some cases, there are restrictions up to the age of 18.

For further information, see the guidelines and the relevant LEA.

Children as offenders or victims

Under the Children and Young Persons Acts 1933 and 1967 (England and Wales), it is an offence to publish the names and addresses of children under 17 involved in court proceedings or to publish any information which may lead to their identity being revealed. Similar rulings apply to Scotland and Northern Ireland. Broadcasting such information in any medium (including the press) is prohibited unless a judge lifts the restriction. The BBC Editorial Guidelines have specific guidance on children and the law in the media.

Child protection: DBS and safeguarding

The Protection of Children Act 1978 makes it an offence to take indecent photographs, videos or film of children under 16 or for children to take part in such material even when their own role is not indecent. Under such circumstances, it is also illegal for actors over 16 to portray under-age children. The Sexual Offences Act 2003 increased the age of a child to 18. Various more recent amendments include electronic images of children.

The Protection of Children Act 1999 created the system identifying people considered unsuitable to work with children, leading to the National Criminal Records Bureau (CRB) – now the DBS (Disclosure and Barring Service).

After the Jimmy Savile scandal and Operation Yewtree (launched September 2012 by the Metropolitan Police to investigate alleged sexual abuse primarily against children), several celebrities have been arrested and tried for abusing children from the 1960s.

Anybody working in the media must expect to have an enhanced check especially if there is any chance of working with children. Of course, if someone hasn't been convicted as, for instance, a paedophile, the check could still be clean. A CRB/DBS only highlights what was recorded up to the date it was checked.

Any organisation in contact with children must have a safeguarding policy in place. Should anything untoward happen, this will be scrutinised. After the Jimmy Savile exposé, the BBC revised its safeguarding policy to include guidance for *online* safeguarding of children.

For children involved in sex cases, according to the Editors' Code of Practice (2013), 'the press must not, even if legally free to do so, identify children under 16 who are victims or witnesses in cases involving sex offences'. Also, 'in any press report of a case involving a sexual offence against a child – the child must not be identified'.

Children as viewers

All the regulatory bodies are keen to ensure that children are not upset or inadvertently influenced by programmes aimed at them. The use of bad language before the watershed (generally accepted as 9pm until 5am), and especially during programmes specifically aimed at children, is a case in point but so is the choice of subject matter. Violence, the use of guns and offensive weapons, crime, drugs and solvent abuse, anything harmful that may be imitated must not be broadcast when children are listening or watching. Ofcom's guidance is found in Section 1, protecting the under 18s. The BBC issues advice throughout its guidelines.

Contempt of court

The reasons why video cameras are not permitted in trials at British courts is because the law of contempt ensures a temporary embargo on the publication or broadcast of information which might influence the course of official proceedings. The government is constantly reviewing whether to allow cameras into courts, and they are now allowed in some courts of appeal, after, of course, the initial trial has taken place.

Contempt of court is a criminal offence with a maximum penalty of two years' imprisonment and an unlimited fine. In April 2013, two men were arrested in Basildon Magistrates' Court for filming on their mobile phone. It is not only people who can be in breach of this law but also broadcasts and newspaper reports which, if they are found to interfere with the course of justice (by vilifying a defendant, for instance), constitute contempt.

In October 2012, the *Daily Mirror* and *Daily Mail* were fined £10,000 each for contempt of court for publishing articles after Levi Bellfield was convicted for the abduction and murder of Milly Dowler. The stories were published after the guilty verdicts for murder but while jurors were still deliberating a separate charge.

Legal advice should be sought if there is any risk that a comment, photograph or interview is in contempt of court.

Contracts

An employment contract is binding by law. The casting and personnel departments are obviously the first port of call for any employment queries. Equity, PACT, BECTU, the MU and other trade unions can be contacted for advice.

Release forms are effectively a type of contract recording people's permission to be filmed or supply their services. See the regulatory codes of practice.

Copyright (see also Chapters 5 and 7)

Copyright is the intellectual rights to any creative work. According to the Copyright, Designs and Patents Act 1988, the categories of works which are the subject of copyright protection include: books, photographs, paintings, drawings, architectural drawings, music, poetry, films, broadcasts, sound recordings and magazine and newspaper articles, amongst others. Anything that has been created is 'owned' by someone who must be paid for the right to reproduce (or copy) it. Hence 'the right to copy' or *copyright*.

Copyright can be transferred by inheritance or by being bought and sold although some rights may be retained which is what makes the copyright issue so complicated. I keep repeating this but never think that because something is on the internet it is copyright free. No! Annually, billions of pounds are lost to authors, composers, publishers and film makers via the internet.

In 1996, European legislation extended the length of copyright from 50 to 70 years after the death of the author (in the case of two authors, 70 years after the death of the last author to die).

The copyright for sound recordings and broadcasts at the moment is 50 years after recording although this is under review. The copyright on computer-generated works last for 50 years.

Ideas cannot be copyrighted although formats can (see Chapter 2).

Photocopying – over the past few years, the Copyright Licensing Agency (CLA) and the Authors' Licensing and Collecting Society (ALCS) have attempted to raise the profile of the illegality of wholesale photocopying. The ALCS and CLA act as collecting and redistribution agencies similar to PRS for Music. However, photocopying is difficult to police and many companies, not surprisingly, prefer to risk prosecution.

Names – there is no copyright on a name or a title. Trademarks are an exception and some programme titles have been trademarked. Also, beware of using characters' names from *Coronation Street* or other programmes. In 1997, the

BBC threatened to sue British Telecom for using several *EastEnders* actors, 'playing themselves' in an advert. The BBC claimed that, by using the actors collectively, they were seen as soap opera characters, not actors. BT paid the BBC an undisclosed sum and the BBC withdrew its action.

Novels, poetry, plays and the spoken word – adapting novels for the screen and the purchase of the rights to do so are not in the province of the researcher or the day-to-day life of a journalist. However, quoting from novels, poetry or plays may well be.

It is permissible under copyright law to quote as long as it isn't a 'substantial part' of the text. Unfortunately, copyright law does not define a 'substantial part'. One short quotation from a long novel is safe. For poetry, for instance, a court case ruled that the quotation of four lines from a 32-line poem was a substantial part. Be aware when quoting song lyrics that record companies charge for very short extracts and the cost may be considerable.

If a work is old enough to be out of copyright and in the public domain, this affords no problems whatsoever. However, if the intention is to film the text and put that on screen, the typography of the book may be in copyright depending on when the book was printed. In other words, Charles Dickens' work is out of copyright but the typeface of the latest Penguin edition of *Oliver Twist* and its preface is not. Typography copyright lasts for 25 years from the end of the year in which the edition was first published.

Similarly, quoting Wordsworth's *Daffodils* is fine, but quoting something when the author has died within the last 70 years is not. The fee for quoting poetry depends on how many lines are to be used, the importance or fame of the poet and the territory (e.g. the world, UK and Commonwealth). For newspapers, local papers with smaller print runs may pay less than nationals. A programme intended for sale abroad will cost more than a local programme. Refer to the publisher for permission to quote. If the poem or extract is to be published in a newspaper, the copyright owner might demand a credit.

Letters are different. The letter itself belongs to the recipient but the copyright belongs to the writer. However, if the letters have been assigned to a library then the library is the owner. Quoting from a letter requires at least two phone calls or emails and still may not be straightforward.

Both the playwright and the publisher have a vested interest in the fees for quoting from *plays*. J.M. Barrie, the author of *Peter Pan*, left the rights to Great Ormond Street Hospital for Sick Children. As a huge amount of the hospital's income was derived from *Peter Pan*, it took an Act of Parliament to renew the copyright and ensure the continuance of the royalties (part of the Copyright, Designs and Patents Act 1988).

Some authors ensure that the lyrics of their songs cannot be parodied or treated derogatorily. This is the *right of integrity*. See Chapter 7 for music and Chapter 5 for photos, pictures and film clips.

A useful guide to copyright and permissions is published by the Society of Authors.

Coin of the realm – it is illegal to reproduce or photocopy bank notes or coins of the realm as this infringes copyright and, of course, is forgery. If a large facsimile bank note is required, permission must be sought from the Bank of England.

Company logos, trademarks, Disney characters, video games designs – unlike copyright, trademarks go on forever; consider the trademark *Coca-Cola*, reputedly the most famous and international logo in the world and over a century old. Trademarks can be registered and once registered, last in perpetuity. *Coca-Cola* has not only registered its name as a trademark but also registered the design of the bottle. Registered trademarks are distinguished by the ® sign.

Video game characters and images such as Lara Croft and Pokémon are trademarked. Characters invented by Disney, for instance, are all licensed, as are J.K. Rowling's Harry Potter characters. Thus, if a company wants to put Disney's Snow White on its pyjamas, they have to clear copyright with Disney and buy a licence to reproduce the character. These marketing off-shoots are extremely lucrative. The anomaly is, of course, that Snow White, being a fairy tale character, is in the public domain but the Disney image of her is not. Mickey Mouse's copyright is expected to expire in 2023 with that of Snow White not long after. It will be interesting to see Disney's take on this . . . it polices its trademarks very aggressively.

Showing one of these characters on television (unless governed by the fair trading rules) is reproducing a trademark and should be cleared with a fee if required. News programmes and newspapers are exempt. Check with the editor.

Using company logos such as the shell of the eponymous oil company in investigative documentaries, news programmes and newspaper articles is an exception to copyright infringements, as it is *fair dealing* (see later) for the purpose of criticism or reporting current events.

Defamation: libel and slander

Effectively, libel is when a defamatory statement is published or broadcast. Slander is when a defamatory statement is spoken. The reason why defamation on television, radio and social media (Facebook, Twitter and blogs, for instance) is termed *libel* (and not slander) is because it is in a permanent form even if, in social media terms, the message is quickly deleted.

Current affairs, news programmes, newspapers and magazines are most likely to be faced with issues of libel but gossip in chat shows may also cause concern. When in doubt, the first stop is to refer the problematic statement to the producer or editor. When in further doubt, the producer or editor will refer to a higher authority. All television and newspaper companies have media lawyers whose province covers libel and when in doubt, the script, transcript of a pre-recorded interview or the newspaper copy can be referred on to them. Lawyers are overprotective, erring on the side of caution so that an 'exciting, gritty controversial' idea may become weak and toothless.

An explanation can be given that a contributor's contentious opinion is not that of the newspaper or programme maker. However, if the situation blows up out of all proportion, the producer and production company or the journalist and editor may be sued for compensation.

Blogging, Facebook and Twitter are covered under the Defamation Act 2013 which became UK law in April 2013. This amends the law of defamation to include social media, thus ensuring that malicious false gossip spread by, for instance, anonymous trolls can be prosecuted.

The Malicious Communications Act 1988 covers the sending of malicious letters and telecommunications (including electronically) which covers cyber bullies. Found guilty, the maximum term of imprisonment is six months plus a fine.

Effectively, people cannot hide behind their anonymity and social media sites must reveal their names to the authorities. All computers leave digital foot-prints. In media terms, by spreading *unsubstantiated* rumour or 'gossip' obtained from social media websites, media professionals can also be prosecuted. In May 2013, after a highly publicised case, Sally Bercow, the wife of the Speaker of the House of Commons, was convicted of libel after posting a tweet consisting of seven words about Lord McAlpine. The courts are taking a strong line on how social media operate and, in the words of Sally Bercow, 'Things can be held to be seriously defamatory, even when you do not intend them to be defamatory and do not make any express accusation'. Cheeky statements made on social media may be seen as 'pushing boundaries' but can lead to defamation accusations and not only can the perpetrator be fined but they can also be sent to jail. Liam Stacey was jailed for 56 days for racist comments about footballer Fabrice Muamba in 2012.

The Crown Prosecution Service (CPS) published interim guidelines on prosecutions involving communications sent via social media in December 2012. www.meejalaw.org has discussions on the use of social media sites. Also visit the BBC College of Journalism website which has a good summary on the law of defamation. Twitter publishes its own rules. For a guide to the law for Twitter users, see www.bbc.co.uk/news/magazine-20782257.

D notices – Defence Advisory Notes and Official Secrets Act

There may be times when a television programme or newspaper touches on matters of national security. Media professionals working in this province need to be aware of the Official Secrets Acts of 1911 and 1989. The Official Secrets Act 1989 removed 'the public interest defence' from the 1911 Act after Clive Ponting was acquitted at his trial in 1985 for passing secret papers about the Falklands War to an MP. His defence? Public interest.

In September 2000, David Shayler, former *Sunday Times* journalist who later joined MI5, was charged with breaching the Official Secrets Act 1989 for leaking sensitive information to a national newspaper. Found guilty, he was sentenced to six months in jail in 2002. The court did not accept his 'public interest' claim.

Defence Advisory Notes, 'D notices' for short, are issued by the Defence, Press and Broadcasting Advisory Committee and are designed to advise the media that if they broadcast or publish certain information, it may damage national security. They are voluntary notices and do not have the force of law but even if an item is cleared from a D notice, there still might be a legal risk should the item be broadcast. D notices were issued to the BBC, other TV stations and national newspapers in June 2013 after Edward Snowden's whistle blowing. Editors were asked not to publish anything which may 'jeopardise both national security and possibly UK personnel'. Presumably, as we all know about this (the Guido Fawkes blog first revealed the story), the media did not adhere to the notice . . .

Senior executives will be involved with all decisions should a D notice be applied.

Ethnic minorities

The NUJ's code of conduct states that a journalist 'produces no material likely to lead to hatred or discrimination on the grounds of a person's age, gender, race, colour, creed, legal status, disability, marital status, or sexual orientation'. NUJ guidelines can be found on www.dochas.ie/Shared/Files/7/Guidelines_on_Race_Reporting.pdf.

It is an offence to incite racial hatred. Sections 21 and 22 of the Race Relations Act 1976 refer specifically to broadcasting.

Fair use, fair dealing, fair practice

The concept of fair use in copyright is to prevent copyright from stifling free speech, etc. It covers certain use of copyright material without it being regarded as infringement of the work. Showing front pages of newspapers or trademarks on the news or current affairs programmes is an example of fair dealing.

Fair dealing in newspaper reviews applies to quotations illustrating comment about the work. They cannot be used to comment about the author.

For fair dealing, you do not need to ask permission although you must consider how important the quotations and the length are in comparison with the actual review itself. See copyright entry above.

Hacking

Hacking is the illegal intervention of computer systems, phone calls, answerphones and voicemail. In October 2012, several high-profile (and not so high-profile) people took the Mirror Group (publishers of the *Daily Mirror*, *Sunday Mirror* and the *People*) to court, alleging they were victims of hacking. They included *Coronation Street* actress Shobna Gulati and Sven-Göran Eriksson, the former England football manager. Ultimately, the hacking scandal closed the *News of the World*, brought the newspaper industry and the media into serious disrepute and resulted in the Leveson Inquiry (2011–2012). The way in which the media will be regulated in the future – either by legislation or self-regulation – is still, at the time of writing, in debate with the closure of the PCC to be replaced possibly by the IPSO or a Royal Charter.

Hacking into computers is illegal and high-profile cases abound of the US government demanding extradition of those accused of hacking into their security systems, etc. as happened with the UK's Gary McKinnon. However, companies, law firms and governments (see Edward Snowden's revelations) also engage in it . . .

Also see *Privacy*.

Impartiality and bias

In the summer of 2013, the BBC came under attack for 'left-wing bias' when John Humphrys was accused of breaching the impartiality rules in *The Future of Welfare*, a documentary about welfare reform which he had written and presented. The BBC Trust said that the programme had failed to substantiate its claims with statistics. The ensuing furore both backed and disputed Humphrys with several commentators suggesting that BBC journalists should be allowed to express their own views – currently forbidden in the BBC Editorial Guidelines which advocate impartiality.

All broadcast regulatory bodies regard impartiality as crucial and there is a legal element to this in the Communications Act of 2003 and Article 10 of the European Convention of Human Rights, both affecting broadcasting. See the BBC's Guidelines and Ofcom Broadcast Codes for guidance on how these should be interpreted and adhered to. To quote Ofcom guidelines from Section 5.1: 'News, in whatever form, must be reported with due accuracy and presented with due impartiality'.

Newspapers, of course, have their own agenda and it is well known which newspaper 'promotes' which political party. The NUJ Code of Conduct states that a journalist should strive 'to ensure that information disseminated is honestly conveyed, accurate and fair' (Point 2). This is not the same as being impartial.

Insurance

Media companies have woken up to their liability towards their staff, contributors and the general public. Gone are the days, I hope, when members of the general public embark on a dangerous stunt when, if there is a nasty accident, it is discovered that there was no insurance. Risk assessment is crucial and in many companies an integral part of getting permission to film or broadcast. Equity insists in its agreements that insurance is in place. Producers and editors can be prosecuted for serious breach of health and safety.

The HSE gives plentiful guidance.

Language and obscenity

Television and radio are often criticised for the use of bad language; for instance, Chris Moyles on Radio 1 in 2006. Many newspapers asterisk out what they consider offensive words. The watershed curtails the use of unsuitable subject matter, obscene language and violence before 9pm but there are increasing complaints that sexual and moral topics unsuitable for family viewing are creeping into daytime scheduling in soap operas and shows like *This Morning* and *Jeremy Kyle*.

Radio 4 is not averse to including four-letter words in its daytime drama and current affairs programmes.

Ofcom's ruling on the use of offensive language is found in Section 2, Harm and Offence in its programme codes and in Section 5, Harm and Offence, Language in the BBC's Editorial Guidelines. The main ruling is that it must be 'editorially justified'.

The same guidelines apply to sex and nudity. In other words, if the scenes are portrayed with tact and discretion, 'justified by the context' (both BBC and Ofcom guidelines under Harm and Offence), can be defended as integral to the programme, and as long as sexual intercourse isn't represented before 9pm, these can be transmitted. Again, approval must be sought from a senior executive.

Privacy

According to Articles 8 and 10 of the European Convention on Human Rights, everyone has a right to privacy for private and family life and the right to freedom of expression. This was incorporated into UK law in the Human Rights Act 1998. This legislation is integral to all codes of practice which give guidance on scenes of extreme suffering and distress, set-up situations, interviewing children, interviews without prior arrangement, video news releases and the use of recording telephone interviews, hidden microphones and cameras. However, in the light of the phone hacking scandals first highlighted by the 2007 jailing of *News of the World* royal editor Clive Goodman, and private investigator Glenn Mulcaire for illegal interception of phone messages, i.e. hacking and the Leveson Inquiry (2011–2012, published November 2012), this law is increasingly important.

Although journalists will quote 'in the public interest', they must be increasingly aware of how intrusion into grief, for instance, is perceived (a) by the judiciary and (b) by the public. It was public disgust at the hacking accusations which spelt the demise of the *News of the World*. The *Sun's* handling of the Hillsborough disaster resulted in its boycott in Liverpool for years.

The Leveson Inquiry recommended a replacement for the PCC to regulate the press which, at the moment, may take the guise of either a government-preferred Royal Charter or industry-preferred IPSO. The press vigorously opposed the Royal Charter, insisting that it spells the demise of the freedom of the press because of potential governmental interference. It had other objections such as complainants (members of the public) having to pay an administration fee. Previously, arbitration by the PCC was free for complainants. The press is also unhappy with the level of financial sanctions which could be taken against it for contravening the Charter although, if the Royal Charter is established, local newspapers may opt out of the arbitration scheme should the system prove it causes them 'serious financial harm'. The Media Standards Trust and Hacked Off (two charities fighting for higher news standards on behalf of the public) regard IPSO as a cynical rebranding exercise of the PCC. Whichever body takes over the regulation of the press, best practice is to adhere to its rules. See *Hacking*.

The Leveson Inquiry also made recommendations on the Data Protection Act and to the Information Commissioner's Office (responsible for compliance with various Acts such as Data Protection and Freedom of Information).

Public domain

Anything out of copyright is technically in the public domain and can be used without payment. Be aware that, although Shakespeare's works are in the public domain, a publisher of his plays may copyright the layout, font and any notes published with it. The same may apply to a painting in the public domain held, for instance, in an art gallery. See *Copyright*.

Further reading

Carey, Peter, *Media Law*, 5th edn, Sweet and Maxwell, 2010

Copyright, Designs and Patents Act 1988, HSMO

Creech, Kenneth C., *Electronic Media Law and Regulation*, 6th edn, Routledge, 2013

Crook, Tim, *The UK Media Law Pocketbook*, Routledge, 2013

Davies, Gillian, *Copyright Law for Writers, Editors and Publishers* (Essential Guides), A & C Black, 2011

Hanna, Mark and Dodd, Mike, *McNae's Essential Law for Journalists*, 21st edn, OUP, 2012 (generally updated annually)

Patching, Roger and Hirst, Martin, *Journalism Ethics: Arguments and Cases for the Twenty-First Century*, Routledge, 2013

Quinn, Frances, *Law for Journalists*, 4th edn, Pearson, 2013

Writers' and Artists' Yearbook published annually by A & C Black, has chapters on copyright, libel, slander and BBC broadcasting rights and terms

Websites

Authors' Licensing and Collection Agency (ALCS): www.alcs.co.uk

BBC College of Journalism: www.bbc.co.uk/academy/journalism

BBC College of Production: www.bbc.co.uk/academy/production

BBC Editorial Guidelines: www.bbc.co.uk/guidelines/editorialguidelines

Channel 4 Producers Handbook, useful sections on media law including defamation: www.channel4.com/producers-handbook

Communications Act 2003, Section 320: www.legislation.gov.uk/ukpga/2003/21/section/320

Copyright Licensing Agency (CLA): www.cla.co.uk

Copyright for the USA: www.copyright.gov

Crown Prosecution Service (CPS) gives guidelines on use of social media and when they will prosecute: www.cps.gov.uk

Guardian editorial code: www.theguardian.com/info/guardian-editorial-code

Hacked Off, charity representing some victims of phone hacking: http://hackinginquiry.org

Health and Safety Executive (HSE): www.hse.gov.uk

Media Standards Trust, an organisation fostering high transparent standards in reporting: http://mediastandardstrust.org

Meeja Law, news, resources and discussion for digital publishers: www.meejalaw.com

National Union of Journalists (NUJ): www.nuj.org.uk

NUJ race reporting guidelines: www.dochas.ie/Shared/Files/7/Guidelines_on_Race_Reporting.pdf

Ofcom broadcast codes: www.ofcom.org.uk

Official Secrets Act 1989: www.legislation.gov.uk/ukpga/1989/6/contents

Society of Authors for copyright and permissions information: www.societyofauthors.org

Twitter users, guide to the law by the BBC: www.bbc.co.uk/news/magazine-20782257

Organisations and websites from all chapters

AA, for driving abroad, etc.: www.theaa.com
AIM, Association of Independent Music: www.musicindie.com
Airport hand luggage restrictions: www.gov.uk/hand-luggage-restrictions/overview
ALCS Authors' Licensing and Collection Agency: www.alcs.co.uk
All Music, music resource: www.allmusic.com
Amazon: www.amazon.co.uk
Archive.org, internet archive: www.archive.org
ATA carnets: www.hmrc.gov.uk, and search ATA carnets
Athletics events and athletes' biographies: www.britishathletics.org.uk
BAPLA, British Association of Picture Libraries and Agencies: www.bapla.org.uk
BASCA, British Academy of Songwriters, Composers and Authors: www.basca.org.uk
BBC: www.bbc.co.uk
BBC College of Journalism: www.bbc.co.uk/academy/journalism
BBC College of Production: www.bbc.co.uk/academy/production
BBC Editorial Guidelines: www.bbc.co.uk/guidelines/editorialguidelines
BBC Motion Gallery: www.bbcmotiongallery.com
BBC network: www.bbc.co.uk/filmnetwork
BBC Photo Library: http://bbcphotosales.co.uk
BBC Worldwide: www.bbcworldwide.com
BECTU, trade union: www.bectu.org.uk
Benn's Media Guide World www.wlrstore.com
British Film Commission: www.britishfilmcommission.org.uk
British Guild of Travel Writers: www.bgtw.org
British Library: www.bl.uk
British Library sound archive: http://sounds.blu.uk
British Newspaper Archive: www.britishnewspaperarchive.co.uk
British Pathé News: www.britishpathe.com
British Recorded Music Industry Ltd (formerly BPI): www.bpi.co.uk
British Tourist Office: www.visitbritain.com
British Universities Film and Video Council: www.bufvc.ac.uk
Broadcast Production Guide, subscription: www.theproductionguide.co.uk
Celebrity Bulletin: www.fens.com

Celebrity Intelligence: www.celebrityintelligence.com

Channel 4: www.channel4.com

Channel 4 Producers Handbook: www.channel4.com/producers-handbook

Civil Aviation Authority: www.caa.co.uk

CLA, Copyright Licensing Agency: www.cla.co.uk

Communications Act 2003, Section 320: www.legislation.gov.uk/ukpga/2003/21/section/320

Copyright for the USA: www.copyright.gov

CPS, Crown Prosecution Service: www.cps.gov.uk

Creative Commons: www.creativecommons.org

Creative England, agency supporting film and production: www.creativeengland.co.uk

Creative Skillset: www.creativeskillset.org

Debrett's: www.debretts.com

Drama UK: www.dramauk.co.uk

DueDil database: www.duedil.com

eBay: www.ebay.com

Editors' Code of Practice: www.editorscode.org.uk

EHIC: www.ehic.org.uk

Equity, the actors' union: www.equity.org.uk

ESTA, information and application: https://esta.cbp.dhs.gov/esta

Facebook and Facebook Follow: www.facebook.com

Foreign Office: www.fco.gov.uk

Frontline Club: www.frontlineclub.com

Google Books: www.books.google.co.uk

Guardian Editorial Code: www.theguardian.com/info/guardian-editorial-code

Gumtree: www.gumtree.com

Hacked Off, charity representing some victims of phone hacking: http://hacking inquiry.org

The Handbook: www.thehandbook.com

HSE, Health and Safety Executive, supervises health and safety in the UK. There are several useful guides on its internet site referring to filming, working with animals in the entertainment industries, and safety in broadcasting sports events. It also publishes leaflets on manual handing, electricity, and the working environment: www.hse.gov.uk

IMDb, International Movie Database: www.imdb.com

IMG Worldwide: www.img.com

Imperial War Museum: www.iwm.org.uk

Intellectual Property Office UK: www.ipo.gov.uk

International Federation of Journalists: www.ifj.org

Internet Archive: https://archive.org

IRN, Independent Radio News: www.irn.co.uk

ITN source, for ITN footage: www.itnsource.com

ITV: www.itv.com

Kaleidoscope: www.kaleidoscope.org.uk

Kaleidoscope Publishing: www.kaleidoscopepublishing.co.uk

KFTV, film and TV directory: www.kftv.com

The Knowledge, production directory: www.theknowledgeonline.com

Kobal Collection and Art Archive, picture agency: www.picture-desk.com

Leveson Inquiry: www.levesoninquiry.org.uk

London Chamber of Commerce and Industry: www.londonchamber.co.uk

London Sound Survey: www.soundsurvey.org.uk

Magic Circle, magicians' trade association: www.themagiccircle.co.uk

Mandy's Film and Television Production Directory: www.mandy.com

Mary Evans Picture Library: www.maryevans.com

Media Standards Trust: http://mediastandardstrust.org

Meeja Law, news, resources and discussion for digital publishers: www.meejalaw.com

Movietone, digital news archive: www.movietone.com

Musicians' Union: www.musiciansunion.org.uk

Network Rail: www.networkrail.co.uk

Newspaper Society, representing local and regional newspapers: www.newspapersoc.
    org.uk

NAPCS, North American Conference of Press Clippings Services: http://nacpcs.com

NBC Universal Archives: www.nbcuniversalarchives.com

NCTJ, National Council for the Training of Journalists: www.nctj.com

NLA, Newspaper Licensing Agency, lists the media monitoring agencies: www.nla
    mediaaccess.com

NUJ, National Union of Journalists: www.nuj.org.uk

Ofcom, for broadcast codes and compliance. Crucial regulatory body for the broadcast
    industry, radio, TV, telecommunications and the internet: www.ofcom.org.uk

Official Secrets Act 1989: www.legislation.gov.uk/ukpga/1989/6/contents

Oral History Society: www.ohs.org.uk

Own it, intellectual property advice service with downloadable resources: www.own-
    it.org

PACT, Producers Alliance for Cinema and Television: www.pact.co.uk

Personal Managers' Association: www.thepma.com

Pinterest: www.pinterest.com

PhonepayPlus, regulatory body for premium phone lines: www.phonepayplus.org.uk

PPL, Phonographic Performance Ltd, and VPL, Video Performance Ltd: www.ppluk.
    com

Press Association: www.pressassociation.com

Press Complaints Commission: www.pcc.org.uk

Project Gutenberg: www.gutenberg.org

PRS for Music and MCPS: www.prsformusic.com

RAC, driving abroad, licences and regulations, etc.: www.rac.co.uk

Radio Academy: www.radioacademy.org

Scotland Screen Commission for filming in Scotland: www.creativescotlandlocations.
    com

Shooting People, general filming, forms and crewing, crowdfunding: www.shooting
    people.org

Society of Authors, copyright and permissions information: www.societyofauthors.org

Sound Cloud, 'YouTube' of sound: www.soundcloud.com

Sport England: www.sportengland.org

Spotify, Swedish music streaming company: www.spotify.com

Spotlight, directory for actors, choreographers, directors and presenters: www.spotlight.com

Storyful, news agency for social media: www.storyful.com

TinEye, reverse image search: www.tineye.com

Twitter: www.twitter.com

Whitaker's Almanack online: http://whitakersalmanack.com

The White Book, events, production news and feature service: www.whitebook.co.uk

Who's Who: www.ukwhoswho.com

World Intellectual Property Organisation: www.wipo.int

Writers' and Artists' Yearbook: www.writersandartists.co.uk

All websites and URLs were correct at the time of writing.

Glossary

AD   assistant director; there are up to three assistant directors on a large drama production, the 1st AD acting in the same role as that performed by the floor manager in a television studio. The 2nd and 3rd ADs are the 1st AD's assistants.

Ad lib   off the cuff, unscripted remark.

Ads   advertisements and commercials.

Agreements   contracts stipulating conditions on the use of recorded music or actors, etc.

AIM   Association of Independent Music.

ALCS   Authors' Licensing and Collection Agency.

AP   assistant producer or associate producer.

A&R   Artists and Repertoire, the department in a recording company which finds and looks after the careers of singers and groups.

As live   pre-recording a programme as if it were live so that the first take is usually the one used. If there is a severe technical problem, the tape is rewound and taped over. Pre-recording usually takes place very shortly before transmission. A half-hour 'as live' production theoretically will be recorded in half an hour. There is no editing.

ASM   assistant stage manager.

Aston   a type of caption generator. See *Captions*.

Atmos   atmosphere, background sound effects giving the impression of an environment.

Autocue   an electronic prompt device from which newsreaders and presenters read the script; other makes include Portaprompt and Teleprompter.

BA broadcast assistant (radio's equivalent of production assistant).

BAPLA British Association of Picture Libraries and Agencies.

BASCA British Academy of Songwriters, Composers and Authors, representing music writers.

BCU big close-up, a camera shot.

BECTU Broadcasting, Entertainment, Cinematograph and Theatre Union, one of the industry's trade unions.

BPI British Phonographic Industry, association of UK recorded music companies. Now renamed the British Recorded Music Industry Ltd.

Buy-out clauses in a contract of employment, 'buying out' overtime by paying an overall fee for the job.

Byline the author of an article in a magazine or newspaper. By . . . followed by name.

C/A cutaway, a camera shot, usually a close-up where the sequence 'cuts away' from the master shot to telescope time or as an explanation. For example, when something is being referred to verbally, it is shown in close-up.

CAA Civil Aviation Authority.

Call sheet an information sheet explaining where and when filming will take place so everyone knows where to go and when.

Cam camera.

Captions the names of contributors shown on screen but also includes opening titles and end credits and any other on-screen writing. Generated by a caption or character generator colloquially referred to as a capgen. In newspapers, the caption is the writing underneath a photograph explaining what is happening.

Carnet a transit certificate for equipment (like a passport).

CGI computer-generated image.

Chopper shots colloquial term for shots filmed from a helicopter.

Churnalism 'churning' out stories from press releases by just repeating the content.

CLA Copyright Licensing Agency.

Clearance see *Copyright clearance*.

Clip short extract from a longer item, an excerpt.

Clippings/cuttings   press clippings or cuttings taken from newspapers.

Copy   the text for, e.g., a newspaper. A copywriter in advertising writes the copy (text) for display adverts and television/radio adverts.

Copyright   the ownership or the right to reproduce any artistic work such as a book, film, play, photograph or piece of music.

Copyright clearance   the means by which permission is sought for copyrighted material to be reproduced.

Corporates/corporate videos   non-broadcast products made by small independent production companies for training, staff information or promotional purposes.

Crowdsourcing   sourcing new ideas by asking the company workforce to suggest them or making an internet appeal to the internet community to solve a problem of some kind.

CU   close-up, a camera shot.

Cue   pre-arranged signal to start.

Cue light   a small light in a voiceover or sound studio giving the cueing signal.

Cue sheet   the paperwork giving technical information and script for a programme or insert.

Cume   cumulative, as in running order time, the total running time up to that point.

DBS   Disclosure and Barring Service – replaces the Criminal Records Bureau (CRB).

EDL   edit decision list, the order in which a film is cut. Also called a 'paper edit' or cutting order.

Embargo   a restriction on when information can be disclosed.

ENG   electronic news gathering, pronounced 'enj' or 'E-N-G', depending on the station. Electronic news gathering is a type of lightweight video camera and sound recording system.

Estab shot   establishing shot, usually a long wide shot, the first shot in a sequence to establish where the action is taking place.

exif   exchangeable image file format – a system giving camera data which can be used to verify photographs.

Flash fees   payment for 'flashing' a photograph or picture on television, a royalty payment.

Freelance   self-employed and not on a permanent contract.

Futures desk   the desk filing stories for possible future coverage in a programme or newspaper. May be called 'planning'.

FX   effects, as in sound effects or special effects.

Genny   short for the generator used for supplying electricity on location or for an OB.

GV or gvs   general view(s), a camera shot.

Hand-held   shots when a tripod is not used. The camera is often supported by the camera operator's shoulder. A bad hand-held shot is nicknamed 'wobbly-scope'.

Hand-held cams   cameras light enough to be taken off the tripod and used 'hand-held', i.e. on the shoulder or held low down for tracking.

HSE   Health and Safety Executive, the government body regulating health and safety in the UK.

In cue   the first words of an insert, although it can be music (the 'out cue' are the last words).

Independent producers   small production houses outside the BBC or main ITV companies. Commonly referred to as 'indies'.

Insert   a short item (e.g. a live or tape insert) to be inserted into a radio or TV programme.

Intro   short for 'introduction', i.e. the intro at the beginning of a programme or before a new item. The 'outro' is at the end.

IPSO   Independent Press Standards Organisation; this was proposed at the time of writing to act as a press regulator replacing the Press Complaints Commission (PCC).

IRN   Independent Radio News.

ISDN   Integrated Services over a Digital Network. A digital signal used for both voice and non-voice data over the public telephone system. It does not have the crackle of standard telephone lines but, of course, is more expensive. ISDN via satellite is used by field reporters around the world.

ISM   Incorporated Society of Musicians, professional association for performers, composers and teachers.

LE   light entertainment, a non-serious programme such as quiz, chat/game show, music programme or the department producing it.

Links   inserts to join items; they can be either spoken by presenters on air or to camera, or short 'animated' stings.

Listings   a list of events, cinema, theatre, radio, music, television – in other words, what's on where. Listings magazines include *Radio Times* and *TV Times*.

MCPS   Mechanical Copyright Protection Society Ltd, an agency collecting royalties on behalf of composers and publishers whenever their work is recorded.

MCU   medium close-up, a camera shot, often referred to as 'head and shoulders', used conventionally in interviews and for newsreaders.

MEP   Member of the European Parliament.

Mic/mike   microphone.

Montage   either a sequence of short shots usually cut to music or sfx or the actual cut of the film – in France, the monteur is the editor.

Moral rights   the right of an author of a work to keep the integrity of how it is used or seen.

MU   Musicians' Union, trade union representing musicians.

Multi-platform crossing   between radio, television and internet. An article written for multi-platform use would include a piece to camera for TV, a radio item and copy with photographs for the internet.

Network   nationwide. Programmes going out 'network' are going out all over the country.

NIBS   news in brief; short one or two paragraphs on a news item.

NUJ   National Union of Journalists, a trade union representing journalists working on newspapers, radio and television.

OB   outside broadcast, a live or recorded programme for television or radio made on location for large events; effectively a travelling studio.

Ofcom   Office of Communication, the regulatory body for all broadcast media, radio, television, internet and communications systems.

ONS   Office for National Statistics, which also conducts the census.

OOV   out of vision, similar to a voiceover.

Out cue   the last words of an insert, but can be music. Knowing what the last words are acts as a cue for the studio presenter to get ready to speak and a mic cue for the engineers.

Outro   'outro'duction, the last statement in a programme, opposite to intro.

PA   production assistant, Press Association, a news agency or public address system.

Packages   in radio, pre-recorded edited inserts 'packaged' up and including links, music and actuality.

PACT   Producers Alliance for Cinema and Television, the UK film and television trade's main professional organisation.

Panning shots   a pan is when the camera is fixed to the ground, i.e. on a tripod, but is swivelled, panned from left to right or right to left (see *Tracking shots*).

Paper edit   also known as the edit decision list, EDL or cutting order, a list of shots put into order so that the editor has an idea of what they have to cut.

P as Bs   programme as broadcast, notes to show what music, length, film, etc., is included on the programme for future payment purposes, usually compiled by the BA or PA.

PCC   Press Complaints Commission, a self-regulated organisation policing the press. At the time of writing, this was under recommendation to be replaced, possibly by the IPSO.

Peds   pedestal cameras, heavy cameras on wheels used in OBs and studios.

PPL   Phonographic Performance Ltd, licenses recorded music played in public or broadcast on the radio or TV and distributes the fees to its performer and record company members.

Press release   an information sheet about a special event sent to local TV and radio stations and newspaper offices in order to receive publicity. Also called news releases.

Primary research   basic first-hand research such as going on a recce, interviewing people, phoning them up.

PRO   Public Record Office, at Kew, London, where UK public records are stored.

Promo   short for 'promotion', a trailer for a forthcoming programme.

PR   public relations.

PRS for Music   Performing Rights Society for Music, collects royalties on behalf of music creators and publishers for public performance and broadcast. Shares offices with MCPS.

PSC   portable single camera, video not film.

Public liability   insurance to cover accidents befalling the general public, e.g. if a passer-by falls over a tripod in a street.

Recce   short for 'reconnaissance', a visit to a potential location to check filming and recording suitability and conditions.

Release form   forms signed by programme contributors indicating their permission to be recorded, edited and transmitted on television or radio.

Royalties   the payment to a copyright holder for the use of their work.

Running order   shortened to RO, the items and timings of a programme listed in transmission (or recording) order. Running orders on daily programmes like the news are moveable feasts depending on the importance of items.

Running time   shortened to RT, the length of a programme or insert.

Run-through   a rehearsal.

Rushes   the unedited shots from a camera. In the States, they are called the 'dailies' because they are traditionally viewed at the start of each day before filming resumes. In the UK, film was 'rushed' to the lab for overnight processing and 'rushed' back for viewing the following day.

SB   short for 'simultaneous broadcast', a broadcast transmitted simultaneously on radio and television, for instance the BBC Proms.

Scanner   mobile OB truck containing the control rooms for production, vision and sound.

Script   the complete text of a programme or insert. A camera script includes all the camera shots and movements.

Secondary research   taken 'second-hand' from someone else's first-hand research, i.e. a newspaper report (see *Primary research*).

Segue   pronounced 'segway', the running together of two items directly after each other without a pause or presenter's link, especially used for music when the transition between the two tracks should be smooth.

Sfx   sound effects or special effects.

Simulrec   simultaneous recording.

SOT   sound on tape.

Sound bite   short pithy phrase either on video or audio summing up a particular point of view. It can usually stand alone, e.g. Tony Blair in October 1996 said, 'Ask me my three main priorities for government, and I tell you: education, education, education'.

Spark   colloquial term for electrician.

Steadicam   trademarked name for a camera on a harness used to stabilise hand-held shots. The term is used for all similar cameras.

Stings and logos   five-second graphic inserts to act as buffers and links and for dramatic effect.

Stock-shots   short generic film clips, e.g. 'woods' or 'gardens' or 'the Blackpool Tower', bought in from a film library or in-house picture library.

Stringer   a freelance contributor paid by the item, often a journalist or cameraman based abroad where UK staff are not employed although stringers do work in the UK.

Synopsis   a précis of the basic story line.

Talkback   a communication system from control room to studio floor.

Talking head   colloquial term for someone talking in vision. It is generally regarded that too many talking heads make poor television.

Timecode   electronic system numbering each individual frame of video and used for accurate editing.

Tracking shots   in tracking, the camera is physically moved (either on tracks or when the cameraman walks with the camera) from left to right or forwards or backwards. A camera moving from left to right or right to left is a crab right or crab left. See *Panning shots*.

Trail/trailer   a short 'advertisement' for a forthcoming programme, also called 'promo', short for promotion.

Tranny   transparency (photographic slide) unlikely to be used nowadays with digital images.

Treatment   how an idea will be worked for the programme.

TS   technical supervisor, the engineer in charge of the TV studio or OB.

TX   short for 'transmission', when the programme is broadcast.

UGC   user-generated content, content supplied by the general public and included in the newspaper, television or radio programme, includes, e.g., mobile phone/Flickr/Instagram photos, tweets, emails and SMS texts.

V/O or voiceover   as in narration, when the speaker cannot be seen. In radio, the narration may be over low-level music.

VOD   video on demand.

Vox pop   vox populi, 'voice of the people', a short composite recording of several people's views recorded in the street or other public place. Alan Whicker (1925–2013) was regarded as the 'inventor' of the vox pop.

VPL   the sister company of PPL and specifically dealing with licensing of music videos.

VT   video tape. Also video-tape inserts in a show.

Warm-up/warm-up man   provides an introduction and chats to the audience to relax them before recording. If there is no specially employed warm-up man to do this, the presenter, producer or floor manager will do it.

Watershed   generally accepted as a time between 9pm and 5am in which material unsuitable for children (violence, language, sexual themes) should not be transmitted. Enforceable by Ofcom.

Wild/wild track   the recording of atmosphere, actuality or sound effects without picture. Also called the 'buzz track' or 'actuality'.

Wind-up   visual signal to warn of the approaching end of the programme or contribution. The signal can either be the index finger rotating vertically or a flashing cue light.

Wrap   either a short piece of actuality and back announcement (back anno) 'wrapped around' by a vocal piece, or 'it's a wrap', originally coming from the film term 'wind, roll and print' but now meaning filming has finished, it's time to wrap up the equipment and leave.

Index